P9-DFL-042

1,001 Things You Always Wanted to Know About the Bible

(But Never Thought to Ask)

J. Stephen Lang

OLIVER
NELSON

THOMAS NELSON PUBLISHERS
Nashville

Copyright © 1999 by J. Stephen Lang

All rights reserved. Written permission must be secured from the publisher to use or reproduce any part of this book, except for brief quotations in critical reviews or articles.

Published in Nashville, Tennessee, by Thomas Nelson, Inc.

Unless otherwise noted, Scripture quotations are from THE NEW KING JAMES VERSION. Copyright © 1979, 1980, 1982, Thomas Nelson, Inc., Publishers.

Scripture quotations noted KJV are from the KING JAMES VERSION of the Holy Bible.

Scripture quotations noted NIV are from the HOLY BIBLE: NEW INTERNATIONAL VERSION®. Copyright © 1973, 1978, 1984 by International Bible Society. Used by permission of Zondervan Publishing House. All rights reserved.

Library of Congress Cataloging-in-Publication Data

Lang, J. Stephen
    1,001 things you always wanted to know about the Bible : but never thought to ask / J. Stephen Lang.
      p. cm.
    Includes index.
    ISBN 0-7852-7346-8 (pbk.)
    1. Bible—Miscellanea. I. Title. II. Title: One thousand and one things you always wanted to know about the Bible. III. Title: One thousand one things you always wanted to know about the Bible.
BS615.L36   1998
220—dc 21   98-44531
                                                   CIP

Printed in the United States of America.

2 3 4 5 6 QPK 04 03 02 01 00 99

To
Wightman Weese

Contents

1

Familiar Phrases

1. eat, drink, and be merry

Yes, it's a phrase from the Bible. It's found in Jesus' "parable of the rich fool," a cautionary tale about being too attached to one's possessions. The rich fool said to himself, "You have many goods laid up for many years; take your ease; eat, drink, and be merry." But then God said to him, "Fool! This night your soul will be required of you; then whose will those things be which you have provided?" (Luke 12:13–21).

2. scapegoat

In the original sense it was a real goat. On the annual Day of Atonement, Israel's high priest would lay his hands on a goat, symbolically transferring the people's sins to it, then drive it away into the wilderness. The scapegoat fared better than the other Day of Atonement goat, which was sacrificed as a sin offering.

The word has come to mean "someone who takes the blame for others."

See 666 (atonement).

3. fat of the land

This familiar phrase is first used in Genesis 45:18, where Joseph tells his eleven brothers, "I will give you the best of the land of Egypt, and you will eat the fat of the land."

4. wolf in sheep's clothing

This familiar phrase is from the lips of Jesus: "Beware of false prophets, who come to you in sheep's clothing, but inwardly they are ravenous wolves" (Matt. 7:15). He was referring to religious teachers who appear good on the surface but are hypocrites.

5. the skin of my teeth

Meaning "just barely" or "by a very narrow margin," the phrase comes from Job 19:20, "My bone clings to my skin and to my flesh, and I have escaped by the skin of my teeth."

6. eye for an eye

Yes, the idea of "eye for an eye, tooth for a tooth" really is in the Bible: "If a man causes disfigurement of his neighbor, as he has done, so shall it be done to him—fracture for fracture, eye for eye, tooth for tooth; as he has caused disfigurement of a man, so shall it be done to him" (Lev. 24:19–20).

This law from the Old Testament strikes us as spiteful and vindictive (or "mean-spirited," to use the now popular phrase). In the New Testament, Jesus taught a higher ethic: "You have heard that it was said, 'An eye for an eye and a tooth for a tooth.' But I tell you not to resist an evil person. But whoever slaps you on your right cheek, turn the other to him also" (Matt. 5:38–39).

Isn't that better—more "Christian"?

For the record, the Old Testament law was pretty compassionate. "Eye for eye, tooth for tooth" was a *limit*. It meant "tit for tat"—but no more. The common custom (human nature never changes!) was (and is) to get *more* than even. But the enlightened law in Leviticus said, No, if you're injured you can't take two teeth because you lost one tooth. It was actually a progressive law. Jesus took it a step further.

How would the Bible authors view personal injury lawsuits today?

7. fire and brimstone

People often refer to "fire-and-brimstone preachers" without knowing just what brimstone is. It is an old name for sulfur, something common in volcanic areas. When Genesis reports that God destroyed the immoral cities of Sodom and Gomorrah with fire and brimstone, it may be referring to a volcano (Gen. 19:24). The book of Revelation says that

3

at the end of the world Satan and all nonbelievers will be cast into a lake of fire and brimstone where they will burn eternally (Rev. 14:10; 19:20; 21:8). This is why "fire and brimstone" is another way of saying "the fires of hell."

8. beautiful

William Tyndale produced his English translation of the New Testament in 1524. It was the first English Bible produced on a printing press. It was also the first English Bible to include a word we now use every day: *beautiful.* It was still a fairly new word at the time, and some people were amazed that Tyndale would use such a "novel" word in the Bible.

9. the blind leading the blind

This is one of many biblical phrases that have become part of the language. In Matthew 15:14 Jesus says, "If the blind leads the blind, both will fall into a ditch." He was referring to false teachers who lead people astray.

10. can a leopard change his spots?

Jeremiah (13:23) raised the questions, "Can the Ethiopian change his skin or the leopard its spots?" The leopard question passed into common usage.

11. feet of clay

This expression comes from Daniel 2, where Daniel interprets the strange dream of the Babylonian king Nebuchadnezzar. In the dream a statue of a man is composed of various metals, but its feet are clay—or, to be precise, clay mixed with iron. "Feet of clay" has come to mean a personal flaw that isn't readily apparent.

12. brother's keeper

Cain, first child of Adam and Eve, killed the second child, his brother, Abel. According to Genesis 4:9, "The LORD said to Cain, 'Where is Abel your brother?' He said, 'I do not know. Am I my brother's keeper?'"

13. thorn in one's side

This familiar phrase comes from the apostle Paul, who admitted that he suffered because "a thorn in the flesh was given to me, a messenger of Satan to buffet me . . . Concerning this thing I pleaded with the Lord three times that it might depart from me. And He said to me, 'My grace is sufficient for you, for My strength is made perfect in weakness'" (2 Cor. 12:7–9). Paul may have been referring to some physical ailment, though we can't be sure.

14. keeping the faith

This expression has become so common that we forget it originated in the Bible, where it refers to *the* faith, faith in Christ. The apostle Paul, who apparently expected to die soon, wrote to his young friend Timothy, "I have fought the good fight, I have finished the race, I have kept the faith" (2 Tim. 4:7). "Fight the good fight" has also passed into common usage.

15. maudlin

Webster's defines it as "weakly and effusively sentimental." The word *maudlin* actually comes from *Magdalene,* referring to Mary Magdalene in the Gospels. Mary, one of the devoted women followers of Jesus, was usually presented in artwork as weeping over her sins, so being "maudlin" came to mean "overdoing it emotionally."

See 519 (Mary Magdalene).

16. salt of the earth

The phrase appears in Jesus' famous Sermon on the Mount (Matt. 5–7). Matthew 5:13 states, "You are the salt of the earth." Jesus was telling His disciples that they were to serve as both a seasoning and a preservative in the world. If they were not doing this, they were useless.

Salt was a valuable commodity in the ancient world. Some people, including many Roman soldiers, were paid their wages in salt instead of money. Our word *salary* comes from the Latin word *salarium,* meaning "salt money."

When Jesus referred to His followers as "salt," He wasn't referring to a cheap everyday item, but to something valuable and important.

See 393 (Sermon on the Mount).

17. the handwriting on the wall

Daniel 5 presents one of the Bible's most colorful stories, set at a feast given by the Babylonian ruler Belshazzar. The king was drinking from vessels plundered from the Jewish temple at Jerusalem. During the feast, a strange disembodied hand appeared and wrote mysterious words on the palace wall: MENE, MENE, TEKEL, UPHARSIN. Belshazzar was so terrified that "his knees knocked against each other." The faithful Jew Daniel appeared and interpreted the message, which meant that God had brought the Babylonian Empire to an end and given it over to the Medes and Persians. That very night Belshazzar, king of Babylon, was killed, and Darius the Mede took over the kingdom.

Artists have delighted in capturing this story on canvas, and the great Rembrandt's painting *Belshazzar's Feast* is only one of many.

18. forbidden fruit

According to Genesis, the original man and woman had an ideal existence in the Garden of Eden, with only one rule that God imposed on them: "Of the tree of the knowledge of good and evil you shall not eat, for in the day that you eat of it you shall surely die" (Gen. 2:17). The fruit of that one tree was the "forbidden fruit." The serpent tempted

Eve (who then tempted Adam) into eating the fruit by telling Eve a lie: "You will not surely die. For God knows that in the day you eat of it your eyes will be opened, and you will be like God, knowing good and evil" (Gen. 3:4–5). Adam and Eve disobeyed God, leading to their own punishment, and the serpent's as well.

The tradition that the fruit was an apple has no basis in the Bible. We don't know what kind of fruit it was, except that it was the one that should have been avoided.

19. Adam's apple

According to an ancient tradition, when Adam ate the fruit from the tree that God had declared off-limits (Gen. 3), a piece of it stuck in his throat forever. The Bible doesn't actually say that the forbidden fruit was an apple. The legend does provide an amusing explanation for why men (more so than women) have a bulge in the center of the throat.

20. money is the root of all evil

Is it? The Bible never says so. What Paul says in 1 Timothy 6:10 is "the love of money is a root of all kinds of evil." Money itself is not evil—_loving_ it is. Note something else: Money is not the root of _all evil,_ but the root of _all kinds of evil._

21. Woe is me!

Jeremiah, the "weeping prophet," used the phrase several times, but the most familiar "woe" was in the vision of

Isaiah, who was awestruck at encountering the Almighty in the temple: "Woe is me, for I am undone! Because I am a man of unclean lips; and I dwell in the midst of a people of unclean lips; for my eyes have seen the King, the LORD of hosts" (Isa. 6:5).

See 214 (Isaiah's vision).

22. sweating blood

Luke's gospel tells of Jesus' anguish in the Garden of Gethsemane. Knowing He would soon be arrested and executed, He prayed to His Father, and "being in agony, He prayed more earnestly. Then His sweat became like great drops of blood falling down to the ground" (Luke 22:44).

23. spare the rod and spoil the child

According to Proverbs 13:24, "He who spares his rod hates his son, but he who loves him disciplines him promptly." This bit of ancient wisdom passed into English as "spare the rod and spoil the child." The ancient Hebrews took a view of corporal punishment different from that of many modern parents.

24. a drop in the bucket

Probably one of the most commonly used phrases from the Bible, it is found in Isaiah, who claimed that God was not impressed with mighty empires: "The nations are as a drop in a bucket, and are counted as the small dust on the scales" (40:15).

25. holier than thou

Today we connect the phrase with self-righteousness—a "holier-than-thou" attitude. In the Bible God condemned this attitude and mocked the words of self-righteous people: "I have spread out my hands all the day unto a rebellious people, which walketh in a way that was not good, after their own thoughts; a people that provoketh me to anger continually to my face; . . . which say, 'Stand by thyself, come not near to me; for I am holier than thou'" (Isa. 65:2–5 KJV).

26. shibboleth

Judges 12 relates that this word was pronounced differently on the two sides of the Jordan River. The judge Jephthah used the word as a test to determine if the speaker was friend or foe. ("Sibboleth" was the pronunciation that led to execution.) The word passed into our language as meaning a custom that a group uses to distinguish itself from another group, usually for purposes of snobbery.

27. jeremiad

A lament or song of sorrow is called a jeremiad after the prophet Jeremiah, the "weeping prophet," who was also the author of Lamentations, the sad reflection on the city of Jerusalem, devastated by the Babylonians.

28. land of milk and honey

The phrase means "a rich, fertile land" or even "a nice place to live." It is used many times in the Old Testament to refer to Canaan, the land God promised the Israelites after they left their slavery in Egypt.

See 879 (Canaan).

29. Job's comforters

In the book of Job, poor Job suffers all kinds of calamities. Three close friends come to (supposedly) comfort him but, in fact, insist that he must have done something horrible to bring the disasters on himself. The expression "Job's comforters" refers to people who discourage or depress while claiming to be consoling.

30. Jehu

God was appalled at the wickedness of Israel's King Ahab and his family, and His instrument of punishment was one of Ahab's military men, Jehu. God ordered the prophet Elisha to anoint Jehu king, and Jehu proceeded to wipe out (in brutal fashion) Ahab's entire clan, including Ahab's wicked wife, Jezebel, who was devoured by dogs. Jehu then tricked the worshipers of the false god Baal into a trap and killed them all. So Jehu destroyed Baal worship in Israel (2 Kings 10:28).

A "Jehu" has come to mean a fast and furious driver. This is based on 2 Kings 9:20: "The driving is like the driving of Jehu . . . for he driveth furiously" (KJV).

31. a lamb to the slaughter

Isaiah 53:7 describes God's chosen servant, who "was led as a lamb to the slaughter, and as a sheep before its shearers is silent, so He opened not His mouth." The early Christians saw this as a prophecy of Jesus, condemned to death but passively accepting His fate. "Lamb to the slaughter" has come to mean any innocent victim.

32. lusting in one's heart

This gained fame in 1976, when presidential candidate Jimmy Carter admitted in an interview that he had never committed adultery, except "in his heart." He was referring to Jesus' words on adultery: "You have heard that it was said to those of old, 'You shall not commit adultery.' But I say to you that whoever looks at a woman to lust for her has already committed adultery with her in his heart" (Matt. 5:27–28). Jesus did not mean that lustful looks were _the same as adultery,_ but that our thoughts are as important to God as our actual deeds are.

33. anathema

"Something or someone odious" is the dictionary definition of this Aramaic word found in Paul's epistles. _Anathema_ is translated "accursed" (Rom. 9:3) and "let him be accursed" (1 Cor. 16:22; Gal. 1:9). As the church grew and councils met to decide questions of doctrine, a false teaching would be pronounced _anathema._

34. apple of the eye

The Hebrew words that we translate "apple of the eye" refer to the center of the eye, the pupil. But the expression also refers to someone who is highly valued by another (as in "his son is the apple of his eye"). The phrase occurs several times in the Bible. Deuteronomy 32:10 says that God guarded Israel "as the apple of His eye." The prayer of Psalm 17:8 implores God, "Keep me as the apple of Your eye; hide me under the shadow of Your wings."

35. a little wine for the stomach

These words are often used in jest, and most people have no idea they are from the Bible. In his first letter to Timothy, Paul advised the young pastor, "No longer drink only water, but use a little wine for your stomach's sake and your frequent infirmities" (5:23).

36. what God hath joined together

Traditional marriage ceremonies contain these words spoken by the minister: "What therefore God hath joined together, let not man put asunder" (Mark 10:9 KJV). The words are those of Jesus, who was speaking of the permanence of marriage.

37. God helps those who help themselves

Many people believe this oft-quoted proverb is in the Bible. It definitely is not. John F. Kennedy made it famous in one of his speeches, but the words actually are not Kennedy's but are from another noted American, Benjamin Franklin.

38. we reap what we sow

The phrase is so much a part of our language and thought that we forget it originated in the New Testament: "Do not be deceived, God is not mocked; for whatever a man sows, that he will also reap" (Gal. 6:7).

39. pride goeth before a fall

It isn't quoted as often as it once was (meaning we are more accepting of pride?), but for centuries it was part of the English language. It is found in full in Proverbs 16:18: "Pride goeth before destruction, and an haughty spirit before a fall" (KJV).

40. fly in the ointment

We use it to mean something vile that ruins something good. The phrase comes from Ecclesiastes 10:1: "Dead flies putrefy the perfumer's ointment, and cause it to give off a foul odor."

41. gird up one's loins

It means to prepare for action, to muster one's resources. Literally, it meant that a person's loose garments would be tucked in with a belt so the person was ready to fight. It occurs many times in the Bible (Ex. 12:11 [KJV]; 1 Kings 18:46; Job 38:3 [KJV]; Prov. 31:17 [KJV]).

42. the spirit is willing

We are all familiar with "the spirit is willing, but the flesh is weak." It summarizes the human dilemma of having good intentions but not the will to follow through. Matthew 26:36–56 tells of Jesus' agony in Gethsemane just before Judas betrayed Him to the authorities. While He was praying, His disciples fell asleep, and when He found them He said, "Watch and pray, lest you enter into temptation. The spirit indeed is willing, but the flesh is weak."

43. seek and ye shall find

In Jesus' Sermon on the Mount, He told His followers, "Ask, and it will be given to you; seek, and you will find; knock, and it will be opened to you" (Matt. 7:7). He was driving home the point that God's children should approach God hopefully in prayer.

44. faith to move mountains

Jesus did not intend His followers to go around rearranging the landscape. Still, He did speak (figuratively) about faith that could move mountains: "If you have faith as small as a mustard seed, you can say to this mountain, 'Move from here to there' and it will move. Nothing will be impossible for you" (Matt. 17:20 NIV).

45. the powers that be

The phrase comes from Paul, speaking of the need to submit to worldly authorities: "Let every soul be subject unto the higher powers. For there is no power but of God: the powers that be are ordained of God" (Rom. 13:1 KJV). This verse has aroused much controversy, since it says, in essence, if you are living under a horrible, cruel government, submit to it. Is it ever right to disobey the "powers that be"? The New Testament has another view, heard when the apostles were on trial for preaching the gospel: "We ought to obey God rather than men" (Acts 5:29).

46. Armageddon

The dictionary defines it as "a vast decisive conflict or confrontation." Ronald Reagan used it this way in a presidential address. The reference is to Revelation 16:14–16, which speaks of kings gathering together for the "battle of that great day of God Almighty . . . And they gathered them together to the place called in Hebrew, Armageddon." Revelation is describing some horrible conflict at the end of the world.

47. sabbatical

We use the word to refer to a leave of absence, some change from a normal work routine. The word comes from the biblical word *Sabbath*. According to Leviticus 25, every seventh year was to be a "sabbath year" or "sabbatical year," a year in which land was to lie fallow instead of being farmed.

During the sabbatical year, whatever grew on the land was for the poor to glean. The Sabbath was so important in Israel's life that the sabbatical year was a reminder that not just the people but the land itself was to "take time off" from the usual routine.

48. with God all things are possible

These often-quoted words are spoken by Jesus, who told His disciples how difficult it is for the rich to enter heaven. The disciples asked, "Who then can be saved?" Jesus replied, "With men this is impossible, but with God all things are possible" (Matt. 19:25–26).

49. Laodiceans

People who are lukewarm or indifferent in regard to religion or politics are called Laodiceans. Revelation 3:14–22 records a statement to the Christians in the city of Laodicea. The city was wealthy, and the Christians there were smug, self-satisfied people, at ease in their wealth, "lukewarm" in spiritual matters. Jesus said to the Laodiceans, "because you are lukewarm, and neither cold nor hot, I will vomit you out of My mouth." Later He said, "As many as I love, I rebuke and chasten. Therefore be zealous and repent."

50. wine bottles

For reasons no one can remember, several jumbo sizes of wine containers were named for Old Testament characters, including Jeroboam, Joram, and Methuselah.

51. the voice of the turtle

Do turtles sing? According to the Song of Solomon (in the King James Version), "The time of the singing of birds is come, and the voice of the turtle is heard in our land" (2:12). The "turtle" is the turtledove, not a singing reptile. American author John Van Druten titled one of his plays *The Voice of the Turtle* (and the movie version starred an actor named Ronald Reagan).

2

In America

52. Christopher Columbus (1451–1506)

The old rhyme goes "In 1492 Columbus sailed the ocean blue." Why did he sail, when people called him a crackpot for his idea of reaching Asia by sailing west? Curiously, Columbus embarked on his famous voyage guided by the Bible. He believed his voyage across the Atlantic fulfilled a prophecy from Isaiah (46:11) about God summoning one "from the east, the man who executes My counsel, from a far country." Columbus was wrong in one respect: He never reached Asia, even though he was convinced he had. After his third voyage to the New World, Columbus wrote *A Book of Prophecies*. In it he explained how his voyages had fulfilled many prophecies in the Bible. He was convinced that "neither logic nor mathematics aided me. Rather, the prophecy of Isaiah was completely fulfilled."

53. the Bay Psalm Book

The first book printed in America was not the Bible, since English law required that all Bibles be printed in England. But the first American book was Bible-related—it was *The Whole Book of Psalms Faithfully Translated into English Metre*. Since it was printed in the Massachusetts Bay colony, it became known as the Bay Psalm Book (certainly easier to say). Several ministers had made the translation of the Psalms into English rhyme. Stephen Day printed the book in 1640, and the book was so well liked that Day was given three hundred acres of land in Cambridge, Massachusetts, for "being the first that set upon printing."

The New England Puritans did not approve of singing any hymns except the words of the Bible, and the Bay Psalm Book qualified. Its verses were not only read but also sung, so it was America's first book *and* its first hymnal.

54. *The Day of Doom*

This long poem, based on the Bible's images of the Last Judgment, was published in 1662 by New England poet Michael Wigglesworth. It was America's first best-seller.

55. America's first Bible

Not English, but the Algonquin Indian language, was the language of America's first Bible. John Eliot, colonial pastor and "apostle to the Indians," published his Algonquin Bible in 1662. At that time, law required that all English Bibles be printed in England.

56. Pennsylvania, the Bible state

Pennsylvania probably holds the record for places with Bible names. Many of the state's early settlers were deeply religious Quakers, Amish, and German Reformed Christians who believed they were building a new "holy land" in America.

57. Samuel Sewall (1652–1730)

He was a noted statesman in colonial New England and is famous for writing America's first antislavery book, *The Selling of Joseph*. It takes its title from Genesis 37, the story of young Joseph sold as a slave by his jealous brothers.

See 75 (abolitionists).

58. *The New England Primer*

One of America's first best-sellers was this textbook used to teach the alphabet. It reflects the Puritan atmosphere of New England, as in, for example:

"A—In Adam's fall / We sinned all.

"B—Thy life to mend / This Book [with a picture of a Bible] attend."

The popular pocket-size book, published in 1727, also included the prayer "Now I Lay Me Down to Sleep," along with stories of Christians martyred for their faith.

59. American but not English

The first Bible printed in America *in a European language* was not in English but German. Christopher Sauer of Pennsylvania published in 1743 an edition of Martin Luther's German Bible. Britain's law requiring all Bibles in English to come from England did not apply to German Bibles.

60. Jonathan Edwards (1703–1758)

Edwards was the greatest theologian in colonial America, and a noted preacher in the revival movement known as the Great Awakening. Edwards wrote many volumes of theology, but is probably best known for one vivid "hellfire sermon," "Sinners in the Hands of an Angry God." He did not base his sermon on any of the Bible's references to hell, but on a short passage in Deuteronomy 32:35: "Their foot shall slide in due time: for the day of their calamity is at hand" (KJV).

61. Benjamin Franklin (1706–1790)

One of America's greats was, like many men of his age, caught up in the intellectual movement called the Enlightenment, which took a dim view of Christianity and the Bible. Like Thomas Jefferson and others among the Founding Fathers, Franklin called himself a deist, believing in God but not believing Jesus was divine. He wrote in his famous *Autobiography* that it was wise to "imitate Jesus and Socrates." Like many Enlightenment thinkers, Franklin taught that "nature" (whatever that meant) was a better guide to life than the Bible. Even so, he also wrote that "no one ever did himself harm from reading the Book."

62. the Boston Bibles

English law required that American colonists read only Bibles printed in England. Sometime around 1750 two Boston printing firms—Rogers & Fowle, and Kneeland & Green—"pirated" the King James Version by printing it in their shops and giving it a London imprint.

63. Thomas Jefferson (1743–1826)

America's third president, author of the Declaration of Independence, and noted political philosopher, Jefferson had no use for traditional Christianity. Like many educated men of his day, he was a deist, believing in a God who pretty much left man to his own affairs. Not believing in miracles, Jefferson created his own version of the Gospels, *The Life and Morals of Jesus of Nazareth*, in which he deleted all the miracles. His Jesus was a wise teacher and role model, but not a Savior or Lord. Though he was a popular president, Jefferson was frequently criticized for his religious views.

Jefferson is on the record as writing, "The studious perusal of the Sacred Volume will make better citizens, better fathers, and better husbands."

64. 1777

One year after the Declaration of Independence, the Continental Congress authorized Robert Aitken, printer to Congress, to print the first American Bible in the English language. It was the King James Version, but it omitted the traditional dedication page to the king (for obvious reasons).

65. Ethan Allen (1738–1789)

The leader of Vermont's Green Mountain Boys in colonial days, Allen was also a religious skeptic. His one book, *Reason the Only Oracle of Man,* taught that science and logic, not the Bible, were mankind's only safe guides.

66. the Liberty Bell

Millions of tourists have seen it in Philadelphia, complete with its famous crack. The famous artifact from the American Revolution is inscribed with a quotation from the book of Leviticus (25:10): "Proclaim liberty throughout all the land unto all the inhabitants thereof" (KJV).

67. "Alexander the coppersmith"

Paul, in 2 Timothy 4:14, said that "Alexander the coppersmith did me much harm." Centuries later, someone remembered this obscure character: Alexander Hamilton, America's first Secretary of the Treasury (his picture is on

the ten-dollar bill), was nicknamed "Alexander the copper-smith" for his effort to introduce the copper penny.

68. first translation by an American

The first English Bible translation by an American was done by Charles Thomson, secretary of the Continental Congress from 1775 to 1783. He found a copy of the Septuagint (the Old Testament in Greek) at a book auction and translated it and the Greek New Testament into English. It was published in 1808.

69. the American Bible Society

This nondenominational group is noted for making free or inexpensive Bibles available. It was founded in 1816 in New York, and America's first Chief Justice of the Supreme Court, John Jay, was one of its presidents. The ABS sponsored the modern translation known as the Good News Bible (or Today's English Version).

70. Noah Webster (1758–1843)

The words *Webster* and *dictionary* will forever be connected. The Connecticut schoolteacher's fame rests on his *American Dictionary of the English Language*, published in two volumes in 1828. Webster wanted to prove that America was its own country, not dependent on the traditions (or language) of England. So he published an American version of the King James Bible, calling it a "corrected" Bible, in 1833. It altered some British spellings ("colour" became "color," for example) and eliminated some of the old-fashioned wording of the King James Version. Webster realized that English had changed dramatically since the King James Version was published in 1611.

71. Parson Weems (1759–1825)

Mason Locke Weems invented the famous tale of George Washington chopping down the cherry tree. "Parson" Weems was an evangelist and Bible salesman, and around 1800 he wrote to his publisher, "This is the very season and age of the Bible. Bible dictionaries, Bible tales, Bible stories, Bibles plain or paraphrased—so wide is the crater of public appetite at this time!"

72. fonetik byebuls

The Bible is full of words and names that can be hard to pronounce. Americans are a practical people, and several Americans have tried to make Bible reading easier by publishing "phonetic" Bibles. In 1848 Andrew Comstock of "Filadelfia" published a Bible with a "purfekt alfabet." In 1855 the Longley brothers of "Sinsinati" produced a Bible with "fonetik spelin."

73. McGuffey's Readers

In 1836 William and Alexander McGuffey began publishing their "Eclectic Series" of textbooks, better known as *McGuffey's Readers*. The books sold more than 120 million copies worldwide and have recently become popular again with home schoolers. The McGuffeys were devout Christians, and the *Readers* taught morals as well as language. Lessons in the Readers included "The Bible the Best of Classics," "Respect for the Sabbath Rewarded," and many other Bible-based moral lessons.

74. John Brown (1800–1859)

American abolitionist Brown was a saint—or a crackpot, depending on your point of view. He and his followers took violent measures against supporters of slavery, hacking them up with swords and claiming it was the Lord's will. Brown was considered a religious prophet, and he quoted the Old Testament often. But his religion was one of vengeance and bloodshed, not mercy and compassion. After his failed attempt to raid the federal arsenal at Harper's Ferry, Virginia, Brown was executed, and some sympathizers compared him to Christ.

75. abolitionists

Abolitionists opposed slavery in the U.S., but, as their opponents pointed out, the Bible does *not* condemn slavery. It was an accepted part of life in Bible times, and in the New Testament Paul counseled Christian slaves to work hard and show kindness to their masters. As centuries passed, most Christian nations outlawed slavery, and many Christians led the fight to abolish slavery in America. Abolitionists pointed to Paul's words in Galatians 3:28: "There is neither Jew nor Greek . . . slave nor free . . . male nor female; for you are all one in Christ Jesus." But in another letter Paul stated, "Were you called while a slave? Do not be concerned about it; but if you can be made free, rather use it. For he who is called in the Lord while a slave is the Lord's freedman. Likewise he who is called while free is Christ's slave" (1 Cor. 7:21–22). Pro-slavery authors made some fanciful interpretations of Genesis 9:24–27, saying that Africans were the descendants of Canaan, cursed to always be slaves.

76. Beecher's Bibles

Boston preacher Henry Ward Beecher was the brother of Harriet Beecher Stowe, author of the famous antislavery novel, _Uncle Tom's Cabin_. Beecher preached love for God and man, but when it came to fighting slavery, he was willing to support violence. He and his followers shipped crates of rifles to Kansas, which had bloody conflicts between antislavery and pro-slavery forces. Beecher sneakily shipped the rifles in crates marked "Bibles," but in time people figured out what "Beecher's Bibles" really were.

77. Abraham Lincoln (1809–1865)

America's sixteenth president, who died on a Good Friday, was a devoted Bible reader but never joined a church. In a youth of near poverty, the Bible was one of the few books Lincoln owned. When he became president, its words and phrases found their way into many of his speeches.

Earlier, a broken engagement had caused him much pain, and Lincoln declared that his Bible was "the best cure for the blues." Lincoln also said that "this Great Book is the best gift God has given to man." When his wife, Mary, urged harsh measures for the defeated Confederacy, Lincoln quoted Jesus' words to her, "Judge not, lest ye be judged."

78. "a house divided"

Lincoln's famous words, speaking of the slavery issue in America, were, "A house divided against itself cannot stand." He was quoting from Luke 11:17, in which Jesus' enemies claimed Jesus could cast out demons because He was in league with the devil himself. Jesus replied, "Every kingdom divided against itself is brought to desolation; and a house divided against a house falleth" (KJV).

79. Thomas "Stonewall" Jackson (1824–1863)

The revered Confederate general was a devout Christian, a deacon and Sunday school teacher before the Civil War began. Jackson was noted for praying before battles and for his aversion to fighting on Sundays. The saintly man was also an incredibly ferocious fighter. Before one battle, he announced to his men, "The blessed God, the God of the Bible, is the God of peace, but for now we ask His blessing upon our battle."

80. Blue vs. Gray

During the Civil War, the American Bible Society, head-quartered in New York, supplied Bibles to Union *and*

Confederate soldiers. The South had its own Confederate Bible Society also.

81. the Emancipation Proclamation

President Lincoln was a devoted Bible reader. He claimed the Bible moved him to issue his Emancipation Proclamation, freeing America's slaves, in 1863. He noted especially the words of Exodus 6:5: "I [God] have also heard the groaning of the children of Israel, whom the Egyptians keep in bondage" (KJV).

82. the Great Agnostic

The Republican party has recently welcomed Christian conservatives. In the past the party was not so accepting. Robert Ingersoll (1833–1899), a Republican orator, was known as "the Great Agnostic," and one of his life's missions was to shake people's belief in the Bible and Christianity. Ingersoll wrote such books as *The Mistakes of Moses, Superstition,* and *Why I Am an Agnostic.* His views on religion didn't hurt him in the eyes of Republicans, for he gave the nominating address for the presidential candidate at the 1876 convention.

Ingersoll unintentionally was the reason the novel *Ben-Hur* (later made into a blockbuster movie) was written. Ingersoll was riding on a train with retired Civil War general Lew Wallace, and the two discussed their hostility toward Christianity and the Bible. Following their conversation, Wallace decided to study the life of Jesus and then write a book proving Christianity was false. He ended up becoming a Christian and writing the pro-Christian novel *Ben-Hur*.

See 778 (*Ben-Hur*).

83. woman as translator

The first woman to independently translate the entire Bible was Julia E. Smith of Connecticut. Her translation was published in 1876.

84. the hotel room Bible people

Say the word *Bible* and some people immediately think *Gideons*. Since 1899 the Gideons have been distributing free Bibles and New Testaments to hotels, prisons, soldiers, and schoolchildren. (Thanks to the fuss about "separation of church and state," public schools no longer allow the Gideons to distribute to children.) John Nicholson, Samuel Hill, and W. J. Knight organized the group of Christian business- and professional men, naming themselves "Gideons" after the Israelite leader Gideon, who led a small band of Israelites to victory over the Midianites (Judg. 6–8). The small jug that is the Gideon logo is based on the account in Judges 7 of the clever device Gideon used to startle the Midianites. He and his men created a ruckus by breaking empty jars, and the Midianites fled in panic.

85. the Bible on America's map

Every state in the union has numerous towns, villages, rivers, and other sites named for places in the Bible. The most popular Bible names are Bethel, Salem, Bethlehem, Athens, Abilene, Alexandria, Antioch, Bethany, Carmel, Goshen, Lebanon, Rome, Smyrna, and Zion. The largest city with a biblical name is Philadelphia, Pennsylvania.

86. Mary Baker Eddy (1821–1910)

The founder of Christian Science was a deeply religious woman, reared in traditional Christianity. Suffering from many physical ailments, she was finally cured (via hypnotism) by a blacksmith, "Doctor" Phineas Quimby. Combining "Quimbyism" with her understanding of Christianity, she gave birth to her "Divine Science of Healing." She claimed her book, *Science and Health, with a Key to the Scriptures,* was dictated to her by God. Christian Scientists accept both that book and the Bible as inspired, though the two books contradict each other in many ways.

87. D. L. Moody (1837–1899)

A former shoe salesman who was never ordained, Moody became one of America's best-known evangelists, also taking his crusades to Britain. Preaching in a simple, homey style, Moody won millions of converts, aided by his music director, Ira D. Sankey. In an era when liberals and conservatives fought over interpreting the Bible, Moody managed to steer clear of controversy. Moody was involved in charitable work, particularly in his base city, Chicago. He founded the Chicago Evangelization Society, later known as the Moody Bible Institute, which publishes *Moody Magazine.*

On one occasion Moody said, "I know the Bible is inspired because it inspires me."

88. C. I. Scofield (1843–1921)

Scofield's study Bible has been around since 1909 and is still being printed in various editions. Scofield himself was a Confederate army veteran, then a lawyer who turned to the ministry and worked with the famous D. L. Moody. He organized Bible conferences in the U.S. and abroad, but his chief claim to fame is the *Scofield Reference Bible* with its notes reflecting the position known as dispensationalism (see 722).

89. the Bible Belt

This term, usually used by those who frown on the Bible, used to refer to areas of the U.S. that took a conservative view of the Bible and believed its moral standards were still in force. The Deep South was usually thought of as the "Bible Belt." As more and more Americans relocate, "Bible Belt" now refers not to a place so much as a state of mind.

90. Benjamin B. Warfield (1851–1921)

A professor at Princeton Theological Seminary, Warfield was the nation's most noted defender of the Bible's inerrancy. Warfield defined *inerrancy* in this way: All the Bible's statements are true *if interpreted according to the sense in which their authors intended them.* In this way of looking at the Bible, the truth of Genesis 1 (the truth that its authors wanted to communicate) was not that the world was created in six twenty-four-hour days, but that God purposefully made all things for His pleasure, including man. In matters of faith and morals, the Bible's truths are "absolutely errorless, and binding the faith and obedience of men."

Conservative as he was, Warfield believed his view of the Bible could accommodate the theory of evolution. He wrote, "I do not think there is any general statement in the Bible . . . that need be opposed to evolution."

91. "the Great Commoner"

Statesman William Jennings Bryan (1860–1925) was a curious mix: a political liberal and theological conservative. Bryan was a Cabinet member and three-time presidential candidate. As a fundamentalist Christian he found himself involved in the notorious Scopes "monkey trial" in 1925. He successfully prosecuted John Scopes for teaching evolution in a Tennessee school. But Scopes's lawyer, Clarence Darrow, succeeded in making Bryan (and Christians in general) look backward and foolish. During the trial Darrow asked Bryan if he truly believed Jonah had been swallowed by a whale. Bryan replied that, no, the Bible claimed it was a "great fish," not a whale.

92. Little Jerusalem

Americans can see the Holy Land without going abroad. Ave Maria Grotto, near Cullman, Alabama, contains miniature replicas of sites in Jerusalem, Bethlehem, and

Nazareth. The Catholic monks who created the replicas used items ranging from stone to shells to beads to cold-cream jars.

93. Music City and Bible Town

Nashville, "Music City," the home of country music, used to be called "the buckle on the Bible Belt" because several large Christian publishers are located there. It is home to the enormous Southern Baptist Sunday School Board and several other religious publishers and agencies (including the one that publishes the book you are now reading).

94. H. L. Mencken (1880–1956)

The noted journalist and critic Mencken despised Christians, particularly those who took the Bible seriously. But then, Mencken despised almost everyone. He attacked Christians, Jews, blacks, the Klan, and practically everyone else. He hated middle-class Americans, whom he called the "booboisie." His columns and books were widely read, and he covered the famous 1925 evolution trial in Tennessee, which gave him a chance to write viciously about funda-mentalist Christians.

95. the huge commandments

You can't post the Ten Commandments in a public school, but you can post them on private property. On a moun-tainside at Fields of the Wood, North Carolina, are the Ten Commandments—carved in stone in letters five feet high (probably the grand example of a large-print Bible). A border around the commandments measures the length of a football field.

96. the Revised Standard Version

Sponsored by the National Council of Churches, this popular version was published in 1952. Like many earlier versions in English, it was a revision of the King James Version. It met with a lot of resistance from older readers who preferred to stick with the King James. The "nonsexist" revision, the New Revised Standard Version, was published in 1989.

97. Madalyn Murray O'Hair

In 1963 the U.S. Supreme Court ruled that laws requiring Bible reading in public schools were unconstitutional. A key agitator for this landmark decision was atheist activist Madalyn Murray O'Hair.

Her son, William Murray, became an evangelical Christian.

98. Dick Van Dyke

The popular actor-comedian published the book *Faith, Hope, and Hilarity,* based on his experiences as a Sunday school teacher. The book is a play on the apostle Paul's list of the "three greatest things" in 1 Corinthians 13—faith, hope, and charity.

99. *The Living Bible*

America's best-selling nonfiction book in 1972 and 1973 was *The Living Bible,* one of the most popular versions of the twentieth century. It is not an actual translation but a paraphrase, by Dr. Kenneth N. Taylor. Its simplicity gave it a wide appeal.

100. the Good News Bible

Also known as Today's English Version, this highly readable translation was sponsored by the American Bible Society. It has been very popular with people unfamiliar with the "churchy" language of other translations. Part of its popularity is due to the appealing pen-and-ink illustrations by a Swiss artist, Annie Vallotton.

101. *The Cotton Patch Versions*

Clarence Jordan did some interesting paraphrases of the New Testament, presented in the style of Southern black farmers, published in the 1970s. These came out in several volumes with interesting titles like *Luke and Acts: Jesus' Doings and the Happenings.*

102. Harold Lindsell

He was editor of the evangelical magazine *Christianity Today* in 1976 when he published his book *The Battle for the Bible.* Lindsell argued that evangelicals were beginning to abandon their belief in the Bible's inerrancy. His own denomination, the Southern Baptists, has indeed struggled with that issue in recent years.

103. the New International Version

This is on its way to becoming *the* Bible of American evangelicals. Published in 1978, it managed—quite amazingly—to displace the beloved King James Version as evangelicals' favorite. It is a clear and readable translation and—the translators were wise—it does retain the wording of the King James wherever it was accurate.

104. *Stone vs. Graham*

In 1980 the U.S. Supreme Court ruled that the state of Kentucky (or any other state) could not require the posting of the Ten Commandments in any public school classroom.

105. the Bible for Jewish Christians

For Jews who accept Jesus as Messiah there is a version of the New Testament: *May Your Name Be Inscribed in the Book of Life: A Messianic Jewish Version of the New Covenant Scriptures.* It was published in 1981 by the Messianic Vision.

106. the Reader's Digest Bible

It had to happen—a condensed Bible, from the people famous for condensing books. Published in 1982, the Reader's Digest Bible is based on the Revised Standard

Version. It omits the chapter and verse divisions found in all Bibles (which makes it useless for reference purposes) and has no footnotes, just the straight text. It omits duplicate material (for example, the parts of 1 and 2 Chronicles that duplicate parts of 1 and 2 Kings).

107. The New King James Version

Published in 1982, the NKJV is popular with the many people who still love and respect the great King James Version of 1611. It eliminates many of the dated words and "Englishisms" of the old version.

108. the Equal Access Law

Congress passed this law in 1984, giving public school students the right to hold religious meetings, including Bible study groups, in school buildings—*after* class hours.

109. Steve Allen

Former *Tonight Show* host and also host of the stimulating PBS *Meeting of Minds* series, Allen is a comic but also a very intelligent man. In 1990 he published *Steve Allen on the Bible, Religion, and Morality,* an alphabetical "mini-encyclopedia" that looks at key Bible teachings and people. The genial Allen is skeptical about the Bible, but his book is an interesting read.

110. the name bank

In the last three hundred years in America and Britain, the most popular Bible names for men and women have been some of the most popular names in general. For men: John, James, Thomas, Samuel, Benjamin, Joseph, and, more recently, David, Stephen, Paul, Michael, Matthew, and Mark. For women: Mary, Elizabeth, Deborah, Sarah, Rebecca, and Ruth.

111. Allan Bloom

Bloom's best-selling 1987 book, *The Closing of the American Mind*, looked at the shallowness of America's educational system. Bloom was not a Christian, but he lamented that familiarity with the Bible is no longer a part of an education: "The Bible is not the only means to furnish a mind, but without a book of similar gravity, read with the gravity of the potential believer, it will remain unfurnished."

112. Bill Moyers

The veteran journalist proved in 1996 that people still find the Bible interesting. He hosted a popular PBS series, *Genesis: A Living Conversation*, presenting roundtable discussions involving Christians and Jews of various theological persuasions.

113. Gallup polls

The respected Gallup organization has been polling America on thousands of topics for decades. In the area of religion, polls show that Americans by and large define themselves as religious people, and the majority identify themselves as Christian.

But polls also show that people (including those who consider themselves Christian) are amazingly ignorant of the Bible, unfamiliar with its most important people and teachings.

This contrast has been apparent in the polls for decades. Yes, Americans are (or claim to be) religious. No, they do not know much about the Bible.

3

People of the Book: Jews and Christians

Israel's Religion

114. ark of the covenant

The movie *Raiders of the Lost Ark* was about a modern quest for the ark of the covenant. The ark seen in the movie does fit the description found in the Bible (Ex. 25:10–22). It was a gold-covered wooden chest, carried on two poles. Its solid-gold lid had images of two winged creatures (the "cherubim") facing each other. The ark signified God's presence among the Israelites. They did not actually worship the ark (since the Ten Commandments forbid worshiping anything but God), but they did consider it sacred. The ark was the centerpiece of the tabernacle, the large tent where Moses went to meet with God.

Miracles were associated with the ark: crossing the Jordan River on dry land (Josh. 3), the crumbling of the walls of Jericho (Josh. 6), and the harm the ark did when the pagan Philistines captured it and placed it in their god Dagon's temple (1 Sam. 5). After the ark brought a plague on the Philistines, they returned it to Israel.

When King David made Jerusalem his capital, he brought the ark there. During the reign of his son Solomon, the ark's resting place was the great temple that Solomon built (1 Kings 8:3–9). Inside the ark were the stone tablets of the Ten Commandments.

What became of the ark? *Raiders of the Lost Ark* was correct in claiming that it mysteriously disappeared. Most likely it was captured when the Babylonians destroyed the temple in 586 B.C. The Apocrypha contains the legend that the prophet Jeremiah hid the ark away in a cave somewhere (2 Macc. 2:5).

Ark, by the way, simply means "chest" or "large box."

115. tabernacle / Tent of Meeting

God is everywhere, but most religions have some concept of a "holy place" where God is present. Before Israel had the temple in Jerusalem, this place was portable—a tent, known as the tabernacle (or, in some translations, the Tent of Meeting). Not long after the Israelites were led out of Egypt by Moses, God gave Moses detailed instructions on the tabernacle and the rituals connected with it. It is described in Exodus 26–27. It included an altar for sacrificing animals, a table for the "showbread" (twelve loaves of bread representing Israel's twelve tribes), and a seven-branched lamp stand, the menorah.

The most holy part of the tabernacle was off-limits to everyone except Israel's high priest. This was the Holy of Holies (see 116).

The tabernacle, large but portable, served as Israel's center of worship and sacrifice until King Solomon built the temple in Jerusalem.

116. Holy of Holies

The innermost part of the tabernacle, a section about fifteen feet square, was the Holy of Holies, or Most Holy Place. It contained only one object, the ark of the covenant (see 114), the sacred gold-covered chest that symbolized the presence of God. Only on very special ceremonial occasions would Israel's high priest enter the Holy of Holies, notably on the annual Day of Atonement, when he would sprinkle blood on the ark's lid, a symbol of sacrifice for the people's sins.

Later, Israel's rituals were transferred from the Tent of Meeting to the temple in Jerusalem, which also contained a Holy of Holies housing the ark.

117. Torah

This Hebrew word is usually translated "law," but the meaning is more like "direction" or "instruction." The Jews use the word to refer to the first five books of the Bible: Genesis, Exodus, Leviticus, Numbers, and Deuteronomy. They still consider it the most important part of their Bible. All five books of the Torah are referred to as the "books of Moses," since he is the main character.

In the New Testament period, a definite difference existed between the Jewish groups known as the Sadducees and the Pharisees. The Sadducees believed that only the five books of the Torah were sacred. The Pharisees accepted the Torah as sacred, but also accepted the Prophets (the historical books beginning with Joshua, plus the prophetic books from Isaiah to Malachi), and the Writings (the other books of the Old Testament, including Psalms, Proverbs, and Job).

118. circumcision

It's a common and simple surgical procedure today, done for reasons of hygiene. In Bible times it was more: a visible sign to the people of Israel that they were God's chosen people. The Bible traces the practice to Abraham, the ancestor of the Hebrews/Jews. According to Genesis 17, God commanded Abraham that every male child be circumcised when eight days old—a practice Jews still observe. Many nations besides Israel practiced circumcision, but only Israel gave it a spiritual significance. The warlike Philistines, a constant thorn in Israel's side, were notorious for not practicing circumcision, and the Old Testament refers to them as "the uncircumcised."

Later in the Old Testament, the prophets warned the people of Israel that outward signs of religion were not enough: A person's heart had to be right with God and with others. More than one of the prophets spoke of the necessity of being circumcised "inside"—not just the physical operation, but the more important change of the heart turning to God. The prophet Jeremiah told the people to "circumcise your hearts."

A change occurred with Christianity. All the first Christians were Jews, as was Jesus, but the faith began to spread to non-Jews, many of whom were not circumcised. A question arose among the Christians: Must males be circumcised in order to be Christians? There was a danger of a split in the Christianity community, but a council in Jerusalem (see Acts 15) decided that, no, circumcision was not a requirement for Christians. The apostle Paul took a great interest in this discussion, since he was spreading the faith to non-Jews. Writing to Christians in Rome, he said that "circumcision is that of the heart, in the Spirit" (Rom. 2:29). This was a crucial decision: It meant that Christianity was a religion in its own right, not just a kind of "wing" of the Jewish religion.

Muslims (who, like the Jews, consider themselves "children of Abraham") also practice circumcision.

See 429 (council of Jerusalem).

119. a Jewish Old Testament?

Contemporary Jews don't call the Old Testament by that name. Since they don't acknowledge any "newer" testament, they speak of "the Hebrew Bible" or "the Scripture" when referring to those books that Christians call the Old Testament. Jews do not accept the New Testament as inspired or holy.

120. Aaron's breastplate

The high priest Aaron and his successors wore an ornate item called a breastplate ("breastpiece" in some translations). Worn on the chest, it was a square of fine fabric, attached to the priest's clothes with gold chains. Mounted in the breastplate were twelve gems, each representing one of the tribes of Israel and engraved with its name. Thus when the priest entered the Holy of Holies, he would bear the names of the Israelites over his heart. The piece is described in Exodus 28:15–30.

121. usury

Lending money at interest is something we take for granted. But the Old Testament Law prohibited it (Ex. 22:25). However, there was an exception: They could charge a foreigner interest, but not a brother Israelite (Deut. 23:20). In the Middle Ages, laws prohibited Christians from charging interest to other Christians—which is why Jews could serve as moneylenders to Christians (but not to other Jews).

122. Urim and Thummim

Were they a sort of "holy dice"? The Old Testament refers several times to Urim and Thummim as objects Israel's high priest used in determining God's will, but the objects are never actually described. We can assume they functioned in a kind of "heads or tails" manner. (See Ex. 28:30; Lev. 8:8; Ezra 2:63.)

123. ram's horn / shofar

The horn used in Israel was literally a ram's horn, and its sound played a role in the downfall of the city of Jericho (Josh. 6:4) and in temple worship (1 Chron. 15:28; Ps. 81:3). Jews today use the ram's horn, or *shofar,* on certain holy days such as Yom Kippur.

124. kosher

The dietary restrictions still followed by many Jews today are found in Leviticus 11. The laws distinguish between "clean" and "unclean" animals, with "unclean" being prohibited eating. Pork is forbidden, as are shellfish and rabbit. Some of the "unclean" creatures are ones the majority of people would avoid anyway: most insects, vultures, ravens, gulls, owls, storks, bats, rats, weasels, lizards, etc. The prohibitions only affect animals. Any kind of fruit or vegetable is "clean."

Leviticus, Exodus, and Deuteronomy contain rules about how to properly slaughter and prepare meat. Also, there are rigid restrictions against mixing meat and dairy products (which is why some Jewish households have two separate sets of dishes and utensils).

Even though Jesus and His first followers were Jews, the dietary laws were abandoned by Christians. Mark 7 records Jesus' confrontation with the Pharisees, who criticized Him for not being fastidious about the Jewish food laws. Jesus told the people that nothing outside a man can make him "unclean" by going into him. Rather, it is what comes out of a man that makes him "unclean." In saying this, Jesus declared all foods "clean." Acts 10 relates the apostle Peter's vision of a huge cloth holding clean and unclean animals, with God telling Peter, "What God has cleansed you must not call common" (v. 15). As more Gentiles became Christians, the apostles decided that the only dietary restriction on Christians was to avoid meat offered to idols.

The Hebrew word *kosher* means "proper."

125. Tanach

This is the word contemporary Jews use to refer to their Bible, the books that Christians call the Old Testament.

126. altars

In Bible times, all religions used altars, places where animals or other items were sacrificed. The first one mentioned in the Bible was erected by Noah after leaving the ark (Gen. 8:20). God gave Moses specific instructions on constructing the altar used in the tabernacle (Ex. 27). It was made of wood but overlaid with bronze, and at each corner was a "horn," a sort of pointed projection. Like the ark of the covenant, the altar was portable, carried about on poles. Later, when Solomon built Israel's temple, a larger altar was installed. Because some of the kings "polluted" the altar by sacrificing to pagan gods on it, it had to be ritually "cleansed" at times (2 Chron. 29:12–18).

Besides the altar for burnt offerings, there was a smaller altar for burning incense, placed near the Holy of Holies and made of gold (see 127 [incense]).

Altars are not mentioned as part of Christian worship in the New Testament. Jesus is presented as the final sacrifice for sin (Heb. 10:12), so there is no need for animal sacrifice. As time passed, however, the table used for the bread and wine of Communion came to be referred to as an altar. Catholics and others refer to "altar" while some churches prefer to use "table."

127. incense

In a world a lot less sanitized than ours, anything fragrant was highly valued. Small wonder that most world religions, including ancient Israel's, used incense in worship. Israel's law had guidelines for making the special incense used in worship (Ex. 30:34–38). Israel's high priest burned incense daily in the tabernacle. It was burned on an altar of pure gold.

Incense is not mentioned much in the New Testament, although one of the gifts of the magi to the baby Jesus was a form of incense (Matt. 2:11). The book of Revelation speaks of incense in heaven, using it as a symbol: The elders in heaven hold "golden bowls full of incense, which are the prayers of the saints" (5:8). Since the smoke of incense drifts heavenward, it is easy to see how it symbolizes prayer. Some churches still use incense in worship.

128. Pentateuch

This is the same as the Torah (see 117), the first five books of the Bible. The Greek word *Pentateuch* means "five tools." Sometimes Jews use the word *Torah* to refer to their whole body of belief. But Pentateuch refers only to the first five books, traditionally called the "books of Moses" because he is the chief character and, probably, one of the main authors.

129. holocaust

Long before the word referred to the Nazis' extermination of Jews, it meant a burnt offering, a ritual sacrifice in which the whole animal is burned on the altar (Lev. 1). In other offerings, only portions of the animal were consumed by fire. The Greek word *holokaustos* means "burnt whole."

130. the Five Rolls

Five Old Testament books are the *Megilloth,* or "rolls," each one read aloud at a major Jewish festival. Ruth is read at the Feast of Weeks, the Song of Solomon at Passover, Esther at Purim, Ecclesiastes at the Feast of Tabernacles, and Lamentations at the ninth of Ab (commemorating the destruction of the temple).

131. prayer-locks

Hasidic Jews, the most conservative Jews today, are noted for their "prayer-locks," the unclipped locks of hair in front of each ear. The practice is based on Leviticus 19:27: "You shall not shave around the sides of your head, nor shall you disfigure the edges of your beard."

132. synagogue

In the New Testament period, as today, a synagogue was a place of worship for Jews. Before the Babylonian capture of Jerusalem in 586 B.C., the center of worship was the temple built by Solomon. With the temple destroyed and the Jews scattered through Babylon and elsewhere, the Jews developed synagogues as places to meet and study their holy books. By the time of Jesus, Jews lived in cities and towns throughout the Roman Empire, and wherever there were Jews, they formed synagogues. The Jewish group known as the Pharisees were often the leaders of synagogues, since they took a great interest in studying the Scriptures and trying to lead a godly life. In Jesus' day the Jerusalem temple had been rebuilt, and the old system of priests and animal sacrifices was still in operation. But for most Jews, particularly those who lived away from Jerusalem, the synagogue was the center of their spiritual life.

Jesus was brought up in the synagogue of His hometown of Nazareth (Luke 4:16), and as He traveled about teaching and healing, He made the local synagogues His stopping points. Later His apostles did the same. Paul, who traveled widely in spreading the gospel, always tried to connect with his fellow Jews at the obvious place, synagogues. As Christianity spread, many Jews opposed it, and not all synagogues gave a warm welcome to Christian Jews.

133. rabbi

The word means "my teacher," and in the New Testament era it was a title of respect to teachers of the Jewish law.

Several people used it when addressing Jesus—most memorably Judas Iscariot at the time of betrayal: Judas said, "'Greetings, Rabbi!' and kissed Him" (Matt. 26:49). Jesus criticized the Pharisees for putting on religious airs; they loved to be greeted in the marketplaces and to have men call them "Rabbi." "But you, do not be called 'Rabbi'; for One is your Teacher, the Christ, and you are all brethren" (Matt. 23:8).

THE CHURCH

134. Hallelujah

This familiar Hebrew word of praise means, "praise the LORD." It occurs many times in the Psalms (usually as "praise the LORD" instead of "hallelujah"), and it made its way into Greek (which has no letter *H*) as *Alleluia*. It does not appear in the New Testament until Revelation, notably in 19:6: "Alleluia! For the Lord God Omnipotent reigns!" Handel set it to beautiful music as the "Hallelujah Chorus" in his *Messiah*.

135. Amen

"So be it!" or "Yes, indeed!" or "Truly!" are fair translations of this Hebrew word used in both Old and New Testaments. Indicating agreement and affirmation, it often concludes prayers and was and is widely used in worship. Jesus used it when teaching, and it is often translated as "Truly," as in "Truly, truly, I say to you . . ." Some later translations read "I tell you the truth," but either way they're translating "Amen." Revelation 3:14 calls Christ "the Amen, the Faithful and True Witness." And Revelation (and thus the whole Bible) ends in this way: "The grace of our Lord Jesus Christ be with you all. Amen" (22:21).

136. baptism

John the Baptist, Jesus' relative, baptized both Jews and Gentiles as a sign of repentance and washing away of sins. People who came to John for baptism (by immersion in the river) were indicating a new direction in life, a conversion. Jesus Himself was baptized by John (see 392 [Jesus' baptism]). John had told his followers, "I indeed baptize you with water unto repentance, but He who is coming after me . . . will baptize you with the Holy Spirit and fire" (Matt. 3:11). Jesus baptized no one, although His disciples did (John 4:1–2). Before He ascended into heaven, the risen Jesus told His followers, "Go therefore and make disciples of all the nations, baptizing them in the name of the Father and of the Son and of the Holy Spirit" (Matt. 28:19). Acts and the Epistles show that baptism was an essential part of publicly acknowledging oneself as Christian. Paul refers to it many times. For him it was a symbol of dying as Christ died (the immersion under water) and rising up again. Baptism was a symbol of washing away one's sins and of identifying with the dead and risen Christ.

The Bible does not mention baptizing infants—unless some infants are included in the jailer's family of Acts 16:33: "He and all his family were baptized."

All baptisms in the Bible were done by immersion. There is no mention of "sprinkling" or other methods used in churches today.

See 700 (baptism in the Holy Spirit).

137. Hosanna

In Hebrew it means "save now," so it is a short prayer. But when the crowds yelled it as Jesus made His way to Jerusalem (Matt. 21:9; John 12:13), the meaning was more of praise. The Gospels state that the people said, "Hosanna to the Son of David" and "Hosanna in the highest," indicating that they believed they were calling to a great man, perhaps Israel's long-awaited Messiah. The word is still used in worship services.

138. holy, holy, holy

A much-loved Christian hymn has this title, and the Catholic mass uses it. In the Bible it is found in Isaiah's vision in the temple, where he sees seraphs (angels) calling to one another: "Holy, holy, holy is the LORD of hosts; the whole earth is full of His glory!" (Isa. 6:3). A similar vision is found in Revelation 4:8: "Holy, holy, holy, Lord God Almighty, who was and is and is to come!"

139. Nunc Dimittis

This is the Latin name given to the prayer of Simeon, who encounters Mary, Joseph, and the baby Jesus in the temple and recognizes that the child is the Messiah he has waited for all his life. Luke 2:29–32 says, "Lord, now You are letting Your servant depart in peace, according to Your word; for my eyes have seen Your salvation." It has been widely used in church services and has been set to music.

See 620 (presentation of the Lord).

140. the Magnificat

Luke 1 records the visit of the Virgin Mary to her elderly relative Elizabeth, who will soon give birth to John the Baptist (see 616 [the Visitation]). Mary, who will give birth to Jesus, utters a poem of praise to God, often known by its first word in Latin, *Magnificat*. The poem praises God for smiling upon humble people like herself. The Magnificat has been widely used in worship, and has been set to music many times, notably by Johann Sebastian Bach.

141. stations of the cross

Many Catholic churches have, around their walls, fourteen "stations" (sometimes with pictures or carvings) representing Jesus' sorrows from His sentence of death to His being put in the tomb. Based on the four Gospels, the stations are: (1) He is condemned to death by Pilate. (2) He is made to bear His cross. (3) He falls the first time. (4) He meets His sorrowing mother. (5) Simon of Cyrene is forced to carry the cross. (6) A woman (traditionally named Veronica) wipes Jesus' face. (7) He falls a second time. (8) Jesus speaks to the women of Jerusalem. (9) He falls a third time. (10) He is stripped of His garments. (11) He is nailed to the cross. (12) He dies. (13) He is taken from the cross.

(14) He is laid in the tomb. Some of the incidents, like number 6, are based on old traditions, not on the Gospels.

Christian pilgrims to the Holy Land actually walked the "way of the cross" in and near Jerusalem. Churches began setting up the fourteen "stations" so that those who could not actually visit Jerusalem could reenact the pilgrimage as a devotional exercise.

142. reading aloud

In Bible times almost all reading was done aloud. Acts 8:30 refers to the evangelist Philip approaching the Ethiopian eunuch. As he approached he heard the man reading the words of Isaiah the prophet, apparently reading aloud to no one but himself. People in the ancient world assumed that the written word had to be "brought to life" by speech. There was a "community" feeling about written words; books and scrolls were expensive and rare, so the idea of reading silently was an oddity.

143. positions for prayer

Kneeling is the usual position for prayer, along with bowing the head. Is this the "Bible-approved" position? Yes and no. Some people did pray while kneeling. But some people prayed while standing (Jer. 18:20); sitting (2 Sam. 7:18); even lying facedown (Matt. 26:39). Some people prayed with hands lifted up, which is now becoming common again (1 Kings 8:22; 1 Tim. 2:8). People prayed silently (1 Sam. 1:13) and out loud (Ezek. 11:13). They prayed alone (Matt. 6:6) and in groups (Acts 4:31). They prayed in an open field (Gen. 24:11–12); in the temple (2 Kings 19:14); at a riverside (Acts 16:13); on a seashore (Acts 21:5); in bed (Ps. 63:6); and on a battlefield (1 Sam. 7:5).

Only one verse in the Bible hints that people bowed their heads while they prayed: King Hezekiah and his officials "bowed their heads and worshiped" (2 Chron. 29:30). Even in this verse, we aren't sure that bowing the head was actually connected with praying.

What about closing the eyes while praying? The Bible never mentions it. It doesn't mention placing the hands together, either.

144. silent prayer

Praying silently is a standard procedure today. But in Bible times, most people prayed aloud, even when they were alone. Hannah, who gave birth to the great leader Samuel, was accused of being drunk by the priest Eli when he saw her praying silently: Hannah was praying in her heart, and her lips were moving but her voice was not heard. Eli thought she was drunk and scolded her. Hannah replied that she was not drunk but merely pouring out her soul to the Lord (1 Sam. 1:9–15).

145. grace

For many people, the only memory they have of praying is the memory of someone saying the grace or blessing before a meal.

Is this practice in the Bible? Indeed it is. The person most noted for practicing it was Jesus Himself. Several places in the Gospels mention Him giving thanks before eating. The Gospels mention that He "looked up to heaven" when He gave thanks.

146. footwashing

Some churches follow the custom of members washing each other's feet. This is based on John's gospel, chapter 13, in which Jesus washes His disciples' feet and tells them they should continue the practice. Footwashing was a gesture of hospitality in that era of sandals, mud, and dust. It was normally done by a servant, so Jesus used it as a symbol of His followers serving one another.

147. laying on of hands

Laying both hands on another person (usually on their head) had serious meanings in Bible times. It could symbolize a parent bestowing an inheritance (Gen. 48:14–20) or an act of blessing (Matt. 19:13). Jesus and the apostles often laid hands on a person asking to be healed (Mark 5:23). But laying on of hands is most often associated with conferring the gifts and rights of an office—priests, deacons, pastors, missionaries. The ones laying on the hands are respected authority figures who symbolically pass on power and authority to the other person (Acts 6:6; 13:3). The apostles would sometimes lay hands on a person who would then receive the Holy Spirit (Acts 8:17; 19:6).

Laying on of hands is still practiced in churches, used in ordaining pastors and deacons and in confirmation services.

148. gifts of the Spirit

According to the New Testament, all true believers "have the Holy Spirit," meaning that God is actively working in their lives. In 1 Corinthians 12, the apostle Paul lists various "gifts of the Spirit," or "spiritual gifts." These include: wisdom, knowledge, faith, healings, miracles, prophecy, distinguishing between spirits, speaking in tongues, interpretation of tongues. "One and the same Spirit works all these things [gifts], distributing to each one individually as He wills" (12:11). Paul emphasizes that all Christians are members of one body and all should not expect to have the same gifts. He also stresses, in 1 Corinthians 13, that self-giving love is more important than the more demonstrative gifts.

Pentecostal and charismatic Christians place emphasis on spiritual gifts. See 327 (Pentecostals) and 328 (charismatics).

149. speaking in tongues / glossolalia

Speaking in tongues appears in the New Testament in two forms: speaking in languages one does not know, and speaking in a kind of "spirit language" when under the influence of the Holy Spirit. At Pentecost, Jesus' apostles were filled with the Spirit and began to "speak with other tongues" and could be understood by people from other nations (Acts 2:1–12). But more often the New Testament refers to the second meaning of "speaking in tongues," an "unknown tongue" as a way of prophesying and praising God. Acts mentions this several times (Acts 10:46; 19:6), and Paul stated he had spoken in tongues many times. In 1 Corinthians 12 we learn that the Christians at Corinth placed a high value on speaking in tongues. Paul told the Corinthians that this was fine, but that it was only one of many gifts from the Holy Spirit, and not everyone should expect the same gifts.

Pentecostals and charismatic Christians place a high value on gifts of the Spirit, including speaking in tongues. See 327 (Pentecostals) and 328 (charismatics).

For more on gifts of the Spirit, see 148.

150. cross and crucifix

These are the same, except that a crucifix also has an image of the crucified Jesus on it. The cross is mentioned many times in the New Testament, but there is no suggestion that Christians used it as a visual symbol then.

151. revivals

Revivalism is similar to evangelism, except that evangelism focuses on nonbelievers while revivals focus on Christians whose faith needs renewing. The New Testament shows Christianity as a new faith, so it says more about evangelism than revivals. Acts 3:19 refers to "times of refreshing" that come from the Lord, and many preachers have looked upon revivals as "times of refreshing" to revitalize faith.

The Old Testament had its own revivals, as worship and morals were reformed under kings like Hezekiah and Josiah. After the return from exile in Babylon, the scribe Ezra led the Jews in a rededication to their faith.

152. "this is the day the Lord has made"

Many churches begin their Sunday worship with the pastor speaking these words. They are from Psalm 118:24, and the full verse reads: "This is the day the LORD has made; we will rejoice and be glad in it."

153. "the Word of the Lord"

Liturgical denominations such as Catholics and Episcopalians feature Bible readings in each worship service. When the passage is read, the reader concludes by saying, "The Word of the Lord," and the congregation responds, "Thanks be to God."

154. "I know that my Redeemer liveth"

This passage from Job 19:25–26 has been used at countless Christian funeral services. The verse (in the King James Version) reads, "I know that my redeemer liveth, and that he shall stand at the latter day upon the earth: and though after my skin worms destroy this body, yet in my flesh shall I see God." Handel set the verse to beautiful music in his *Messiah*.

155. "lifting up the hands"

Charismatic churches often "lift up hands to the Lord" in their worship services. They base this practice on Psalm 134:2: "Lift up your hands in the sanctuary, and bless the LORD." Also, in the New Testament, Paul states, "I desire therefore that the men pray everywhere, lifting up holy hands" (1 Tim. 2:8).

156. bishops

It comes from the Greek word *episkopos,* which translated literally is "overseer." (It is the root of the word *episcopal.*) Most older Bibles translate the word as "bishop" but newer translations use "overseer." In the course of time, the English word *bishop* came to mean a clergyman who is head over several local pastors. The meaning in the New Testament is more like a local pastor, one who "oversees" the local Christian community, so *overseer* is probably more accurate. Paul, in 1 Timothy and Titus, lists the necessary moral qualifications for overseers.

157. elders

Literally, it means "old ones." In cultures that valued age and experience, elders were honored. The Gospels and Acts mention "the elders of the people" many times, referring to the Jewish religious establishment (which rejected Jesus, showing that age does not necessarily bring wisdom).

As Christianity spread, elders became a feature of the congregations. Acts refers to "the apostles and elders" many times as an authoritative body. Paul and Barnabas, in their missionary travels, appointed elders in each church (Acts 14:23). In 1 Timothy 5 and Titus 1, Paul laid out the moral qualifications for elders.

Elder is a translation of the Greek word *presbuteros,* the root of our *presbyterian.*

158. deacons

Many Christian churches today choose members to serve as deacons. The word in the New Testament refers to "helpers," church officials who are not pastors but who look after other church matters. In 1 Timothy 3, the apostle Paul describes the sort of men who could be deacons, focusing on their moral habits. But the concept of Christian deacons goes back to Acts 6, which shows the Christians choosing seven men to lead in the charitable distribution of food, leaving the apostles free to preach and teach. Their job was important, because the Christians presented the men "before the apostles; and when they had prayed, they laid hands on them" (v. 6). The "laying on of hands" signified spiritual importance. One of the seven was the famous Stephen, who was stoned to death, becoming the first Christian martyr.

The word *deacon* comes from the Greek word *diakonos*, meaning "servant."

159. the fish symbol, ICHTHUS

The familiar "fish" logo seen on a lot of car bumpers is a symbol for Christianity, but even people who know that may wonder what the connection is. The Greek word for "fish" is *ICHTHUS*, with the letters representing *Iesous CHristos THeou Uios Soter*—"Jesus Christ, God's Son, Savior." The symbol is very old and was used widely by Christians as a signal to one another during times of persecution. Archaeologists have found the symbol in ancient tombs, seals, rings, and urns.

160. lectionary

Catholics, Episcopalians, and some other denominations use a lectionary, a list or table of designated Bible passages for each worship service. The practice is very old, going back to Jewish synagogues. Bible passages are chosen to tie in with holy days such as Easter, Christmas, and Pentecost. The theory behind lectionaries is that they require that a church have a public reading of key passages from the Old and New Testaments.

161. *agape* feast

This was a "love feast," a meal in conjunction with the Lord's Supper, held to express the brotherly bond of love (*agape*) among Christians. The New Testament mentions such feasts in 1 Corinthians 11 and Jude 12. This early form of "church supper" was expected to have a dignified feel to it, and Paul criticized the Corinthians for their crudeness at the meals.

As time passed and the church became more institutionalized, the meals were discontinued, though many churches continue to enjoy the warm fellowship of a church supper.

162. Benedictus

Latin for "blessed," it refers to the song of praise of Zechariah at the birth of his son, John the Baptist. It is found in Luke 1:68–79 and begins "Blessed be the Lord God of Israel; for he hath visited and redeemed his people" (KJV). The Benedictus, like the other songs of praise in

Luke's gospel, has been widely used in worship and often set to music.

163. Alpha and Omega

These are the first and last letters of the Greek alphabet. "Alpha and Omega" occur three times in the book of Revelation, each time referring to Christ: "I am the Alpha and the Omega, the Beginning and the End, the First and the Last" (22:13). Put another way, "I am the Eternal One."

164. Agnus Dei

It is Latin for "Lamb of God" (see 661) and refers to John the Baptist's words about Jesus in John 1:29, "Behold! The Lamb of God who takes away the sin of the world!" Set to music and sung, it has been part of Catholic worship for centuries. In its English form, Handel used it in his *Messiah*, setting it to beautiful, almost eerie, music.

165. missions

Christianity has been an evangelistic faith since its beginning (see 691 [evangelism]), following the example of the apostles who could not keep the gospel (meaning "good news") to themselves. The book of Acts shows the faith spreading beyond its birthplace to the Samaritans, to the Roman province of Asia (what we today call Turkey), then jumping into another continent, to Macedonia and Greece, the gospel's introduction to Europe.

Paul, the greatest missionary in the Bible, referred to himself and his coworkers as "ambassadors for Christ" (2 Cor. 5:20).

166. vestments

The Old Testament describes the special garb of Israel's high priest, but the New Testament gives no hint that Christian pastors wore any distinctive clothing. Christian leaders were respected because they appeared to be led by the Spirit, not because they wore any kind of garb or called themselves "Reverend" or "Father" (something Jesus actually condemned, Matt. 20:26; 23:8).

167. the Apostles' Creed

It isn't. The familiar creed probably dates from around A.D. 200. It is called the Apostles' Creed not because Jesus' apostles composed it, but because it is based on beliefs in the New Testament, written by the apostles.

168. descent into hell

The Apostles' Creed, a classic summary of Christian belief, states that between Jesus' burial and resurrection "He descended into hell." This puzzles many people—why would the sinless Jesus be in hell, even if it was only temporary? The problem is one of translation: The Creed, written in Greek, says Christ descended into *Hades,* the Greek word for the region of the dead, not a place of eternal punishment. (It has the same meaning as the Old Testament word *Sheol.* See 869.) Paul, in Ephesians 4:9, says that before He ascended into heaven, Christ "also first descended into the lower parts of the earth." So, "descended into hell" is more accurately translated "descended into Hades" or "descended into the realm of death." Many churches solve the difficulty by simply omitting "descended into hell" from the Creed. But "descended into the realm of death" is important, reminding us that Christ did indeed die a normal human death before God raised Him.

169. gloria in excelsis Deo

This Latin phrase means "glory to God in the highest." It was part of the angels' song to the shepherds as they announced the birth of Jesus (Luke 2:14): "Glory to God in the highest, and on earth peace, goodwill toward men!" The "Gloria" has been set to music hundreds of times, notably as the chorus of the Christmas song "Angels We Have Heard on High."

170. "the sinner's prayer"

An old tradition said that a dying person ought to utter the "sinner's prayer," "God, be merciful to me a sinner!" (Luke 18:13). It is found in Jesus' parable of the proud Pharisee and the tax collector, whose prayer reflected his awareness of his sin.

171. unction

The New Testament refers to anointing the sick with oil as part of the healing process. James speaks of this ritual in his letter: "Is anyone among you sick? Let him call for the elders of the church, and let them pray over him, anointing him with oil in the name of the Lord" (5:14). And Jesus' disciples "anointed with oil many who were sick, and healed them" (Mark 6:13). Catholics refer to the anointing of a dying person as "extreme unction."

172. tentmaker ministry

The great apostle Paul, like most Jewish men of his time, learned a trade, and even after his life's work became spreading the gospel, he continued this trade, tentmaking. His close friends Priscilla and Aquila, a married couple, engaged in the same trade (Acts 18:3). Today people use "tentmaker ministry" to refer to pastors or missionaries who earn their income in a regular job while also working (sometimes for free, or for little pay) in their ministry.

173. IHS

These three letters appear in churches all over the world, usually on pulpits. Does anyone ever explain to the church members what the letters mean? Many people think they mean "In His Spirit" or (for those who know Latin) *Iesus Hominum Salvator* ("Jesus, Savior of man") or *Iesum Habemus Socium* ("We have Jesus as our companion").

The explanation is simpler. The "H" is actually the capital form of the Greek letter *eta*, the Greek "e." "IHS" is, in Greek, the first three letters of Jesus' name. In other words, "IHS" is, simply, "Jesus."

174. fisherman's ring

Peter was a fisherman when he became a follower of Jesus. Catholic tradition says Peter was the first pope, and all popes are said to occupy "the chair of St. Peter." Each pope has a "fisherman's ring," used as a kind of official seal.

175. women as pastors

Paul, the great apostle, has received criticism for his position on women as pastors. In essence, his position was: No. This is explained in 1 Corinthians 14:34–35: "Let your women keep silent in the churches, for they are not permitted to speak; but they are to be submissive, as the law also says. . . . It is shameful for women to speak in church." In 1 Timothy 2:12 he wrote, "I do not permit a woman to teach or have authority over a man, but to be in silence." Some churches and denominations (not many) still follow this to the letter.

176. Ave Maria

It is Latin for "Hail, Mary," and is a common Catholic prayer to her. It is based on the words of the angel Gabriel in Luke 1:28: "Hail, thou that art highly favoured, the Lord is with thee" and the words of Mary's relative Elizabeth in

Luke 1:42: "Blessed art thou among women, and blessed is the fruit of thy womb" (KJV).

The Ave Maria has been set to music countless times and is extremely popular at weddings. Franz Schubert's version may be the most loved.

177. rosary

This refers to the string of beads used, but also to the method of prayer itself. Popular with Catholics, the rosary devotions involve meditating on the fifteen "mysteries" in the life of Jesus and His mother. "Praying the rosary" includes repetition of the Ave Maria ("Hail Mary," see 176 [Ave Maria]) and the Lord's Prayer.

The fifteen "mysteries" are: annunciation, visitation, nativity, presentation, finding the boy Jesus in the temple, agony in Gethsemane, scourging, crown of thorns, carrying the cross, crucifixion, resurrection, ascension, descent of the Spirit, assumption of Mary, coronation of Mary as "queen of heaven." All but the last two are events found in the New Testament, and most are covered elsewhere in this book.

178. stigmata

The apostle Paul stated in Galatians 6:17, "I bear in my body the marks of the Lord Jesus." He was probably referring to scars from the various punishments he endured for his faith. But some Christians, beginning in the Middle Ages, have exhibited marks or wounds on their hands or feet like those of the crucified Jesus. The famous Francis of Assisi supposedly exhibited *stigmata*.

4

In English

179. gospel

The original Greek New Testament refers to the story of Jesus as the *euangelos*—"good news." For hundreds of years the English translation of *euangelos* has been "gospel"—first in the Old English form of *godspel*, later as *gospel*.

180. Caedmon

This poet was an illiterate herdsman who claimed he received divine inspiration to compose Christian poetry. He entered a monastery, where his poetic retellings of Genesis, Exodus, and Daniel were written down in Anglo-Saxon (also called Old English). He produced another long poem, *Christ and Satan*. Caedmon died around 680.

181. Cynewulf

Like Caedmon, Cynewulf was a poet who composed in Anglo-Saxon (Old English). Living sometime in the ninth century, he wrote *The Fate of the Apostles, The Ascension, The Last Judgment, Christ,* and other poems based on the Bible.

182. King Alfred the Great (849–899)

The beloved English king during the Dark Ages was a Bible reader, and his list of laws (known as "the dooms" for some reason) included the Ten Commandments. King Alfred also translated some of the Psalms from Latin into his native language of Anglo-Saxon (also known as Old English).

183. John Wycliffe (d. 1384)

The first notable translator of the Bible into English was Wycliffe. Around 1380 he and some aides produced an English translation. This was before the printing press, so each Bible had to be copied by hand—a long and painstaking process. But many people were eager to read the Bible in English, and Wycliffe's version circulated in manuscript form for 150 years. Church authorities decreed that reading an English Bible was a criminal offense. People read it anyway. With copies rare and expensive, people would pay a "rental fee" to study a copy of the Bible for an hour or so. Common folk like farmers would pay for this privilege with produce. Illiterate folks would gather around while some brave soul read to them the Bible in their own language.

Wycliffe was never in his lifetime punished for doing his English translation. He was put on trial postmortem, forty years after his death. Found guilty, his body was unearthed and burned, with his ashes scattered in a river.

184. thou, thee, thine

You might think of "thou" and "ye" as "Bible language." It's true that older Bible versions like the King James use "thee" and "thou" and "ye" as well as "you." It wasn't just the language of the Bible, though—it was ordinary English then. It was the English used by Shakespeare, whose plays are filled with "thees" and "thous." Modern English is simpler: We use "you" for both singular and plural, both subject and object. This seems like a great improvement—but not necessarily.

In the older versions, the different forms of "you" had different meanings. "Thou" and "thee" were singular, "ye" and "you" were plural. "Thou" and "ye" were subjects, "thee" and "you" were objects. So the four words weren't just all saying the same thing as "you." The words preserved some of the distinctions in the original Hebrew and Greek. In the King James Version, for example, the Ten Commandments in Exodus 20 begin with "Thou shalt"— "thou" is singular, so the Commandments were addressed to each individual person, not just Israel as a whole. All modern versions have "you shall"—which could be plural or singular.

185. William Tyndale (1494–1536)

Tyndale, as he was being burned at the stake, uttered his famous last words: "Lord, open the king of England's eyes!" The king was Henry VIII, who followed the old tradition of not allowing Bibles in the people's language. (The Latin Bible, the Vulgate, was legal, but only priests and scholars read Latin.) Tyndale, a professor, was appalled not only that the people could not have the Bible in their own language, but that many ministers were ignorant of the Bible. He told one priest, "If God spare my life, ere many years pass, I will cause a boy that driveth the plow shall know more of the Scriptures than thou dost." Tyndale set out to make a translation from the Hebrew and Greek. He was opposed by the English church officials, so he did his work in Europe. In 1525 his English New Testament was published in Germany. He translated part of the Old Testament but didn't live to complete it. Agents of Henry VIII arrested him, and he was burned at the stake as a heretic. Ironically, the same king who executed him ordered, years later, that an English Bible be made available in every church in England.

Tyndale is known as the "Father of the English Bible." He was burned, and so were copies of his New Testament, but some remained in circulation and were widely read. The popular and familiar King James Version of 1611 was in many ways just a revision of Tyndale's work. Many of his words and phrases endure in English Bibles.

See 186 (Coverdale).

186. Miles Coverdale (1488–1568)

The "dales" gave us the first English Bible—William Tyndale, who died before he could translate the whole Bible, and Miles Coverdale, who completed the task. Tyndale had translated the entire New Testament and part of the Old (and was executed), and Coverdale finished the Old Testament—not translating from Hebrew, oddly enough, but from Martin Luther's German Bible. It was published in 1535, the first Bible printed entirely in English. It carried a dedication to King Henry VIII—who had ordered the execution of Tyndale.

See 185 (Tyndale).

187. King Henry VIII (1491–1547)

He is best known for having six wives, but he also had a lot to do with the English Bible. In his younger days Henry violently opposed the Protestant Reformation (which emphasized having the Bible in the people's own language), and like most Catholic kings, Henry prohibited any Bible except Latin versions. When he broke England away from the Catholic church, he continued the old ban on English versions. Poor William Tyndale labored in Europe on an English translation but Henry's agents tracked him down and had him burned at the stake. Tyndale's dying prayer was "Lord, open the king of England's eyes!"

The prayer was answered. As he grew older, Henry became slightly more open to Protestant influences, and he authorized an English version, the Great Bible, published in

1539 (see 188). The title page of the Great Bible had a picture of the king.

188. the Great Bible

Its name refers to its size—huge. It was a pulpit Bible, not an everyday household Bible, and it never became popular with the people as did the later Geneva Bible (see 189). This 1539 version, authorized by King Henry VIII, had a picture of the king on its title page, plus the inscription "This is appointed to be read in churches." Indeed, it was the first time in English history that a Bible in the people's own language was available in churches. Most people had never heard the Bible in their own tongue, and they flocked to the churches to read it (or, if they were illiterate, to hear someone read it aloud). Many adults learned to read just so they could have access to the Word of God.

See 187 (Henry VIII).

189. the Geneva Bible

This was the first English Bible that you could read—that is, the first to use the normal typeface that we have today, instead of the pretty (but hard-to-read) "Gothic" letters. It was also the first English Bible divided into verses. One other thing in its favor: It was a reasonable size, while the earlier English version called the Great Bible was so big it was used only in churches.

First printed in Geneva, Switzerland (where it got its name), in 1560, it quickly became the most popular "household" Bible, and was almost certainly the Bible used

by Shakespeare, by the Pilgrims, and by the first English settlers in Virginia. Even after the King James Version was
published in 1611, the Geneva Bible remained popular for
years

190. the Bible as decoration

When the Church of England broke away from the Catholic
church in the 1500s, churches saw a major change in decor.
Instead of stained glass and statues of saints, churches
began to paint or engrave Bible verses on church walls.
After centuries of not being allowed to read the Bible in
English, people were thrilled to see the sacred words on
their church walls. The Ten Commandments were a favorite
Bible passage. When Queen Mary, a Catholic, began to rule
in 1553, she made this illegal. After her death, it became
legal again, and even today many Church of England
churches (which include colonial Episcopal churches in the
U.S.) have the Ten Commandments on the walls.

When you visit someone's home and see a Bible verse on
a plaque or poster or stitched in needlepoint, take note:
Four hundred years ago such things were amazing novel-
ties—the Word of God in the people's own language.

191. the Bishops' Bible

Official doesn't usually mean "popular." The bishops of the
English church were not pleased that the Geneva Bible,
printed abroad, was the most popular Bible in English.
Queen Elizabeth I had several of her bishops produce a new
English Bible, which would be "authorized" (by the queen)

to be read in churches. Published in 1568, the so-called Bishops' Bible had on its title page a portrait of the queen. A curious note: The pages of its New Testament were printed on thicker paper than the Old—on the assumption (probably correct) that the New would be used more.

It had some interesting footnotes, notably this one at Psalm 45:9: "Ophir is thought to be the island in the west coast, of late found by Christopher Columbus."

The Bishops' Bible was the one found in most churches until the King James Version in 1611. But this "official" version achieved no popularity with the people, who preferred the Geneva Bible for their own use. The chief significance of the Bishops' Bible is that it was the version that the King James scholars worked from.

192. the King James Version

The year 1611 saw the publication of the most popular English Bible ever, the Authorized Version, better known as the King James Version (named for the king of England, James I). James did not like the Geneva Bible, the most popular Bible among the people, and he saw that England's "official" Bible, the Bishops' Bible, was never going to be popular. He appointed fifty-four scholars to revise the Bishops' Bible, paying attention to the Greek and Hebrew originals. The team was free to use words and phrases from other translations, including William Tyndale's. The work went on from 1607 (the year the English settled Jamestown, Virginia) until 1611. It carried a dedication "to the most high and mighty Prince James by the Grace of God." It did not become immediately popular, and the Pilgrims who sailed to America in 1620 were readers of the Geneva Bible, not the new King James Version. But in time the "KJV" became *the* Bible in English, the one that generations of Americans and English knew and loved. Its phrases have entered the language permanently, just as phrases from Shakespeare, who lived during the same time.

193. the Rheims-Douai Bible

In the 1500s, Catholics persecuted Protestants and Protestants persecuted Catholics. While Elizabeth I ruled in England, many Catholics fled to Europe, where they worked on an English Bible for Catholics (partly in the hope that England would become Catholic again some day). They followed the Catholic rule that any translation had to use the Latin Vulgate, not the original Greek and Hebrew. It was not a particularly good translation, and priests used it much more than the laity. The New Testament was published in Rheims, France, in 1582 and the Old in Douai, France, in 1609.

The motivation behind this version was that Catholics had learned that the English people liked having the Bible in their own language—but all the previous translations had been by "heretics" (Protestants, that is).

194. the Book of Common Prayer

The Church of England and all the churches that sprang from it (including the Episcopal Church in the U.S.) use the Book of Common Prayer as their worship guide. In large part it consists of Bible passages arranged for use in

Sunday worship, baptisms, weddings, burials, and other rituals. It includes all 150 Psalms and also a lectionary (see 160).

195. the Wicked Bible

In 1632 a printer in London published a Bible that omitted the word *not* from "Thou shalt not commit adultery." Purchasers had a Bible telling them "Thou shalt commit adultery." The printers were fined three hundred pounds for their blunder.

196. creation of the world in 4004 B.C.?

You can still find old editions of the Bible that state, in footnotes, that the creation of the world (found in Gen. 1) occurred in 4004 B.C. That date (which we now know to be wrong, of course) was calculated by a bishop who simply worked backward from the New Testament and used the life spans of men in the Old Testament to conclude that, yes, the world was formed in 4004 B.C. James Ussher (1581–1656) was the chief bishop of Ireland in his day and, in fact, an extremely educated and intelligent man. His dating was accepted for many years before the science of archaeology began to change our view of things.

197. the Soldier's Pocket Bible

Oliver Cromwell (1599–1658) led the antiroyalist forces in England's revolution in the 1640s, leading to the execution of King Charles I. Cromwell came to serve as Lord

Protector of England but refused to be made king. The forces he led were loosely called Puritans, though some were more religious than others. Many of Cromwell's soldiers carried the Soldier's Pocket Bible, printed in 1643. It contained excerpts (mostly Old Testament) from the Geneva Bible, always the most popular version with the Puritans.

198. *Leviathan*

Thomas Hobbes (1588–1679) was an English philosopher, well known as a religious skeptic. His masterpiece, a study of politics (but also of human nature), had a title from the Bible, *Leviathan*. The title page of the book included this Bible quote from Job 41:33, "There is no power on earth that may be compared with him." The Leviathan mentioned in Job and elsewhere in the Bible refers to a mythical sea creature of great strength. Hobbes was one of the first scholars to deny that Moses wrote the first five books of the Bible.

199. John Locke (1632–1704)

America's Founding Fathers were influenced by the Bible, but also deeply influenced by English philosopher Locke, particularly his *Second Treatise on Government*. Locke also wrote a widely read book on religion, *The Reasonableness of Christianity*. Locke considered himself an orthodox Christian, but he downplayed the supernatural elements of the Bible without denying they were true. He was a powerful influence on the Enlightenment (see 583).

200. Tate and Brady

Hard as it is to believe, for many years churches did not sing hymns—except for rhymed versions of the Old Testament Psalms. This was a limited repertoire (there are 150), but some talented people did create some good English poetry from the Psalms. In 1696 a "metrical psalter" was published in England, the work of Nahum Tate (the poet laureate) and Nicholas Brady. It was popular for many years, and almost every hymnal today contains a few of their versified Psalms. Two found in many hymnals are "As pants the heart for cooling stream" (Ps. 42) and "Through all the changing scenes of life" (Ps. 16).

201. Matthew Henry (1662–1714)

Henry was a noted Bible scholar and pastor in England, and the author of the multivolume *Exposition of the Old and New Testaments*. It has been periodically revised (and the language updated) and is still widely sold as *Matthew Henry's Commentary* in one volume. It may be the best-selling commentary of all time.

202. the Vinegar Bible

Bible misprints can be delightful. In 1716 an edition of the Bible was printed in England with the headline "The Parable of the Vinegar" over Luke 20. It should have read "The Parable of the Vineyard." Rare book collectors have paid amazing sums for copies of "the Vinegar Bible."

203. Alexander the Corrector

Poor Alexander Cruden (1701–1770) had a troubled life, in and out of insane asylums and provoking a lot of snickers because he called himself "Alexander the Corrector," guardian of the nation's morals. But, long before computers made indexes and concordances easy, the name Cruden was one that people associated with Bible concordances. Cruden issued his concordance to the King James Version in 1737, and it went through many editions, aiding generations of pastors, students, and Bible readers in general.

See 955 (concordance).

204. "Father of the Sunday School"

Robert Raikes (1735–1811) is known by this name because he worked to establish schools in which poor children would learn not only the Bible and Christian doctrine but also skills needed in emerging industries. By 1787 such schools enrolled a quarter-million students in Britain.

205. the English Revised Version

The King James Version of 1611 was so widely loved that many people could not imagine another English Bible. But languages change, and the Church of England decided it was time for another version. The New Testament of the Revised English Version was published in England and America in 1881. It sold three million copies in the first year. The *Chicago Tribune* published the entire New Testament in its May 22, 1881 issue. The Old Testament appeared in 1885. Not everyone liked having changes in the beloved King James Version. Old habits die hard.

The American edition had some interesting changes from the King James: "Jehovah" instead of "LORD" to translate *YHWH*; "Holy Spirit" instead of "Holy Ghost" (a change that has stuck); and "love" instead of "charity" to translate the Greek *agape*.

206. the New English Bible

In 1970 the churches of England took a radical step: They published an English translation of the Bible that was genuinely new, not just a revision of the beloved King James Version. The version was popular in both Britain and the U.S. Some critics objected that a modern translation still used "thee" and "thou." Some noticed a few quirks that were distinctively British—for example, in Acts the day of *Pentecost* was translated *Whitsunday*, the name the British use for the holiday of Pentecost.

207. William Barclay

A Scot, he was the author of the popular Daily Study Bible series, a devotional commentary on the entire New Testament. He published his own translation of the New Testament in 1969.

208. The Jerusalem Bible

Critics called this the "Yahweh Bible" because it broke with the long tradition of translating the Hebrew *YHWH*, the

name of God, as "the LORD." It actually uses "Yahweh"—
more correct, although some people find it jarring, particularly in familiar passages like Psalm 23, "Yahweh is my
shepherd." The translation itself is well done, and because
it was done in cooperation with Catholic scholars, it
includes the Apocrypha. It also had extensive footnotes and
study helps. First published in 1966, it was revised in 1985.

5

Angels, Devils, and False Gods

ANGELS

209. angels

Angels are now trendy, being featured in books, cards, and calendars. They appear many times in the Bible, but definitely *not* as the cute, pudgy infants that adorn Christmas cards. Our word *angel* comes from the Greek *angelos*, meaning "messenger." In the Bible, angels are messengers from God. Some angels were so humanlike that the people they visited noticed nothing unusual about them, as with the two men who visited Lot in the city of Sodom (Gen. 19). The warrior Gideon didn't realize he had been conversing with an angel until the visitor set a rock on fire by tapping it with a cane (Judg. 6).

Angels are unnamed, with two exceptions: Michael (Dan. 10; Rev. 12) and Gabriel (Luke 1). See 212 (Michael the archangel) and 213 (Gabriel the angel).

Were there *bad* angels? According to 2 Peter 2:4, some rebellious angels were cast out of heaven: "God did not spare the angels who sinned, but cast them down to hell." The fallen angels face a certain doom, described in the book of Revelation (12:9).

See 216 (Satan); 211 (cherubim).

210. Jacob's ladder

The patriarch Jacob led an exciting life. Fleeing his brother Esau (whom he had cheated out of his inheritance), Jacob spent a night in the wilds, using a stone for a pillow. He had a dream of a stairway to heaven, with angels going up and down it. (Older translations read "ladder" instead of "stairway.") Above the stairway God Himself spoke and renewed His covenant with Jacob's grandfather Abraham, promising blessing on Jacob's descendants. Jacob awoke and concluded, "Surely the LORD is in this place . . . This is none other than the house of God, and this is the gate of heaven!" (Gen. 28:16–17). Jacob named the spot Bethel (meaning "house of God") and vowed that if God would guard him on his journey, he would be God's man.

"Jacob's Ladder" is a popular campfire song, and also the name of the rope ladders used on ships.

211. cherubim

Cherubim usually refers to the cute, pudgy angels found on Christmas cards. But in the Bible they are awesome, almost frightening creatures. The prophet Ezekiel had a strange vision of the cherubim (that's plural—one cherub, two cherubim): "Their whole body, with their back, their hands, their wings, and the wheels that the four had, were full of eyes all around. . . . Each one had four faces: the first face was the face of a cherub, the second face the face of a man, the third the face of a lion, and the fourth the face of an eagle" (Ezek. 10:12, 14). Much earlier, cherubim served as sentries, brandishing flaming swords to keep Adam and Eve out once they were banished from Eden.

The most commonly seen cherubim—or, at least, figures of them—were the two on the lid of the ark of the covenant. The ark is described in detail in Exodus 25, including the two winged figures who face each other, their wings touching (portrayed accurately in the movie *Raiders of the Lost Ark*). Israel was prohibited from making images of God Himself, but apparently they thought of the space between the cherubim as the place where God was present: The phrase "LORD Almighty, enthroned between the cherubim" occurs many times. When Solomon built the Lord's temple in Jerusalem, it included several cherubim images.

See 114 (ark of the covenant).

212. Michael the archangel

There are several Michaels in the Bible, but the only important one is the archangel (meaning a sort of "ruling angel," head over other angels). The prophet Daniel mentions him more than once as a "prince," a sort of heavenly protector of Israel (Dan. 10:13, 21; 12:1). The book of Revelation pictures a conflict at the end of time, with Michael and his angels fighting against the dragon, Satan (12:7).

Michael is only one of two angels with names in the Bible, the other being Gabriel.

213. Gabriel the angel

Gabriel played a role in the story of Jesus' birth, and also the birth of His kinsman John the Baptist. Luke 1 tells of the priest Zechariah, who saw the angel in the temple. Gabriel announced that Zechariah's wife, Elizabeth, would bear a son who would "make ready a people prepared for the Lord." Zechariah, who was old, had doubts, and Gabriel, who said he "stands in the presence of God" (v. 19), punished Zechariah with muteness till the birth occurred.

Gabriel went to Mary in Nazareth and told her she was to bear a child, "the Son of the Highest" (v. 32). Mary said she was a virgin, but Gabriel told her, "The Holy Spirit will come upon you, and the power of the Highest will overshadow you; therefore, also, that Holy One who is to be born will be called the Son of God" (v. 35).

Gabriel appears in the book of Daniel as an interpreter of Daniel's mysterious visions.

214. Isaiah's vision

In Isaiah 6 the prophet records his "commissioning" by God, which occurs in a vision in which seraphs (angels) are singing praise to God. Isaiah is so awestruck that he cries out "Woe is me!" lamenting that he is an impure man living among impure people. One of the seraphs takes a live coal from the altar, touches Isaiah's mouth, and declares him purified. Then God asks, "Whom shall I send?" The prophet replies, "Here am I! Send me."

215. seraphim

Like the cherubim (see 211) the seraphim were a sort of angel. ("Seraphim" is plural—one seraph, two seraphim.) Their name means, so far as we know, "burning ones." They are mentioned in Isaiah's vision in the temple, and they made quite an impression: "Each one had six wings: with two he covered his face, with two he covered his feet, and with two he flew" (Isa. 6:2).

THE DEMONIC

216. Satan, devils, demons

The evil being known as Satan or the devil appears very rarely in the Old Testament, but several times in the New. In spite of his being pictured with horns and a pitchfork, the Bible says nothing whatever about his looks. (Since Satan is evil, artists naturally portray him as ugly.) Satan and the devils/demons who serve him are depicted as harmful to mankind, tempting us to do evil things and to reject God. The Bible's last book, Revelation, claims that Satan and his followers will be annihilated at the end of time. For the present, Satan and the devils can lead people astray— but not unless the people are willing. Comedian Flip Wilson's old line, "The devil made me do it," doesn't square with the Bible. In the Bible, Satan doesn't *make* anyone do anything. Human beings are responsible for their own sins. The devil may tempt people, but people themselves choose to do wrong.

See 209 (angels); 231 (sin).

217. Lucifer

The name does not mean "Satan" but actually means "light-bearer." It occurs only once in the Old Testament, in Isaiah 14:12–15: "How art thou fallen from heaven, O Lucifer, son of the morning! how art thou cut down to the ground, which didst weaken the nations! For thou hast said in thine heart, I will ascend into heaven, I will exalt my throne above the stars of God . . . Yet thou shalt be brought down to hell" (KJV). Generations of Bible readers believed that Lucifer was Satan, a proud angel who rebelled against God, and was cast out of heaven.

In the New Testament, Paul mentions that Satan "transforms himself into an angel of light" (2 Cor. 11:14). In speaking to Timothy of the spiritual qualifications for pastors, Paul states that he must not be "a novice, lest being puffed up with pride he fall into the same condemnation as the devil" (1 Tim. 3:6). The early Christians believed that

Satan/Lucifer had become conceited and changed from angel to devil.

218. Beelzebub

The name means "lord of the flies" and refers to a god of the Philistine people of Ekron (2 Kings 1:2). But in the New Testament the name refers to the "prince of demons," Satan. Some of Jesus' enemies attributed His miracles to the power of Beelzebub (Mark 3:22; Luke 11:15).

219. Belial

This was, as Paul used it, another name for Satan (2 Cor. 6:15). The name occurs many times in the King James Version Old Testament, which refers to wicked or worthless people as "of Belial" (Deut. 13:13; Judg. 19:22; 1 Sam. 25:25).

220. the witch of Endor

Dabbling with the occult occurred in Bible times, just as today. Israel's law prohibited such activity, and 1 Samuel 28:3 relates that Saul, Israel's first king, had expelled the mediums and occultists from the land. Ironically, before a fateful battle with the Philistines, Saul consulted a medium (called "witch" in older translations) in the village of Endor. Saul assured her she would not be punished, and at his request she called up the spirit of his dead mentor, Samuel. His spirit, not pleased, asked Saul, "Why have you disturbed me by bringing me up?" Poor Saul explained that he wanted Samuel's advice, since God appeared to have abandoned him. Samuel stated that Saul's kingdom would be handed over to David, and "tomorrow you and your sons will be with me"—that is, dead. As Samuel predicted, Saul and his sons died the following day.

Did anyone ever wonder where a "witchy" TV character got her name of "Endora"?

221. "my name is Legion"

The Gospels show Jesus as one with power to drive demons out of people. Whether these were actual exorcisms or (as some people prefer to believe) Jesus was merely working "psychology" on disturbed people, He had a reputation as a healer of troubled souls. One of the most famous exorcism stories concerns a near-naked demon-possessed man who lived among tombs and threatened passersby. According to Mark 5:5–19, "Night and day, he was in the mountains and in the tombs, crying out and cutting himself with stones." When he saw Jesus, he ran out, begging Jesus, "Son of the Most High God," not to torture him. Jesus asked the demon its name. He—they—replied, "My name is Legion; for we are many." Jesus sent the legion of demons into a nearby herd of pigs—which then drowned themselves in a lake. In a touching scene, the man begged to go with Jesus, but Jesus said, "Go home to your friends, and tell them what great things the Lord has done for you."

222. Elymas the sorcerer

On the isle of Cyprus, missionaries Paul and Barnabas found the governor to be an intelligent man, open to their teaching. But they were opposed by Elymas, a Jewish sorcerer who tried to turn the governor from Christianity. For his opposition to them, Elymas was struck temporarily with blindness, a miracle that led the governor to accept the faith (Acts 13:4–12).

223. the fortune-teller of Philippi

A certain slave girl was possessed by a demon who gave her power to predict the future. This fortune-telling ability made a lot of money for her owners. The apostle Paul drove the demon out of the girl, and her owners were so peeved that they had Paul publicly whipped and thrown into jail (Acts 16:16–24).

FALSE GODS

224. idolatry

Again and again in the Old Testament the prophets condemned idolatry. What was idolatry? Essentially it was worshiping an image—a statue or something that represented a god or goddess. The people of Israel were strictly forbidden to do this. One of the Ten Commandments makes this clear: "You shall not make for yourself a carved image—any likeness of anything that is in heaven above, or that is in the earth beneath" (Ex. 20:4). Israel's religion was based on

the worship of the one and only God, an invisible Spirit—
not an object or a force of nature. Israel was surrounded by
nations that worshiped nature gods, notably the weather-
agriculture god Baal. People concocted elaborate myths
about these humanlike gods and their sexual shenanigans.
Worship of such was often more like an orgy than a church
service.

Today most people don't literally bow down to an idol.
But aren't most people still inclined to _worship_ material
things—cars, homes, bodies (our own or someone else's),
the flashy images in advertising? It was this worship—this
chasing after false gods—that Israel's prophets condemned.
The upshot is this: We are supposed to worship the Creator
(God), not anything created. So we aren't to worship Baal
. . . or a Mercedes or the airbrushed images in pornography,
or gods with names like Wealth and Power and Popularity
and Worldly Satisfaction. The idolatry problem won't go
away.

225. Baal

The name Baal (pronounced like "bail") occurs time after
time in the Old Testament, notably because he was a rival
to Israel's God. Baal is not a name but a title, meaning
"master" or "lord." No sooner were the Israelites settled in
Canaan than they were tempted to worship the local god
Baal. The Canaanites thought of Baal as a sort of chief god,
controlling the weather and the land's fertility. They built
altars to Baal, particularly on high places, and they created
statues of him—something the Ten Commandments strictly
prohibited Israel from doing.

Baal's chief purpose was to make things fertile—land, animals, people. Worship of Baal often involved performing sexual acts at Baal's shrines, staffed with both male and female prostitutes.

Israel's prophets were appalled at Baal worship (particularly the sexual aspects of it), which is why Baal is mentioned so often in the Old Testament. At times Baal was offered human sacrifices—something that horrified the prophets (Jer. 19:5). One of the most notorious Baal worshipers was Jezebel, wife of King Ahab of Israel (see 270).

Baal's female counterpart was Ashtoreth, a fertility goddess (see 226).

226. Asherah / Ashtoreth

Israel had only one God, and no goddesses. Most other nations had many gods and goddesses, and usually there was a sort of "mother goddess" of fertility. One name that occurs again and again in the Old Testament is Asherah (which sometimes appears as Ashtoreth). She was a widely worshiped love/fertility goddess, and the Hebrew prophets constantly preached against worshiping her. One key problem: Worshiping Ashtoreth involved "ritual prostitution," in which both men and women served as prostitutes. Archaeologists have found numerous images of the goddess, and her worship sites often featured an "Asherah pole," something the prophets saw as a symbol of forsaking Israel's true God. There were "revivals" in Israel, when the people would temporarily forsake Ashtoreth worship, but they would usually backslide. Several kings of Israel tore down the Asherah poles and other idols. The last to do so was the great reformer king, Josiah (2 Kings 23). No mention is made of Ashtoreth after Josiah's time.

See 225 (Baal).

227. Moloch / Molech

The Ammonites, a neighbor nation of Israel, worshiped the gruesome god Moloch (his name means "king"). In some worship sites an image of Moloch was heated like a furnace while slaughtered infants were placed in its arms and burned. The sacrifice was accompanied by cymbals and other noises—probably to drown out the children's screams. Most people of Israel—especially the prophets—were appalled at child sacrifice, even though it was fairly common in the ancient world. Many Israelites worshiped Moloch, something the prophets condemned. Some of the kings, even the wise Solomon, set up worship sites for Moloch. The wicked king Manasseh sacrificed his own son to Moloch (2 Kings 21:6).

The favored site for the gruesome worship was the Valley of Ben Hinnom outside Jerusalem. The horrible spot had such a reputation that, in the period between the Old and New Testaments, some Jewish writers claimed that Ben Hinnom was the gateway to hell (see 870 [Gehenna]).

228. Dagon

He was chief god of the Philistines, the coastal people who were such a menace to Israel. His name means "fish," and he was probably shown in statues as a "mer-man"—half man, half fish. The Israelite strongman Samson's last act was to tear down Dagon's temple, killing many Philistines (and himself) in the process. Later, the Philistines captured the Israelites' sacred ark of the covenant and placed it in Dagon's temple. They regretted this, because the next morning they found Dagon's statue fallen over and, the morning after, the head and hands broken off it. Wisely, they returned the ark to Israel. Following a battle with the Israelites, the Philistines cut off the head of Israel's king, Saul, and placed it in Dagon's temple.

229. Artemis / Diana

In Greek mythology the goddess Artemis (also called Diana) was a beautiful but elusive virgin goddess of the woodlands, a kind of divine tomboy. But there was another Artemis, a fertility goddess with many breasts. The book of Acts describes how the apostle Paul visited Ephesus, a center of her worship. The apostles had made many Christian converts in Ephesus, which irked a local silversmith named Demetrius. He and other craftsmen made their living from selling Artemis shrines, and he saw the Christians (who would not worship idols) as a threat to his trade. He instigated a riot, leading the pro-Artemis citizens in shouting "Great is Artemis of the Ephesians!" They kept up the chant for a solid two hours—a kind of religious pep rally (Acts 19:34 NIV).

230. Hermes and Zeus

In Greek mythology, Zeus was the chief god and the god Hermes served as his messenger to human beings and other gods. Acts 14:8–16 tells of how the apostles Paul and Barnabas visited a town where they healed a man who had been crippled from birth. Paul told the man, "Stand up straight on your feet!" and the man jumped up and began to walk. The locals then shouted, "The gods have come down to us in the likeness of men!" They assumed Barnabas was Zeus and Paul (who did most of the talking) was Hermes. The local priest of Zeus offered to sacrifice bulls to the two men. Paul and Barnabas would not accept worship, and they assured the people they were only human.

6

Sins, Crimes, and Villains

231. sin

This is an unpopular, old-fashioned–sounding word today, but it occurs so often in the Bible that you can hardly read a page without coming upon the concept of sin. We think of it as a "killjoy" word—that is, a sin is something we enjoy that God doesn't want us to enjoy—drinking, drugs, sex, maybe even dancing and card playing. But in the Bible, sin is the broad concept of doing something that offends God and that harms others and ourselves. God wants what is best for man and makes His intentions clear, but men consciously disobey Him.

The word *sin* seems dated, but the concept remains: Most people today have the general feeling that we aren't all we're supposed to be. This explains why self-help books, psychologists, diets, exercise programs, etc., are so popular. There is the feeling that *something is wrong with each of us.*

We believe we ought to improve, become better. All the world's religions have this idea: Whatever I am, I am not quite what I was meant to be. According to the people who wrote the Bible, our failure is that we don't honor and love the God who made us. As a result, we do harm to others and to ourselves. Until we "get right with God" (as the old highway signs said), we can't be the people we were meant to be.

The first few chapters of the Bible tell the story of Adam and Eve, the first human beings, who were given a beautiful place to live but who chose to disobey the one rule God imposed on them. According to the Bible, each human being repeats the mistake of Adam and Eve. (For shorthand, we call this beginning of sin "the Fall.") Each of us chooses to disobey God's orders. Sin is universal—every human being sins, even good people. The New Testament says, "All have sinned and fall short of the glory of God" (Rom. 3:23). Sin is not confined to another nation, race, class, gender, or political group. Each of us is in the same boat.

Sin is not just deeds but an attitude—worshiping ourselves instead of giving first honor to God. Sin is connected with the idea of *idolatry*—worshiping something or someone other than God. God wishes to be not only worshiped but also loved—freely, of our own will. We have the freedom not to—that is, we have the freedom to sin, to say no to God. Sin is bad, but it is a sign that God made us capable of choosing. We can choose to love God or snub Him. If we were not capable of sinning, we would be like robots, without free will.

In the Old Testament, when people knew they had offended God by disobeying Him, they had a system of sacrifices—offering an animal as a sign that they were sorry for what they'd done and wanted to make amends. In the New Testament, a new idea was introduced: Instead of repeatedly sacrificing animals to show we wanted a right relationship with God, there was a final sacrifice, Jesus, who was executed by crucifixion. Jesus was the ultimate sacrifice, who restores us to a right relationship with God. Jesus is often called *Savior* because He saves people from their sin.

The Bible is "anti-sin," but, looked at in a more positive way, it is "pro-happiness." In the Bible, we cannot find true happiness or joy in life unless we put God first. The purpose of avoiding sin is to have the most important relationship of all, peace with the Maker and Sustainer of everything. Sin is important in the Bible, but so is joy.

232. the fall of man

This phrase doesn't appear in the Bible, but the concept is present, particularly in Paul's letters. Adam, the original man, yielded to temptation and disobeyed God. His punishment was banishment from Eden and, eventually, death. By one act of disobedience, Adam brought sin into the world, and all his descendants have followed in his footsteps. Thus man "fell" from a happy existence and right relationship with God into a troubled life where he must look forward to death (see Rom. 5).

233. 666

The number is found only in Revelation 13:11–18: "I saw another beast coming up out of the earth . . . Let him who has understanding calculate the number of the beast, for it is the number of a man: His number is 666." Revelation is the most difficult book of the Bible to interpret, and people disagree violently about its visions and symbols. The "beast" refers (probably) to an evil ruler or government persecuting the faithful, but whether past or future no one knows. People have enjoyed trying to connect 666 with some famous person's name, and for centuries probably every notable person was accused by someone of being "the beast." In the Bible six usually represents incompleteness (as opposed to the "good" number, seven). So 666 may mean . . . truth to tell, no one knows. It certainly gained fame in the movie *The Omen* and its sequels.

234. Herod the Great

One of the Bible's nastiest characters is known to history as "the Great." Herod, who was only part Jewish, had made an impression as a leader on the Roman ruler Augustus, who allowed Herod to rule as king over the Jews (though he was still under the Roman thumb). Herod knew the Jews despised him, so he tried to impress them with lavish building projects. His most notable project was rebuilding the temple in Jerusalem, making it much more impressive than the original built by Solomon. (The famous Wailing Wall in Jerusalem is the only part of Herod's temple still standing.)

Herod the Great appears only briefly in the Bible, notably in connection with Jesus' birth. When Jesus was born in the town of Bethlehem, the wise men came "from the east" and asked Herod where to find "the King of the Jews." Paranoid, egotistical Herod considered himself the king of the Jews and wasn't pleased to hear that he had a rival. His aides told him the Messiah (or Christ) would be born in Bethlehem. Herod told the wise men to find the child in Bethlehem and to report back to him. They found Jesus, presented the famous gifts (gold, frankincense, and myrrh), but a dream warned them not to report to Herod. When Herod realized he had been outwitted by the magi, he was furious. He gave orders to kill all the boys in Bethlehem and its vicinity who were two years old and younger. A dream warned Joseph to flee with Mary and Jesus. Herod died not long after, in 4 B.C., and another dream told Joseph that it was safe to return home.

The name Herod appears later in the New Testament, and the authors weren't always careful to note *which* Herod they were discussing. Herod Antipas, Herod Agrippa I, and Herod Agrippa II all appear in the New Testament, sometimes only called by the name Herod.

See 272 (Salome).

235. prostitutes / harlots

Prostitution seems to be universal, and it existed in Israel and the surrounding nations. In ancient times, prostitution could be more than a money matter. Some prostitutes—both female and male—worked in the service of a fertility god or goddess. They were "ritual prostitutes," whose services were not only sexual, but intended to bring on the favor of the god or goddess. Israel's prophets constantly condemned this.

"Prostitution" also had a spiritual meaning. Israel was supposed to be the loyal "wife" of God, who was sometimes presented by the prophets as a faithful husband who resented his "wife" taking other lovers (the pagan gods and goddesses). The prophet Hosea married a prostitute, whose promiscuity was a symbol of Israel's habit of worshiping other gods. Since the worship of other deities could involve sexual acts, it is easy to see how "prostitution" or (as the King James Version puts it) "whoring" could have two meanings at once.

Several notable prostitutes appear in the Bible, the most famous being Rahab, who helped the Israelite leader Joshua capture the city of Jericho (Josh. 2).

236. Sodom and sodomy

The word comes from the immoral city of Sodom (Gen. 19). Lot, a resident of Sodom, entertained two heavenly visitors who were about to bring divine judgment on the place. The men of Sodom surrounded Lot's house and demanded that he make his male visitors available for sex. The King James Version says, "Bring them out unto us, that we may know them" (v. 5). A modern version says, more directly, "Bring them out to us so that we can have sex with them" (NIV). Lot offered the Sodomites an alternative that they refused: his virgin daughters. The lecherous men became enraged and tried to break down the door. Lot's heavenly visitors struck the men with blindness. Lot's family fled and God rained down fire and brimstone on the wicked place.

Sodomy has long been used to refer to homosexuality. The Bible condemns the practice in both the Old and New Testaments (Lev. 18:22; Deut. 23:17; Rom. 1:21–27; 1 Cor. 6:9).

237. simony

Sorcery and the occult were common in Bible days. Acts 8 tells of Simon the sorcerer, who attracted quite a following. He was baptized as a Christian and was impressed that the apostles could, by laying hands on people, give them the Holy Spirit. He offered the apostles money for this ability. Peter was outraged, and told Simon to repent of such wickedness.

Centuries later, when the church became wealthy and church officials were well paid, the word *simony* was used to describe the practice of buying a church position.

238. Naboth's vineyard

Ahab was one of Israel's most wicked kings, as illustrated in his lack of respect for private property. Naboth owned a vineyard near Ahab's palace but refused to sell it. Ahab reacted by pouting, and his evil wife, Jezebel, engineered a plot: Naboth was falsely accused of both blasphemy and treason, then stoned to death (1 Kings 21). Ahab went to look at his new possession, the vineyard, but was met by the prophet Elijah, who condemned the action and prophesied doom for Ahab and Jezebel. Ahab humbled himself—

temporarily—but eventually he and Jezebel both died horribly, as Elijah prophesied.

239. the unpardonable sin

According to Jesus' words in the Gospels, only one sin is unpardonable: "Every sin and blasphemy will be forgiven men, but the blasphemy against the Spirit will not be forgiven men" (Matt. 12:31). People puzzle over what "blasphemy against the Spirit" might mean (and many sensitive souls have asked themselves, "What if I committed the unpardonable sin without meaning to?"). The meaning, so far as we can be certain, seems to be an ongoing hardening of the heart against God—or, possibly, attributing the works of God to Satan. If this second interpretation is correct, then many people who encountered Jesus were guilty of blasphemy against the Spirit, for some of His enemies did attribute His miracles to the power of Satan.

240. the seven deadly sins

Catholic tradition naming the seven goes back to as early as A.D. 600. The Bible never actually lists the seven together, but the New Testament does name, and condemn, all seven. They are: pride, covetousness, lust, anger, gluttony, envy, and sloth.

241. Nero

He didn't fiddle while Rome burned (since fiddles hadn't been invented), but the decadent emperor did watch the fire, which he later blamed on a new religious sect called "Christians." He began Rome's first official persecution of the faithful, and tradition says that both Peter and Paul were martyred under Nero. Ironically, the reason Paul was in Rome was that after his arrest in Jerusalem, he demanded to have his trial in Rome. He used the legal formula available to a citizen of Rome: "I appeal to Caesar" (Acts 25:11). The caesar (emperor) he was appealing to was Nero.

Nero's immorality and cruelty were notorious, and people's revulsion at Rome's moral decline made them receptive to the moral standards of Christianity.

242. smoking

The Bible says nothing at all about tobacco, since the plant (native to America) was not used by any Christians until the English settled Virginia in 1607. King James I (for whom the Bible version was named) opposed smoking and wrote a book against it, but tobacco became popular anyway. While the New Testament emphasizes care for one's body (1 Cor. 6:19), there is nothing in the Bible to suggest that smoking is actually immoral or unchristian. In the past fundamentalist Christians were noted for preaching against smoking, but the antismoking campaign today is in the hands of secular liberals.

243. the Salem witch trials

"Thou shalt not suffer a witch to live" (Ex. 22:18 KJV) sounds cruel, but it is part of the Old Testament's key message of worshiping only God and avoiding the barbarity and immorality of pagan religion (which often involved human sacrifice and ritual prostitution). People who dabbled in the demonic were, as Israel's history shows, a threat to a faith centered on the true God. In contrast, the New Testament shows Christianity spreading in the Roman Empire, where all sorts of religions and magical arts had to coexist. Nothing in the New Testament would condone killing a witch or sorceress. But the devout Christians who settled Massachusetts in the 1600s were bent on preserving a pure religion, and they were willing to exile—and, in a few cases, execute—people who would not conform. The execution of twenty people for witchcraft in Salem, Massachusetts, in 1692, is a blot on Christian history.

244. heresy

We use the word to mean "wrong belief." In the New Testament the Greek word *hairesis* could refer to a philosophical school of thought. It could also refer to a splinter group, and that is how it is used in the New Testament where there was a danger of breaking up the unity of Christian belief and lifestyle. Paul told the Corinthians that the purpose of "splinter groups" was so that believers could learn to recognize right belief (1 Cor. 11:19). But the New Testament also used *hairesis* to mean false belief, as in 2 Peter 2:1: "There will be false teachers among you, who will secretly bring in destructive heresies, even denying the Lord who bought them, and bring on themselves swift destruction."

Over the centuries Christians have persecuted—sometimes even executed—heretics. The New Testament, even though it emphasizes correct belief as well as correct behavior, does not condone harming heretics. The worst punishment for false belief is exclusion from fellowship with Christians.

245. the man of sin

Paul refers to the "man of sin" (or "man of lawlessness") in 2 Thessalonians 2. He is referring to an individual who is the agent of Satan and who will oppose God in every way. Paul does not use the word *Antichrist,* but the same idea is present.

See 248 (Antichrist).

246. dancing

Dancing is universal and most religions practice some kind of "ritual dance." The Old Testament mentions dancing a few times, notably in King David's joyous dancing when the ark of the covenant was brought into Jerusalem (2 Sam. 6:14). Psalms 149 and 150 mention godly dancing: "Let them praise His name with the dance."

Dancing by Christians is not mentioned in the New Testament. We know that early Christians practiced a kind of ritual dancing, but by A.D. 300 some church leaders objected that dancing had suggestions of sensuality and lewdness, so it fell out of use in the church. Stricter Christians have often objected to Christians dancing anywhere.

247. Barabbas

The Romans who governed the Jews had a custom at Passover of releasing one prisoner chosen by the people. It happened that when Jesus was on trial there was another prisoner, a notorious revolutionary and murderer named Barabbas. The Roman governor Pilate asked the Jews whether they wanted Jesus or Barabbas released, and they called for Barabbas. Their choice led to Jesus being crucified.

While Barabbas was a real person, readers have noted the symbolism of his name. It means "son of a father"—in other words, "anybody." So by literally dying in Barabbas's place, the innocent Jesus was dying in the place of every "son of a father"—that is, in place of everyone.

248. Antichrist

The New Testament makes it clear that before the final establishment of God's kingdom, all the forces of evil must do their worst. The "man of sin" (as Paul calls him in 2 Thess. 2:3) is identified with those who deny both God and Christ. The actual word *Antichrist* is found only in John's epistles. There is not just one Antichrist, John says: "As you have heard that the Antichrist is coming, even now many antichrists have come" (1 John 2:18). It could, in fact, be anyone: "Many deceivers have gone out into the world who do not confess Jesus Christ as coming in the flesh. This is a deceiver and an antichrist" (2 John 7).

The book of Revelation, with its visions of the final showdown between God and evil, does not use the name

Antichrist, but it does speak of the Dragon, the two Beasts, and the False Prophet, all of them opposing and persecuting God's people.

Throughout history, Christians have pointed out many historical figures (including other Christians) as the Antichrist: various popes, Martin Luther, Napoleon, Hitler, Stalin, Nero, and so forth. We need to recall John's truth: There are many Antichrists.

249. "thou art the man!"

David, Israel's greatest king, had a colorful life, one of the most colorful (and saddest) incidents being his adultery with Bathsheba, the wife of one of his military men. The king (who already had several wives) saw her bathing, fell in lust, and summoned her to him. Soon after she was pregnant with David's child, to cover himself David brought her husband, Uriah, home for a furlough. But Uriah literally slept on the stoop instead of with his wife. David had Uriah sent to the thick of fighting—where he was killed.

Nathan, David's court prophet, spun the king a fable about a poor man with a pet lamb—which was selfishly taken away by a rich neighbor. David, a man of strong emotions, reacted to the tale with gusto: "The man who has done this shall surely die!" Nathan, spokesman for a righteous God, responded, "You are the man!" Nathan foretold that David's sin would result in his own wives being taken, and the child by Bathsheba would die.

The story is beautifully told in 2 Samuel 12.

250. Absalom's rebellion

He was King David's favorite son, and the most wayward. He was handsome and appealing to both men and women, and had such a mane of hair that whenever he cut it, the clippings weighed five pounds (2 Sam. 14:26). Absalom repaid his doting father by plotting to seize his throne. David and his court had to flee, for it appeared Absalom's popularity was enough to make him king.

Absalom's rebellion almost succeeded, but David still had some fine fighting men. One of them, Joab, found Absalom in a ticklish spot: He had ridden his mule under a tree and his head was caught in the branches. Joab found the would-be king dangling in midair. He threw three spears into Absalom's heart.

David's grief over his son is one of the most tearful stories in the Bible: "O my son Absalom—my son, my son Absalom—if only I had died in your place! O Absalom my son, my son!" (2 Sam. 18:33).

251. Amnon, Tamar, and incest

"Blended families" were a problem even in Bible days. David had children by his many wives, and, human nature being what it is, one of the boys fell in lust with his half sister. David's scapegrace son Amnon lusted for Tamar, a gentle virgin. A friend suggested to Amnon that he play sick and ask Tamar to comfort him. Tamar baked him some bread as he requested, but when she brought it to him, he uttered some of the most disgusting words in the Bible: "Come, lie with me, my sister" (2 Sam. 13:11). Tamar resisted, he raped her, then immediately hated her: "Arise, be gone!" Tamar went into mourning, and her full brother Absalom took her into his home and plotted vengeance on Amnon. He and some cronies got Amnon drunk, then murdered him. Absalom fled, living in exile for three years. "And King David longed to go to Absalom."

252. Rehoboam and Jeroboam

Wise, wealthy King Solomon took Israel to its political peak, but he was a notorious taxer and spender. After his death, his arrogant son Rehoboam announced that he would not lighten the tax load: In fact, he said he would add to their burden—after all, his little finger was thicker than his father's waist (1 Kings 12:10)! The kingdom split in two, with the ten northern tribes following Jeroboam, a former official of Solomon, in setting up the splinter kingdom of Israel. Rehoboam's kingdom, Judah, consisted only of the two tribes of Judah and Benjamin. Jeroboam had the larger, more prosperous chunk of land, but the Lord's temple was in Jerusalem, in Judah. To keep his people from having to travel there, Jeroboam set up worship centers with golden calf idols at Dan and Bethel.

253. hypocrites

Jesus had harsh words for people who liked to *appear* spiritual and religious. He sometimes referred to the Pharisees and scribes as hypocrites, people acting religious so they would win applause from others. Jesus saw that it was possible to be good on the outside but be unmerciful and spiteful on the inside. Jesus was in the tradition of the Hebrew prophets, who condemned people who preferred religious ritual to genuine love for God and man. The Bible makes it clear that "man looks at the outward appearance, but the LORD looks at the heart" (1 Sam. 16:7).

The word comes from the Greek *hypokrinomai*, meaning "acting a part in a play."

254. Judas Iscariot

The "kiss of death" was given to Jesus by one of His own disciples, the treacherous Judas. Since Jesus chose His twelve disciples, we can assume that Judas was, at first, a sincere follower. But the Gospels make it clear that he was, or became, a bad character, thieving from the group's common treasury, which he was in charge of (John 12:6). Judas went to the Jewish priests and offered to lead them to Jesus in a secluded spot, so they could arrest Him without fear of public reaction. The priests gave him thirty pieces of silver. After the Last Supper, while Jesus prayed in the Garden of Gethsemane, Judas led the priests' soldiers to Jesus and identified Him by kissing Him. Judas regretted his action, and he returned his "blood money" to the priests, then went and hanged himself.

In paintings of the Last Supper, Judas is usually portrayed holding a bag with his thirty pieces of silver. His name has passed into the language as meaning "traitor."

255. Cain and Abel

The first two children of Adam and Eve—and one murdered the other. Genesis 4 relates that Cain was born first. He became a farmer, while his younger brother, Abel, was a shepherd. For some reason God accepted Abel's offering of sheep but not Cain's offer of produce. Cain was so angry that he killed Abel in a field. God said that Abel's blood "cries out to Me from the ground" (v. 10). He placed a curse on Cain, making him a fugitive on the earth. Verse 16 says, "Then Cain went out from the presence of the LORD and dwelt in the land of Nod on the east of Eden." Happily for Adam and Eve, they had another son, Seth.

256. Peter's denial

During the Last Supper, Jesus' trusted disciple Peter claimed he would suffer prison or even death for his Master. But Jesus predicted that before the rooster crowed in the morning, Peter would deny three times that he even knew Jesus. That night, after Jesus' arrest, Peter followed at a distance. Warming himself by a fire, Peter encountered three people who swore they had seen him with the arrested Jesus. Peter vehemently denied knowing Jesus, and after the third time the rooster crowed. "So Peter went out and wept bitterly" (Luke 22:31–34, 54–62). All four Gospels tell this sad tale.

257. naked Noah

Noah is best known as the righteous man God preserved from the universal flood, but afterward occurred another curious incident. "Noah began to be a farmer, and he planted a vineyard. Then he drank of the wine and was drunk, and became uncovered in his tent" (Gen. 9:20–21). Ham, one of his three sons, saw his father naked and reported it to the other brothers, Shem and Japheth. These two took a cloth, walked backward toward their father and covered him, "and they did not see their father's nakedness" (v. 23). When Noah awoke from his stupor he pronounced a curse for being seen naked—not on Ham, but on Ham's son Canaan. And he blessed Shem and Japheth, and pronounced that Canaan (again, not Ham) would be their slaves. The Bible scholars still puzzle over the meaning of this story.

258. the death of Herod

Acts 12 records the persecution of Christians by the violent ruler Herod. He killed the apostle James, and had Peter imprisoned for a time. But a dire fate awaited Herod himself. Appearing in his royal robes and giving an eloquent speech before a crowd, Herod made such an impression that the people yelled, "The voice of a god and not of a man!" Perhaps Herod's ego had swelled too big: "Then immediately an angel of the Lord struck him, because he did not give glory to God. And he was eaten by worms and died" (Acts 12:23).

259. the tongue

The Bible has a lot to say about the harm done by gossiping and lying, and one of the Ten Commandments forbids bearing false witness against someone. The classic statement on the harm done by a vicious tongue is in James 3:8. James notes that man can tame every type of creature, "But no man can tame the tongue. It is an unruly evil, full of deadly poison."

260. water from the rock

Numbers 20 records a crucial mistake in Moses' saintly life. The huge throng of Israelites that Moses had led out of Egypt were camped in the wilderness, in a spot with no water. God ordered Moses to speak to a large rock, which would miraculously pour forth water. But instead of speaking to the rock, Moses struck it with his staff. It did pour out water, but God punished Moses for not following His instructions to the letter: After forty years of leading the people from Egypt to Canaan, Moses would not be allowed to enter Canaan himself.

261. Korah's rebellion

Moses was God's appointed man to bring the Israelite slaves from Egypt and lead them to Canaan. But he faced constant griping and occasional rebellion. Korah led a large group in challenging Moses' authority. The rebels were punished by an earthquake that opened a large hole in the earth that swallowed them (Num. 26).

262. the tower of Babel

According to Genesis 11, mankind had one single language. Filled with pride, some of those chose to build a tower "whose top is in the heavens" (v. 4). God took notice, went down, and "[confused] their language" (v. 7). Not being able to understand one another anymore, the builders scattered. By coincidence, "Babel" sounds a lot like "babble."

263. the Flood

Genesis 6–8 records the worldwide deluge, sent by God on account of man's wickedness. The only survivors God chose were the righteous Noah, his wife, his three sons, and their wives. He instructed Noah on building the ark, a huge wooden boat, to contain his family and pairs of all earth's animals. God shut up the group in the ark and rain fell forty days and nights, destroying all mankind except Noah's family. When Noah sent out a dove that returned with an olive branch, he knew the waters had receded enough to leave the ark. Noah (at the age of 601) and his family left the ark, and Noah built an altar to God. God promised that never again would He destroy all living creatures. God established the rainbow as a reminder of this promise.

Skeptics doubt if the entire earth was ever flooded. However, the story crops up in various forms around the world. The key lesson of the story is that God desires to preserve good people even when almost everyone is evil.

264. Jeremiah's dungeon

Saintly people often end up, ironically, in prison, and this happened often in the Bible. The prophet Jeremiah rattled the establishment by preaching against its sins, and he was in and out of prison quite often. His worst imprisonment was in a dungeon with a floor of muck, and Jeremiah "sank in the mire" (Jer. 38:6). The prophet was lowered into it with ropes. One of the king's servants persuaded the king to release Jeremiah from the dungeon, but Jeremiah was still kept in prison.

265. gambling

Many Christians oppose gambling, but in fact the Bible says nothing about the subject. The Gospels report one unpleasant gambling incident connected with Jesus: "The soldiers, when they had crucified Jesus, took His garments and made four parts, to each soldier a part, and also the tunic. Now the tunic was without seam, woven from the top in one piece. They said therefore among themselves, 'Let us not tear it, but cast lots for it, whose it shall be,' that the Scripture might be fulfilled which says: 'They divided My garments among them, and for My clothing they cast lots'" (John 19:23–24). This isn't much to build an antigambling case on.

266. the temptation of Jesus

The Gospels report that after Jesus' baptism by John the Baptist He went into the desert, where for forty days He was tempted by the devil. The three-part temptation is told in Matthew 4 and Luke 4. Jesus was hungry, and the devil suggested, "If You are the Son of God, command that these stones become bread." Jesus replied with a verse from Deuteronomy, "Man shall not live by bread alone, but by every word that proceeds from the mouth of God." In this He was resisting the temptation to be a sort of wonder-worker. The devil then took Him (in a vision, perhaps) to the highest point of the temple and said, "If You are the Son of God, throw Yourself down." The devil then quoted the Bible to the effect that angels would protect Jesus. Jesus replied that God was not to be put to the test this way. Then, from a high mountain, the devil showed Jesus "all the kingdoms of the world and their glory." "All these things I will give You if You will fall down and worship me." Jesus replied, quoting Scripture, "You shall worship the LORD your God, and Him only you shall serve."

By resisting the temptation to be a wonder-worker or a worldly king, Jesus proved He was fit to be the world's Savior. In a sense He undid the temptation of Adam and Eve, who yielded to the temptation to be godlike and powerful.

267. booze

The Bible definitely does *not* prohibit drinking alcohol. The only people who abstained were the Nazirites (see 284), and they were only a small group within Israel. Drunkenness and the dangers it brings are condemned, and Proverbs 20:1 nicely summarizes the Bible's view of drunkenness: "Wine is a mocker, strong drink is a brawler, and whoever is led astray by it is not wise." In other words, don't let drinking turn you into a fool. Proverbs 31:6 reads, "Give strong drink to him who is perishing, and wine to those who are bitter of heart"—a recognition that in the days before pain relievers and anesthetics, alcohol could serve a useful purpose. Jesus' miracle of turning water into wine suggests that He did not disapprove of drinking it (John 2).

The American temperance movement arose in the 1870s, and many Christians were at the front of that movement. In time there was a shift from temperance (which only means moderation) to teetotaling and prohibition. The result was national prohibition from 1919 to 1932—a social experiment that failed.

268. Charles Manson (b. 1934)

The leader of the murderous, drugged-out "Family" that shocked America in 1969 was influenced by the Bible . . . and also by the Beatles, Scientology, LSD, environmentalism, and a life spent mostly in prisons. Manson claimed (sometimes) that he was Christ. His followers believed that Manson/Christ was going to bring about the final world battle in which the Family would emerge to rule. Totally ignoring Jesus' words about forgiveness, mercy, and nonviolence, Manson read the New Testament book of Revelation and connected it with—strangely enough—the Beatles. Manson believed the group's *White Album* was sending him messages about how to launch the world revolution and destroy the Establishment. According to Manson, chapter 9 of Revelation connected with the song "Revolution No. 9" on the *White Album*. The four angels of Revelation 9 were the four Beatles, the "breastplates of iron" were the Beatles' electric guitars, and so on.

Manson was not the first person to get strange ideas from Revelation. The book's symbolism has fascinated and puzzled people for centuries. While the main purpose of Revelation was to bring hope to persecuted Christians, people with twisted minds have often read their own sinister meanings into it and ignored the Bible's message of mercy and love.

269. Athaliah

Judah's only female ruler was a nasty character, the daughter of the wicked Ahab and Jezebel of Israel. She married Judah's king Jehoram, and after he and their son both died, Athaliah took the throne and proceeded to exterminate the whole royal family. But one prince, Joash, was hidden away from the massacre, and six years later the priest Jehoiada plotted to put the boy on the throne. Athaliah entered the temple to see what the ruckus was: Jehoiada had brought out Joash and crowned him, and the people shouted "Long live the king!" Furious, Athaliah tore her clothes, shouting "Treason! Treason!" The murderous woman was dragged from the temple and put to death (2 Kings 11:1–16).

270. Jezebel

A "Jezebel" is, says *Webster's,* "an impudent, shameless, or abandoned woman." Jezebel was the wife of wicked King Ahab of Israel, and a dedicated worshiper of the false god Baal. She encouraged her husband in leading Israel away from God, and her chief opponent was the faithful prophet Elijah. After a showdown between Elijah and Baal's prophets (Elijah won), Jezebel vowed to kill him. Elijah wisely fled. God anointed Jehu to wipe out Ahab's Baal-worshiping clan. Knowing she was about to meet her doom, Jezebel painted her eyes, arranged her hair, and looked out a window. Jehu ordered two servants to throw her from the window. They did, and when they went to bury her, they found nothing except her skull, her feet, and her hands. She had been eaten by dogs (2 Kings 9:30–37).

271. the scarlet woman

In the book of Revelation, John has a vision of a woman sitting on a hideous beast: "The woman was arrayed in purple and scarlet, and adorned with gold and precious stones and pearls, having in her hand a golden cup full of abominations and the filthiness of her fornication." On her forehead was written "MYSTERY, BABYLON THE GREAT, THE MOTHER OF HARLOTS AND OF THE ABOMINA-TIONS OF THE EARTH. I saw the woman, drunk with the blood of the saints" (17:4–6). *Babylon* was a code word for the Roman Empire, which was persecuting believers. But Babylon also symbolized any evil power opposing God's people.

272. Salome

One of the New Testament's most unpleasant stories tells of how the great prophet John the Baptist came to be beheaded by the Jewish ruler Herod. Mark 6:14–29 relates that Herod's wife, Herodias, had earlier been married to Herod's brother, Philip. She divorced Philip and married Herod, a violation of Jewish law. John spoke against this, and Herod threw John into prison, though he hesitated to execute John because the public believed John to be God's prophet. Herodias despised John for calling her and Herod adulterers, and she found a way to bring about John's execution: The daughter by her first marriage fascinated Stepfather Herod, and one evening her dancing pleased Herod so much he offered her anything she wished. She could have had land, palaces, anything. But at her mother's urging she asked for the head of John the Baptist on a platter. Herod granted the wish, then later wondered if Jesus was John the Baptist brought back from the dead.

Herodias's daughter is not named in the Bible. The Jewish historian Josephus tells us her name was Salome. According to legend, her famous dance before Herod was the "Dance of the Seven Veils," in which (we assume) she gradually removed each veil in the manner of a striptease.

See 734 (Oscar Wilde).

273. the temptress

To show that human nature hasn't changed over the centuries, Proverbs 7 presents the sordid picture of the temptress luring the young man into sin. "'Come, let us take our fill of love until morning; let us delight ourselves with love. For my husband is not at home.' . . . With her enticing speech she caused him to yield, with her flattering lips she seduced him" (vv. 18–21).

7

People in Groups

274. the Israelites

The name Israel refers to:

1. The patriarch Jacob, who was given this name after wrestling with a heavenly messenger. The name means "struggles with God" (Gen. 32:28).
2. The nation descended from Jacob and his twelve sons (the ancestors of the "twelve tribes of Israel"). The nation could be referred to as *Israelites, all Israel,* or *children of Israel.*
3. The kingdom formed when the nation Israel divided in two after the death of King Solomon (1 Kings 11). Ten of the twelve tribes of Israel formed the "northern kingdom" of Israel. The two other tribes formed the "southern kingdom," Judah.

In the Bible, "Israel" generally refers more often to the people than to the land itself. The land of Israel in the Bible did not cover precisely the same area as the nation of Israel today.

The modern term *Israeli* refers to the people of the nation Israel. *Israeli* is not found in the Bible.

See 936 (Hebrew).

275. the twelve tribes of Israel

The patriarch Jacob, also named Israel, had twelve sons—Reuben, Simeon, Levi, Judah, Issachar, Zebulun, Gad, Asher, Dan, Naphtali, Joseph, and Benjamin. The twelve "tribes" were clans descended from the twelve sons. When Canaan was settled by the Israelites, the land was divided among the twelve tribes.

If you look at maps of Old Testament times, you won't find Joseph or Levi on the map. You'll find areas named for the other ten tribes. Why? The tribe of Levi (see 280 [Levites]) had no land of its own. It did have certain cities allotted to it. The people of Levi—the Levites—had the duty of serving as priests in the nation. (The great leader Moses was a Levite. So was his brother Aaron, Israel's first high priest.) The tribe of Joseph was divided into two "half-tribes" named for Joseph's two sons, Manasseh and Ephraim. So maps show areas named for Manasseh and Ephraim, but not for their father, Joseph. By eliminating Levi and dividing Joseph in two, we end up with twelve.

Many people believe that when Jesus chose twelve men to be His disciples He was starting a "new Israel"—one based not on blood ties, but on being followers of Christ.

He was establishing a "spiritual Israel" of people—even non-Jews—who chose to commit themselves to God.

276. Semites, Semitic

The name comes from Shem, one of Noah's three sons. Shem was the ancestor of Abraham, who became the ancestor of the Israelites. Anthropologists use "Semites" to refer to a group of ancient peoples with related languages, including the Hebrews, Canaanites, Assyrians, Babylonians, and Arabs.

277. patriarchs

To many feminists, *patriarchy* is a dirty word. They use it to refer to any society dominated by men. (The word originally meant "rule by fathers.") In the Bible, *patriarchs* refers to the ancestors of the chosen people, the nation of Israel. The most important patriarchs were Abraham, the man whom God promised the land of Canaan; Isaac (Abraham's son); and Jacob (Isaac's son, who also had the name Israel). These figures are especially important because of God's promises to them.

Abraham, whose story is told in Genesis 12 through 25, is the patriarch par excellence. Even though it was Abraham's grandson, Jacob, who lent his nickname Israel to the whole nation, Abraham is considered Israel's spiritual father. In most ways he was a more admirable and moral character than Jacob. Abraham was called by God to leave his idol-worshiping homeland of Chaldea and settle in Canaan, "the promised land." Also very important is that

Abraham endured a severe testing of his faith when God asked him to sacrifice his beloved son, Isaac. This story, one of the most dramatic and most touching in the Bible, is found in Genesis 22.

Sometimes "the patriarchs" refers not only to Abraham, Isaac, and Jacob, but also to their distant ancestors in the book of Genesis—Adam, Methuselah, Noah, etc. Also, Jacob's twelve sons—who were the ancestors of the "twelve tribes of Israel"—are referred to as patriarchs.

In brief, the patriarchs were all the important men who preceded the life of Moses.

See 632 (covenant); 274 (Israelites).

278. chosen people

This name applies in the Bible to the people of Israel, who were referred to as Israelites, Hebrews, or Jews. The key idea in the Old Testament is that God chose Israel (the descendants of Abraham) to be the recipients of His moral and spiritual guidance. The idea is expressed many times in the Bible, notably in Deuteronomy 7:6: "You are a holy people to the LORD your God; the LORD your God has chosen you to be a people for Himself, a special treasure above all the peoples on the face of the earth." (This is similar to the idea Americans have that we are a "special" nation dedicated to freedom and equality.) The Bible makes it clear that the "chosen people" are never to be arrogant or cocky because God has chosen them. In fact, because God revealed Himself and His moral law to Israel, the people of Israel will be severely punished when they break the moral law. Being "chosen" was a privilege but also an obligation.

See 632 (covenant); 274 (Israelites).

279. priests

In any religion a priest is a kind of "middleman" between the people and God (or gods). Priests of various religions are mentioned in the Bible. Aaron, Moses' brother, was Israel's first high priest, and the priestly garments are described in Exodus 28–29 and Leviticus 8. Israel's priesthood was connected with the Levites, Moses and Aaron's tribe. In the tabernacle and, later, at the temple in Jerusalem, the priests performed sacrifices and, on behalf of the people, confessed sin and thus reconciled God to His people. In the New Testament, most of the priests were religious officials with no deep spirituality, and they worked to have Jesus executed. Christians began to believe that not only was Jesus the final sacrifice for man's sin (the "Lamb of God") but also the ultimate Priest, making man right with God. The letter to the Hebrews states this theme clearly (Heb. 7–10). The old system of sacrifices and priests is no longer needed. After the Jews' temple was destroyed by the Romans in A.D. 70, the Jewish priesthood ended.

280. Levites

The "twelve tribes of Israel," the descendants of Jacob's twelve sons, divided up the land of Israel among themselves. But the Levites, descendants of Jacob's son Levi, were a special case. Instead of a large chunk of land, the

Levites received certain cities (forty-eight in all) scattered throughout Israel. More important, Levites served as the "priestly tribe," ministering in the temple as priests, aides, and musicians.

Moses and his brother Aaron, Israel's first high priest, were Levites (see 445 [Aaron]).

The Old Testament's book of Leviticus, consisting mostly of ceremonial laws, takes its name from the Levites.

281. Judges

The Hebrew title for what we call the book of Judges is *Shopetim*—not really "judges" in our modern sense, but something more like "liberators" or "military leaders." The period of the judges fell between the Israelite settlement in Canaan and the time when Israel had its first king, Saul. The book of Judges repeats a familiar story: The Israelites forget the true God and worship idols; God allows a neighboring nation to punish them; they beg for a deliverer, and God sends them a mighty man to help quell the enemy. Then the pattern repeats. A total of fifteen judges are listed. The most famous judges were Gideon (see 348 [laying out the fleece]), Samson (see 499), Jephthah (see 469), and the one female judge, Deborah (see 513). The theme of the book is this: "In those days Israel had no king: everyone did as he saw fit" (Judg. 21:25 NIV).

282. Philistines

Palestine, the old name for Israel and the surrounding area, came from a people known as the Philistines. They lived on the coastal plain by the Mediterranean and were a seafaring people, which made them very different from the land-centered Israelites. They were a thorn in Israel's side, a fierce, warlike people, and—an oddity in that region of the world—they did not practice circumcision, something the Israelites sneered at. (Saying "uncircumcised" was practically the same as saying "Philistine.") The book of Judges tells about their wars with the Israelites, who found the mighty Samson to be their best anti-Philistine weapon. Israel's first king, Saul, killed himself after the Philistines wounded him severely.

The English author Matthew Arnold used the word *Philistine* to mean a crude, uncultured person. It passed into the language with that meaning.

283. kings

The word occurs hundreds of times in the Bible, and in some parts of the Old Testament it ought to be taken with a grain of salt. While we think of a king as the ruler of a fairly large nation, many of the "kings" in the Bible (particularly in Genesis) were nothing more than petty rulers of small tribes—more like "chieftains" than "kings" in the usual sense.

284. Nazirites

The name has nothing to do with Jesus' hometown, Nazareth. Rather, they were a specially dedicated group of people who took vows not to touch wine or any grape products, not to cut their hair (either head or beard), and not to touch a dead body. Numbers 6 describes the Nazirite rules in detail. One could choose to be a Nazirite for a period of a month or a lifetime. Whatever the time frame, the vows were taken with great seriousness. Although the Nazirites took vows that made them "separate . . . to the LORD," they did not live apart from other Israelites.

Three Nazirites are significant: Samson, the strongman judge of Israel; Samuel, the judge who crowned Israel's first two kings; and John the Baptist, the only Nazirite in the New Testament. Samson's long hair played a key role in the story of his capture by the Philistines.

See 499 (Samson).

285. Midianites

They were the original "camel jockeys," skilled riders and feared raiders. These nomads occupied the area around the Sinai peninsula. It was Midianite traders who sold Joseph into slavery in Egypt (Gen. 37). When Moses fled from Egypt he lived in Midian, where he married a daughter of the Midianite priest Jethro (Ex. 2). Later, as the Israelites left Egypt and journeyed to Canaan, God commanded Moses to kill the Midianites, who were their enemies (Num. 25:16–18). The judge Gideon had to free Israel from the oppression of the Midianites (Judg. 6–8), who were "like swarms of locusts" that "did not spare a living thing." Gideon's defeat over a much larger Midianite force is well told in Judges 7.

The Midianites were noted not only for their brutality but for their wealth. Judges 8:26 mentions the Midianite kings' purple robes and—an appropriate touch—chains around their camels' necks.

286. Gentiles

The Hebrew word *goyim* was, and still is, used to refer to non-Jews. In most versions of the Bible, *goyim* is translated "Gentiles." Some versions translate it as "the nations" or "heathen," but it always means "non-Jews." In the Old Testament, it is usually a derogatory term, since non-Jews were "outside the covenant"—idol worshipers, people who did not serve the true God, Israel's God. But some of the Hebrew prophets hinted that, in the future, Gentiles would come to serve Israel's God.

This occurs in the New Testament. The first Christians were Jews, but soon the faith attracted Gentiles. Acts 15 describes the fuss made when Jewish Christians insisted that Gentiles be circumcised before they became Christians. In other words, they insisted that being a Christian meant being a Jew also. This was not the position the Christians finally adopted.

The apostle Paul, a Jew, called himself the "apostle to the Gentiles" and traveled around the Roman Empire, preaching the faith to both Jews and Gentiles—but generally being better treated by the Gentiles. The more Gentiles were drawn to Christianity, the more the Jews came to dislike the new faith. Paul insisted that Christianity was the fulfillment of the Jewish religion, and in his letters he spoke of Gentile Christians as being "the new Jews," God's chosen ones. According to Paul, Jesus broke down the old barrier between Jews and Gentiles (Rom. 10:12; Eph. 2:11–18).

Of the many people who wrote the Bible, the only one who was (probably) a Gentile was Luke, author of Acts and the Gospel that bears his name.

See 118 (circumcision).

287. Hittites

The Hittites are a sort of divine joke played on people who doubted the Bible is true. The Old Testament refers to them many times, and one of King David's best soldiers was Uriah the Hittite. But for many years archaeologists found no evidence that the Hittites existed, so skeptics claimed the Hittites were fictional, a tribe invented by the Bible's authors (which suggested that the Bible contained a lot of fictional things). But in 1906 a German archaeologist began digging up Hittite artifacts in the area we now call Turkey. There is now no doubt in anyone's mind that the Hittites really existed.

288. prophets

We think of prophets as fortune-tellers, those who predict the future, psychics. When the Bible refers to a "prophet," prediction may be part of his talents, but only a small part. In the Bible, a prophet was "God's proclaimer," a sort of "mouthpiece" for the words of God. A true prophet (and there were *false* prophets) had no message of his own and did not promote himself. He acted under the impulse of God, taking to the people a clear message from God. Often this took the form of pointing out people's sins and urging them to repentance. The prophet's message was often a prediction of disaster if people did not repent.

Prophets are found throughout the Old Testament. The last section of the Old Testament is called "the Prophets," and it includes books containing the words of some of Israel's greatest prophets—Isaiah, Jeremiah, Ezekiel, Amos, and others. Some of the passages in the prophets' books are among the most inspiring in the Old Testament. Other passages concern ancient political wranglings that have no meaning for modern readers.

The most famous prophet in Israel's history was Elijah, who wrote nothing at all. Elijah (whose story is told from 1 Kings 17 through 2 Kings 2) is a sort of holy man of the wilderness, a miracle worker who dares to confront wicked King Ahab and his equally vile wife, Jezebel. Elijah is "a man on fire for God," and he courageously opposes Ahab and the cult of the false god Baal. Elijah—and God—triumph over the false religion, but not until after Elijah's life has been threatened more than once.

Elijah became *the* symbol of the great prophets of God. The Old Testament's last book, the writings of the prophet Malachi, predicts that Elijah will one day return: "I will send you Elijah the prophet before the coming of the great and dreadful day of the LORD" (Mal 4:5).

The Jews believed that there were no more prophets after the close of the Old Testament. In Jesus' time, many devout Jews wondered if a new prophet might be sent—perhaps the return of Elijah promised in Malachi. Apparently Jesus Himself believed this had occurred: "All the prophets and the law prophesied until John. And if you are willing to receive it, he is Elijah who is to come" (Matt 11:13–14).

The John He is referring to is His relative, John the Baptist, who had baptized Jesus. John, a sort of wilderness man as Elijah had been, was considered by many to be a prophet—the renewal of the prophetic tradition in the land. Jesus shared this belief, claiming that not only was John a prophet, but John was the Elijah they had been expecting to return.

289. Jews

In the earliest parts of the Old Testament, the "chosen people" are called Israelites or Hebrews. Only in the later books—Jeremiah, Ezra, Esther, and others—does the word *Jew* come into use. The word comes from the tribe of Judah, which occupied the largest region of Israel, the region that included Jerusalem, the capital. When the northern tribes were conquered and scattered by the Assyrian Empire, Judah stood out as the most important tribe. *Jew* in the original sense meant "one from Judah."

In the New Testament, the terms *Israelite* and *Hebrew* are hardly ever used. Israel as a political state did not exist, and the name that the ruling Romans gave to the area was "Judea."

290. the Rechabite nature boys

The world's first "back to the land" movement was the Rechabites, a group in Israel. They lived as nomads, in tents instead of houses. They urged fellow Israelites to give up luxury and live simply as a way of getting close to God. (See Jer. 35.)

291. the lost tribes of Israel

A tribe is far too big to lose, of course. In 722 B.C. the Assyrians conquered the kingdom of Israel, which was the ten northern tribes (the other two tribes formed the kingdom of Judah) (2 Kings 17). Many of the people were deported, and foreigners were settled in Israel. The deported Israelites were dispersed around the Assyrian Empire, most of them never to return. They were probably absorbed into the lands they settled in, but many legends have sprung up around the "ten lost tribes." Mormons believe that "lost tribes" settled America.

292. Diaspora

It means "dispersion" or "scattering" and refers to Jews outside Israel. The Diaspora originated when the Assyrians and Babylonians deported the Israelites (related in 2 Kings 17 and 25). Ezra and Nehemiah tell of the return of the Jews from exile—but not all chose to return. Some stayed in Babylon, and by the New Testament period Jews lived in many parts of the Roman Empire, with their religious life centered around synagogues (see 132). When possible they made trips to their spiritual homeland, Jerusalem.

The significance of the Diaspora for Christianity is that as the new faith spread, its missionaries (most of whom were Jews) used the synagogues across the Roman Empire as their first points of contact (a logical thing, since they were preaching the Messiah the Jews had awaited). Diaspora Jews were already proof that the Old Testament faith had moved beyond Israel.

293. Sadducees

These were the wealthiest and most powerful Jews in the New Testament period. They dominated the Sanhedrin (see 296) and the priesthood in Jerusalem. They differed from the common people and the Pharisees in an important respect: They accepted only the Torah, the Bible's first five books, as sacred. And, unlike most Jews in that era, they had no belief in an afterlife. Like the Pharisees, they disapproved of Jesus, and on one occasion they came to Him with a ridiculous question about marriage in the afterlife, which Jesus answered wisely (Matt. 22:23–33).

Acts 23 describes Paul's trial before the Sanhedrin, where he cleverly played off one party against another. Paul, knowing that some of them were Sadducees and the others Pharisees, called out to the Sanhedrin, "Men and brethren, I am a Pharisee, the son of a Pharisee; concerning the hope and resurrection of the dead I am being judged!" (v. 6). When he said this, a dispute broke out between the Pharisees and the Sadducees, and the assembly was divided.

294. Pharisees

This group is mentioned dozens of times in the New Testament—usually with disapproval. They were the most religious of the Jews, striving to follow Israel's law to the letter. But they could be self-righteous and hypocritical, and on many occasions Jesus preached against them (see 398 [the seven woes]). Jesus' concern was that they had created a religion of rules and had forgotten the goal: loving God and one's neighbors. He told His followers that, in this respect, they had to be more righteous than the Pharisees (Matt. 5:20).

Though most Pharisees despised Jesus and worked to bring about His execution, some invited Him to their homes. The most famous Pharisee of all, one who originally persecuted Christians, was Paul, who became Christianity's greatest apostle.

295. scribes

In New Testament times, experts in Jewish law were called "scribes" (or "teachers of the Law" or "lawyers" in some translations). Jesus had harsh words for them, because they (like the Pharisees) were fastidious about adhering to the rules but often forgot the importance of genuinely loving God and other people. They were respected by the people, but Jesus saw that they could be self-righteous and hypocritical, with a religion of rules instead of serving God (Matt. 23; Luke 20). The scribes looked down on Jesus for mixing with the common people and social outcasts.

296. Sanhedrin

This was the Jewish ruling council in the New Testament period. Technically, the land where Jesus walked was under Roman rule, but in religious matters the Sanhedrin was in charge. The group, composed of older and respected Jewish leaders, including priests, was the final court of appeal for questions about Jewish law. It had its own police-military force and could decide whether prophets were true or false, and whether a person was guilty of blasphemy.

The Gospels present the Sanhedrin as a rather nasty group, dedicated to preserving their own position and violently opposed to Jesus. Only one member, Joseph of Arimathea, is described as a good man and a secret follower of Jesus (see 478 [Joseph of Arimathea]).

As the book of Acts shows, the Sanhedrin opposed the first Christians as much as they had opposed Jesus Himself. The apostles Peter and John were jailed and interrogated because they had been preaching that Jesus was raised from the dead (Acts 4). Later, Peter told the council, "We ought to obey God rather than men" (Acts 5:29). One wise member of the council, Gamaliel, advised moderation in dealing with the Christians (see 460 [Gamaliel]). Even so, the Sanhedrin ordered the apostles flogged. Later, the Sanhedrin accused the saintly Stephen of blasphemy, a trial that resulted in Stephen being stoned to death.

Paul ran afoul of the Sanhedrin when he was accused (falsely) of taking a Gentile into the Jewish temple courts. Paul took advantage of a theological split in the council (the Sadducees and Pharisees differed on several issues) and caused a riot in the council. Even so, the Sanhedrin regrouped and plotted to kill Paul, and would have succeeded had he not been under Roman protection.

297. Zealots

The great world power in the New Testament era was Rome, and most of the people Rome conquered resented their status. In Israel, a Jewish patriotic party came into being, the Zealots. They weren't above resorting to violence, even assassination, and their actions eventually led to all-out war with Rome. Rome won, naturally, and one result of the war was the destruction, in A.D. 70, of the temple in Jerusalem.

One of Jesus' twelve disciples was Simon the Zealot (Luke 6:15). The twelve were a mixed bag, since another disciple was the tax collector Matthew, a man whose job required collaboration with the Romans.

298. publicans

In the New Testament, these were tax collectors working for the Roman Empire. They were unpopular people, and Jewish publicans were despised by fellow Jews, who saw them as collaborators with the hated Romans. Many of them were dishonest, scouring off extra funds for their own pockets. Though they were social outcasts, Jesus chose to socialize with them, and He even chose one (Matthew) as one of His twelve disciples. Zacchaeus was a publican whom Jesus visited and blessed (Luke 19). Jesus also told a parable of a humble publican who could only pray, "God, be merciful to me a sinner!" (Luke 18:13).

Jesus' compassionate outreach to publicans provoked criticism from the Jewish religious establishment.

299. disciples / apostles

Jesus selected His "dream team," twelve men who were to be His special followers. He had more than twelve (there is a group referred to as the Seventy), but the Twelve had a special master-pupil relationship with Him. These were the *disciples,* and the New Testament sometimes refers to them simply as "the Twelve." A disciple is a pupil, one who learns.

After Jesus' death and resurrection, the disciples (minus the traitor Judas Iscariot, who killed himself after betraying Jesus) were always referred to as *apostles*—that is, ambassadors on someone else's behalf (Jesus', that is). While Jesus was on earth He used the title to distinguish the Twelve from His other followers: "He called His disciples to Himself; and from them He chose twelve whom He also named apostles" (Luke 6:13).

The book of Acts, which follows the four Gospels, is sometimes called the Acts of the Apostles. But in fact, Acts doesn't tell the doings of all twelve apostles. It focuses on a select few, like Peter, and even on some non-apostles (like the martyr Stephen and the deacon Philip). And the chief player in Acts is not one of the Twelve at all, but the great missionary and teacher Paul. As far as we know, Paul, unlike the Twelve, had never known Jesus personally—at least, not until the risen Jesus appeared to Paul as he was on a Christian-persecuting mission. In his many letters that make up a huge part of the New Testament, Paul frequently referred to himself as "an apostle." In terms of energy, enthusiasm, travel, and influence, none of the original Twelve held a candle to the apostle Paul.

See 996 (twelve).

300. the Seventy

Jesus chose twelve men as His close group of disciples, but Luke's gospel also mentions disciples in a larger group, "the Seventy." "The Lord appointed seventy others also, and sent them two by two before His face into every city and place where He Himself was about to go." Apparently they had some success in their ministry: "The seventy returned with joy, saying, 'Lord, even the demons are subject to us in Your name'" (Luke 10:1–17).

301. Samaritans

The warlike Assyrians captured the northern kingdom of Israel in 722 B.C., deported its inhabitants, and settled the area with foreigners. Some Israelites remained there and intermarried with the foreigners, creating a mixed stock. According to 2 Kings 17:33, this resulted in a mixed religion—serving God, but also serving false gods. The people were known as Samaritans, after Israel's former capital, Samaria (see 905).

When the Jews of the southern kingdom returned from their exile in Babylon, they locked horns with the Samaritans. The Jews saw themselves as the keepers of the true faith, but the Samaritans wanted a part in restoring Jerusalem's temple. The Jews refused, not wanting the help of a mixed-race (and mixed-religion) people. The Samaritans built their own temple on Mount Gerizim. The Samaritans and Jews were now two separate peoples, with similar—but different—religious practices.

The New Testament depicts the hostility between Jews and Samaritans. The Romans had created the province of Samaria between Galilee and Judea, and the Jewish inhabitants of those two regions disliked traveling through Samaria, bypassing it when they could. *Samaritan* was a slur word on Jewish lips, and Jesus' enemies accused Him of being one (John 8:48). John 4 records a remarkable dialogue between Jesus and a woman in Samaria, a dialogue that makes it clear that Christ had compassion for Samaritans. The book of Acts records that Christianity was preached and accepted in Samaria, so the new faith broke down the wall between Samaritan and Jew. The old Samaritan religion still exists, by the way.

The most famous Samaritan was the compassionate one in Jesus' best-known parable (see 397 [the good Samaritan]).

302. eunuchs

Kings in the ancient world often used castrated men to work in their royal harems. In time, the word came to refer to royal officials in general, whether or not they were castrated. Israel's law prohibited physical eunuchs from being part of the faith community.

The most interesting Bible reference to physical eunuchs is the statement of Jesus that some were eunuchs because they were born that way, others were made that way by men, and others made themselves eunuchs because of the kingdom of heaven. "He who is able to accept it, let him accept it" (Matt. 19:11–12). His meaning seems to be that some people (like Jesus Himself) can live a celibate life, particularly if they have a spiritual motivation. He did not mean that a man should castrate himself, though some have interpreted it that way.

See 457 (the Ethiopian eunuch).

303. the Evangelists

Evangelists (capital *E*) refers to Matthew, Mark, Luke, and John, authors of the four Gospels. Because each of them presented to the world the "good news" of Jesus (the Greek word is *euangelos,* meaning "good news" but usually translated "gospel"), each is called Evangelist. Artworks sometimes refer to them as St. John the Evangelist, St. Mark the Evangelist, and so on.

304. Christians

The New Testament is a Christian book but the name Christian doesn't appear in it much. Acts 11:26 says that "the disciples were first called Christians in Antioch," a city in Syria. The apostle Paul preached his faith before the Jewish ruler Agrippa, who referred to "[becoming] a Christian" (Acts 26:28). Enduring persecution as a Christian is mentioned in 1 Peter 4:16.

Much more common are the words *brothers* and *believers,* which have the same meaning as "fellow Christians."

305. proselytes

The Jewish religion is not evangelistic, but many people in the ancient world were attracted to certain features of it: belief in one righteous God, high moral standards, emphasis on close family ties. In the New Testament period many people, including some Roman officials, became followers of the Jews' religion, and these were known as *proselytes.* Technically, Gentile proselytes could never actually *be* Jews (since being a Jew requires being *born* a Jew), but some proselyte men went so far as to have themselves circumcised.

Some Gentiles who were drawn to the Jews' religion were known as "God-fearers." These included the devout Roman centurion Jesus encountered, and another centurion, Cornelius, who became a Christian after meeting the apostle Peter (Acts 10–11). There was no clear distinction between God-fearers and proselytes; both terms applied to Gentiles who in some way followed the faith of the Jews.

Because proselytes *chose* the Jewish religion, they were sometimes more devout than the Jews themselves.

Some Bible translations use "converts to Judaism" or "devout converts" instead of "proselytes."

306. Epicureans and Stoics

In the New Testament period these were two popular philosophies. Epicureans were skeptical about God or gods and believed the goal of life was pleasure—not necessarily wild living, but peace and tranquillity, surrounded by beautiful things. Stoics believed in one God who pervaded everything. They emphasized logic and rationality, and most of them preached detachment from worldly things and learning to rise above passing emotions. Stoics and Epicureans are mentioned in Acts 17:18, where Paul the apostle is preaching Christianity in Athens (see 928), the center of Greek philosophy. He does not get a warm reception from the intellectuals, who refer to him as a "babbler."

307. the Bereans

Paul and the other apostles got mixed results in their missions—some people accepted the gospel, some ignored it, others became violent. The Jews in the Greek town of Berea were "fair-minded" people who "received the word with all readiness, and searched the Scriptures" to determine if the apostles' preaching was true (Acts 17:10–12).

GROUPS CONNECTED WITH THE BIBLE

308. People of the Book

Muslims refer to Jews and Christians with this term, also calling them "People of the Covenant." In Muslim eyes, People of the Book are more highly regarded than pagan idol worshipers. Muslims believe that Jews and Christians received holy scriptures from God (Allah) but these scriptures were later corrupted, which is why (so Muslims say) the Bible disagrees with the Koran (which they believe is error-free and holy).

309. Falasha Jews

This Jewish sect living in Ethiopia traces its descent from Israel's King Solomon and the queen of Sheba (1 Kings 10). The former Ethiopian emperor Haile Selassie, deposed in 1974, also traced his descent from Solomon and the queen.

310. flagellants

Paul the apostle reported that "I beat my body and make it my slave so that after I have preached to others, I myself will not be disqualified for the prize" (1 Cor. 9:27 NIV). The "prize" refers to eternal life, and he is referring to achieving a victory over fleshly desires. But over the centuries some Christians took his words in a literal way, whipping or scourging themselves. These are known as the flagellants, from the Latin word *flagellum*, meaning "whip." This practice (which most Christians find absurd) brings to mind Jesus being scourged by the Romans (John 19:1).

311. the Carmelites

They were and still are a major order of nuns and monks in the Catholic church. The order was founded on the biblical Mount Carmel (see 901) by Europeans in 1154, but the Carmelites claimed they were descendants of the band of prophets that followed Elijah. When the Holy Land was occupied by the Muslims, the Carmelites went to Europe.

312. mendicants

The Latin word means "beggars." The mendicants were Christians who took seriously the words of Jesus to His disciples in Matthew 10. Jesus instructed them to travel to the towns and villages, carrying the fewest possible possessions, and preach the kingdom of God. In the Middle Ages, Francis of Assisi (see 563) and others established groups of mendicants, known as friars (meaning "brothers"). What little they needed, they begged. Like monks, they took vows of chastity and poverty, but unlike the monks, who lived in monasteries, friars traveled about, preaching and teaching.

313. "the Poor in Spirit"

In the 1100s, Peter Waldo of France, a wealthy man, was deeply affected by Jesus' words in Matthew 19:21: "If you want to be perfect, go, sell what you have and give to the poor, and you will have treasure in heaven." Waldo gave away his wealth and began preaching poverty and simplicity as the way to follow Christ. The wealthy and corrupt church of that day excommunicated him. Waldo attracted followers who organized themselves into a church with its own ministers. Attempting to go "back to the Bible," they rejected such nonbiblical teachings as purgatory, transubstantiation, and prayers for the dead. Calling themselves the "Poor in Spirit" (after Matt. 5:3), they promoted high moral standards, and the movement—also known as the Waldensians—spread throughout Europe. The pope ordered a crusade against them, but they took refuge in remote places in Switzerland. Three hundred years later, they happily joined the Protestants.

314. the Anabaptists

The Protestant Reformation in the 1500s was a major split from the Catholic church. A further split occurred as some Christians believed the Protestants were not faithful enough to the New Testament. These became known as the

Anabaptists, meaning "rebaptizers," insisting on baptizing adults who made a profession of faith. This rattled both Protestants and Catholics, who insisted that infant baptism was the norm. The Anabaptists stated—correctly—that infant baptism is never mentioned in the Bible. They insisted that in other areas the New Testament teachings should be obeyed, so they followed a high moral standard based on the Sermon on the Mount. They were harshly persecuted by both Catholics and Protestants.

The Mennonites were a subgroup of the Anabaptists, and the best-known group of Mennonites are the Amish (see 315).

315. the Amish

They are a strict branch of the Mennonites, and certainly the best known, because of their distinctive dress and shying away from modern conveniences. The Amish claim to take the Bible literally, particularly the Sermon on the Mount with its strong stand on nonviolence. The Amish more than any other Christians have followed the New Testament standards of avoiding worldliness. As in the New Testament, they meet for worship and fellowship in each other's homes, not in churches.

316. Freemasons

The Masons claim (without basis) to trace their organization to the builder Hiram of Tyre, who aided Solomon in building the Lord's temple (1 Kings 7). Most likely the group originated centuries later, in the guilds of English stonemasons.

317. Pilgrims

A pilgrim is one on a journey to a holy place. The New Testament refers to Christians as "strangers and pilgrims on the earth" (Heb. 11:13), and 1 Peter 2:11 uses almost the same words. The first Christians believed their destination was a holy place, heaven, so their time on earth was only a journey.

The English Puritans who settled at Plymouth, Massachusetts, in 1620 became known as the Pilgrims because they believed they had left the corrupt church in England to live in a new land and build a holy society.

318. the Quakers

The movement begun by George Fox (1624–1691) called itself the Society of Friends, but they are better known as Quakers. They took their name from John 15:15, where Jesus told His disciples, "No longer do I call you servants . . . but I have called you friends." The Friends believed that Christian worship was overly ritualized and dry, and that the true Christian life consisted of living according to the Bible and also by the "Inner Light," the guidance of the Holy Spirit. The idea of the Spirit as daily guide is a sound one (John 14:15–26; 16:5–15; Luke 12:12; Matt. 10:20), but the Friends suffered incredible persecution, as have most Christians who pursued a simple lifestyle and attempted to take Jesus' teaching literally.

Like the Mennonites, the Quakers advocate nonviolence and are often associated with pacifism (723).

319. Baptists

Almost all Baptist churches practice "adults-only" Baptism—more accurately, "believers' baptism," meaning they only baptize persons old enough to voluntarily ask for baptism and make a profession of faith in Christ. In practice, this can happen as young as five years old. Baptists point out that infant baptism is involuntary on the part of the child, who is not making a conscious choice to become a Christian. They point out—correctly—that baptisms in the New Testament were performed on believers, not on infants.

320. Swedenborgians

Emanuel Swedenborg (1688–1772) was a scientist, theologian, and philosopher. He became Sweden's most noted scientist, but in midlife he turned to studying the Bible and developing his unique philosophy. In books like *Heavenly Secrets* and *The True Christian Religion* he described his experiences in the spirit world. He believed the churches had corrupted the original truth of Christianity and the Bible, and his many books were his effort to "correct" the faith. He claimed the "inspired" Bible included only five books of the New Testament and twenty-nine of the Old Testament. After his death followers established the New Jerusalem Church.

321. the Methodists

The Methodists began with a university group, the Holy Club, that included brothers John and Charles Wesley. In the 1700s the Church of England was spiritually slumbering, but the Methodists took the faith seriously and emphasized meeting for prayer, fellowship, and Bible study. John Wesley defined a *Methodist* as "one who lives according to the method laid down in the Bible." The Methodists found the people of England and America eager for a richer, deeper faith, and the Methodist revival was an astounding phenomenon of the 1700s.

322. the Mormons

The Church of Jesus Christ of Latter-day Saints, better known as the Mormons, accepts the Bible as sacred but also accepts several later books: the Book of Mormon, the Doctrine and Covenants, and the Pearl of Great Price. Joseph Smith, the church's founder, claimed he found the Book of Mormon in 1822 and translated it into English. Many readers see an obvious resemblance between the language of the book and the language of the King James Version of the Bible, the version Smith would have been familiar with. The Bible and the Book of Mormon disagree on certain key beliefs, but the Mormons give precedence to their book.

323. Seventh-day Adventists

William Miller, an American pastor, predicted that Christ would return to earth on October 22, 1844. His followers gathered in their churches on that day to worship and wait. They experienced the Great Disappointment, as it was later called, and Miller disconnected from the movement he started. But the faithful followers claimed they received later revelations, notably from Ellen White. Like many people in the mid-1850s, she was diet- and health-conscious (does any of this sound familiar?). She urged Miller's former followers to follow the Old Testament dietary laws and to keep the Sabbath as God intended—on Saturday, that is.

The Seventh-day Adventists today use the Bible as their guide and are most noted (as their name indicates) for worshiping on Saturday. Most still follow the kosher laws in Leviticus 11, and some are strict vegetarians (a practice the Bible says nothing about, by the way).

324. Jehovah's Witnesses

"Bible Students" was the original name of the group, which was started by Charles Taze Russell in the 1870s. Russell established the organization's publishing house, the Watchtower Bible and Tract Society, which publishes their version of the Bible, the New World Translation. While the Witnesses claim their source of authority is the Bible, the New World Translation alters the Bible's teaching in some important areas, notably in the divinity of Jesus, which Witnesses deny. The Witnesses are, true to their name, very evangelistic

325. the Campbellites

Alexander Campbell (1788–1866) and his father were pastors on the American frontier. They were disturbed at how denominations seemed to compete with each other, so they called for a restoration of New Testament Christianity, dropping all the denominational differences and emphasizing the simple faith of the first Christians. The descendants of the "Campbellites" did, nonetheless, become denominations: the Disciples of Christ and the Churches of Christ. The Churches of Christ have been the more conservative group, sticking close to the Bible in their worship practices.

326. the Oneida Community

John Humphrey Noyes (1811–1886) was not only a minister but also a "perfectionist" who believed true Christians were free from all sin. Declaring himself sinless, he found some other (supposedly) sinless people and formed a commune at Oneida, New York. Noyes read Acts 2:44—"all who believed were together, and had all things in common"—and applied it to his "perfect" community. The people had all things in common—including spouses. Noyes quoted Mark 12:25 and claimed his people had transcended normal marriage and were "like angels in heaven." The commune (also known as the "Bible Communists") prospered materially, but because of the group's questionable morals, Noyes had to flee the U.S., and he died in Canada.

327. Pentecostals

Pentecostal Christians take their name from Acts 2 and its description of the baptism of the Holy Spirit, which occurred among Jesus' disciples at Pentecost. For Pentecostals, this baptism of the Spirit is essential in the life of each Christian, more important than the symbolic baptism in water. The book of Acts reports that baptism in the Spirit was a key feature of the early Christians' experience. In 1 Corinthians 12, Paul describes the various "spiritual gifts" Christians have, including speaking in tongues. These gifts are important to Pentecostals and are evidence of having been baptized by the Spirit.

Many denominations consider themselves Pentecostals, including the fast-growing Assemblies of God. Pentecostals are similar in many ways to charismatics (see 328).

328. charismatics

The name comes from the Greek *charismata,* meaning "gifts." These are spiritual gifts, bestowed upon Christians through the working of the Holy Spirit. Paul lists and describes these various gifts in 1 Corinthians 12 and 14 and Romans 12:6–8. Churches have often become so mired in ritual and social issues that they neglect teaching about spiritual gifts, including speaking in tongues. The charismatic movement in American churches began in the 1960s as people sought a more emotional spiritual life and deeper intimacy with God. Charismatics are similar in many ways to Pentecostals (see 327), and it is possible to be both. But Pentecostals tend to form their own denominations, while charismatics are scattered throughout many denominations, including Catholics.

329. the holiness movement

There have always been groups of Christians who sought a deeper spirituality, something more demanding than just attending church and appearing "nice." In America, several groups in the mid-1800s spun off from the Methodists, whose founder, John Wesley, wrote *A Plain Account of Christian Perfection*. Wesley's book claims that the Bible holds up a standard of perfection in the Christian life, so that a person can live without deliberate sin. A National Holiness Association was formed, and there is now some overlap of holiness groups and Pentecostals (see 327). Both groups emphasize the baptism in the Holy Spirit (see 700) and the importance of sanctification in the person's life (see 681 [sanctification]).

330. Bible-thumpers

This derogatory word has been around since the 1920s, when intellectuals enjoyed putting down conservative Christians. Fundamentalist Christians have the habit (so their opponents believe) of constantly pointing to the Bible—"thumping it"—to support their moral standards. Some evangelists do, admittedly, "thump" the Bible—and why not, if it is the basis of their message?

331. the YMCA

The "Y" today is mostly a recreation center, but originally it really was a Young Men's Christian Association. Its founder, George Williams, was concerned about the moral and spiritual welfare of young men moving from small towns into London. In 1844 he started Bible classes and Christian lectures for young men in his own home. The movement spread to other countries, and in many locales dormitories provided homes away from home, with an emphasis on Christian fellowship and Bible study.

332. Church of the Nazarene

This denomination, founded in 1908 in Texas, takes its name from Jesus' hometown, Nazareth. As a native of Nazareth, Jesus was called a Nazarene.

333. fundamentalists

The name comes from The Fundamentals, a series of twelve booklets defending traditional Christian teachings. These were published from 1910 to 1915 and sent free to thousands of pastors and theology students. They were a response to new findings in science and social thought that seemed to make Christianity outdated. Some church leaders were willing to accept new ideas (such as evolution), while others resisted, leading to a modernist-fundamentalist split in many churches. The authors of The Fundamentals defended such teachings as Jesus' miracles, His virgin birth, His resurrection from the dead, and the historical reliability of the Bible. The name fundamentalists has come to apply to people who take a conservative approach to the Bible and morality.

Curiously, some of the original authors of The Fundamentals were open to the possibility that evolution might be true.

Today, fundamentalists get a bad press, but they are a powerful social and political force. There is a line (a thin one, some would say) between fundamentalists and those who call themselves evangelicals (see 337).

334. the InterVarsity Christian Fellowship

This organization was founded in 1927 to foster fellowship among evangelical college students and encourage a Christian presence on college campuses. The InterVarsity Press publishes a wide range of Bible study materials and studies in Christian doctrine.

335. Wycliffe Bible Translators

How do you translate into a language that has never been written down? Christian missionaries faced this problem centuries ago, and in many locations they invented alphabets just so they could give the native people a Bible. In 1931 in Guatemala, Cameron Townsend and his wife produced a New Testament in the Cakchiquel Indian language—after learning the language and writing down words that had only been spoken aloud, never written. This venture led to the founding of Wycliffe Bible Translators, named for the great English translator of the Middle Ages,

John Wycliffe. Portions of the Bible have been translated into more than three hundred languages.

336. the Unification Church

Often called the "Moonies" after founder Sun Myung Moon, the Unification Church is officially called the Holy Spirit Association for the Unification of World Christianity. Moon, a Korean, claimed that Jesus appeared to him on Easter 1936 and told him to establish the kingdom of God on earth. Although the church is theoretically Christian, Moon's book *Divine Principle* diverges in many ways from the Bible. Moon has claimed to have communicated with Moses, Jesus, and Buddha, and to be able to "travel in the spirit world."

337. evangelicals

In America, the term *evangelical* refers to a Christian who takes a conservative view of the Bible and Christian morality. Like fundamentalists (see 333), evangelicals believe in the overall historical reliability of the Bible, accepting Jesus' resurrection, miracles, etc. Like fundamentalists, they try to base a lifestyle on the New Testament's moral teachings, and both groups emphasize the need to be "born again." One can, in fact, be both an evangelical and a fundamentalist. But beginning in the 1950s some Christians began to call themselves "evangelicals," represented by magazines such as *Christianity Today* and the Billy Graham Association—conservative in teaching, but also intellectually respectable and socially concerned.

Because of the candidacy of Jimmy Carter, *Time* magazine called 1976 the "year of the evangelical."

338. Youth for Christ

Known for its teen evangelism and high school Bible clubs, Youth for Christ was founded in 1945. It publishes *Campus Life* magazine.

339. United Bible Societies

This international group was founded in 1946 and is dedicated to making the Bible available in as many languages as possible. The UBS has sponsored more than 1,600 language translations. The group publishes a Greek New Testament that is used as the basis of its many New Testament translations.

340. Campus Crusade for Christ

Founded by Bill Bright in 1951, Campus Crusade provides outreach and fellowship on college campuses. It publishes guides to the Bible and Christian doctrine, and is probably most famous for its "Four Spiritual Laws" used in personal evangelism.

8

Some Miraculous Highlights

341. the burning bush

Moses' first encounter with God is described in Exodus 3. Moses, living as a shepherd in Midian, saw a bush that was on fire but did not burn up. He approached, and God called him by name and told him he was standing on holy ground. Fearful, Moses hid his face, while God told him He had seen the sorrow of the Israelite slaves in Egypt and was sending Moses to lead the people out. Moses replied, "Who am I that I should go to Pharaoh?" but God said, "I will certainly be with you."

At this first encounter, Moses asked God His name. God replied, "I AM WHO I AM . . . the LORD God of your fathers, the God of Abraham, the God of Isaac, and the God of Jacob." God promised that He would lead them to Canaan, "a land flowing with milk and honey."

This is one of the most famous incidents in the Bible, since it was Moses' "commissioning" by God, and the first time God revealed His name to anyone.

342. the ten plagues of Egypt

The movie *The Ten Commandments* has made many people familiar with the plagues God sent on the Egyptians. Moses, God's appointed leader of Israel, continually relayed to Pharaoh, "Let My people go," but Pharaoh was stubborn. The ten plagues were: turning the waters to blood, frogs, lice, flies, a disease on the cattle, boils on man and beast, hail, locusts, darkness, and, the crowning blow, the death of the firstborn. The tenth plague finally moved Pharaoh to free the slaves, although he changed his mind and sent troops after them, leading to their drowning in the Red Sea, which God had parted for the Israelites.

The plagues affected only the Egyptians, not the Israelite slaves living in the region of Goshen.

There are, some say, "natural" explanations for most or all of the plagues. It can hardly be coincidence that the ten occurred so close together, or that the Israelites were not affected.

343. the food from heaven, manna

This was the miraculous food God provided the Israelites after they left Egypt. Since they were crossing a desert area, God was doing them a kindness. Exodus 16:31 describes it as like white coriander seed and tasting like wafers made with honey. Later generations looked back and saw the forty years of manna as part of the great miracle of deliverance from Egypt and moving on to Canaan (Ps. 78:24).

Manna was literally "bread from heaven." In John 6, Jesus refers to Himself as, figuratively, "the bread which came down from heaven. . . . Your fathers ate the manna in the wilderness, and are dead. . . . He who eats this bread will live forever" (vv. 41, 49, 58).

344. the pillar of fire

When the Israelites left Egypt, God guided them through the wilderness with a pillar of cloud by day and a pillar of fire by night. The pillar of cloud stood over the tabernacle (see 115) whenever God met Moses there. As Moses went into the tent, the pillar of cloud would come down and stay at the entrance while the Lord spoke with Moses (Ex. 33:9).

345. Moses' bronze serpent

The Israelites journeyed in the wilderness forty years after leaving Egypt. They endured various hardships, one being venomous snakes that killed many of them. God told Moses to make a bronze snake on a pole. Moses did, and "if a serpent had bitten anyone, when he looked at the bronze serpent, he lived" (Num. 21:9). The bronze snake was preserved, and later turned into an idol, for 2 Kings 18:4 reports that the Israelites had been burning incense to it.

Jesus referred to the bronze snake on one occasion: "As Moses lifted up the serpent in the wilderness, even so must the Son of Man be lifted up" (John 3:14). The early

Christians probably noticed the parallel: Moses' bronze snake, lifted up on a pole, saved people from death, and Jesus, lifted up on a cross, saved people from eternal death.

346. Balaam's ass

A donkey that can speak? The prophet Balaam had such an animal, at least on one occasion. As the Israelites journeyed from Egypt to their home in Canaan, they passed through the hostile land of Moab. The Moabite king sent his prophet Balaam to place a curse on Israel. God specifically told Balaam not to do this, but he rode out anyway, and as he rode toward the Israelites his donkey saw an angel with a drawn sword in the road. The donkey veered off, and Balaam beat her, not seeing the angel himself. The poor beast finally lay down, and Balaam beat her again. This time she spoke: "What have I done to you, that you have struck me these three times?" (Num. 22:28). God then opened Balaam's eyes and he saw the angel and fell facedown. He changed his plans (naturally), and instead of cursing the Israelites, he prophesied that they would be a great nation, blessed by God (Num. 22–24).

347. "Joshua fit de battle of Jericho"

The old spiritual is based on Joshua 5:13–27. Joshua, leader of the Israelites after Moses died, was told by an angel how to capture the strongly fortified city of Jericho. Instead of attacking, the Israelites were to march around the city for six days, carrying the ark of the covenant. On the seventh day, priests were to blow trumpets and the people were to shout. When they did this, the city walls fell (as the song says, "and de walls come tumblin' down"), and the Israelites captured the city.

348. laying out the fleece

Gideon, who had been chosen by God to lead Israel's armies, wanted a sign that God really was with him. He laid out a fleece on the ground and told God to give him a sign: If, the next morning, the fleece was wet and the ground around it dry, he would believe. God did so, and Gideon wrung out a bowlful of water from the fleece. Then he asked God to do the opposite: At night, leave the fleece dry but make the ground around it wet with dew. God did, and Gideon believed. (See Judg. 6:36–40.) The expression "laying out the fleece" refers to this kind of testing of someone.

349. chariots of fire

The great prophet Elijah did not die, according to 2 Kings 2. He was with his successor, the prophet Elisha, when "suddenly a chariot of fire appeared with horses of fire, and separated the two of them; and Elijah went up by a whirlwind into heaven" (v. 11).

Chariots of fire appeared for Elisha in another incident. He was wanted by the king of Aram, who sent a mighty force to capture him. Elisha's servant saw the Aramean troops coming and was terrified. Elisha said to him, "Those who are with us are more than those who are with them." And then the Lord opened the servant's eyes and he saw "the mountain was full of horses and chariots of fire all around Elisha." Apparently the fiery troops did not have to fight, because Elisha struck the Arameans with blindness (2 Kings 6:8–18).

350. Naaman the Syrian

He was commander of the armies of Syria (or "Aram" in some versions) but had that loathsome disease, leprosy. Naaman's wife's maid suggested he visit Israel's prophet Elisha, who told Naaman to wash seven times in the Jordan River. Naaman was skeptical, but the cure indeed worked, and he sang the praises of Israel's God (2 Kings 5). Naaman asked for some soil from Israel to take home—to put in the temple of his god Rimmon.

See 976 (leprosy).

351. Nebuchadnezzar's dream

Nebuchadnezzar, king of Babylon, is a prominent character in the book of Daniel. The mighty king, who conquered Jerusalem and carried off most of its citizens to exile in Babylon, had a strange dream that none of his court magicians could interpret. The young Jewish man Daniel, who was serving as a court official, learned from God the meaning of the dream and reported it to the king. Nebuchadnezzar dreamed of a huge statue of himself, with a head of gold, chest and arms of silver, belly of bronze, legs of iron, and feet of iron mingled with clay. Daniel explained that the gold head represented Nebuchadnezzar himself and the kingdom of Babylon. The silver part represented a later, and inferior kingdom, the bronze another, and so on. The "feet of clay" represented a kingdom that would not stay united.

Historians and Bible readers have had a field day trying to connect the dream with world empires. Some say the iron legs represent the Roman Empire, but hundreds of other possibilities (none of which can be proved) have been put forward.

352. Shadrach, Meshach, and Abed-Nego

This trio of names (which, for some reason, people often give to pets) is from the Bible. In the book of Daniel, Daniel and three friends are, like many other Jews, living in exile in Babylon, where King Nebuchadnezzar reigns. The four young men are chosen to serve in the king's palace, and a court official changes their Hebrew names to Babylonian ones. Daniel's three companions were renamed Shadrach, Meshach, and Abed-Nego (Dan. 1:7).

According to Daniel 3, the proud Babylonian king set up a gold image of himself and required everyone to worship it. Shadrach, Meshach, and Abed-Nego, being faithful Jews, would not bow down to an idol. The furious king ordered them thrown into a fiery furnace, heated seven times hotter than usual. The three friends were tied up and thrown into the furnace, but God miraculously preserved them from harm. The Babylonians saw not only the three men walking around in the fire, but also a fourth man, who looked like "the Son of God." Nebuchadnezzar was so awed that he ordered that no one be allowed to slander the Jews' God.

353. Daniel in the lions' den

The book of Daniel has always been a favorite for reading to children, and for artists, probably because it has picturesque stories like the fiery furnace, Nebuchadnezzar's statue, and Daniel in the lions' den. Daniel 6 tells how the Persian ruler Darius decreed that no one should pray to any god or man except to Darius himself. Some of Daniel's enemies hoped that the faithful Daniel, who prayed to no one except the true God, would be in trouble. They got their wish, and Darius (who liked Daniel), reluctantly ordered him thrown into a den of lions. The next morning Daniel was found miraculously preserved, not even scratched. The enemies who plotted against Daniel were thrown into the den and devoured.

354. Jonah and the whale

Even people unfamiliar with the Bible have heard of Jonah, the prophet who was swallowed by a whale and lived to tell about it. Fact or fiction? Well, it is scientific fact that people have been swallowed by whales and escaped to tell of it. Did it actually happen to Jonah? Each reader must judge for himself.

Jonah was a reluctant prophet. God sent him to the pagan city of Nineveh to preach repentance. Jonah ran away from the Lord by boarding a ship. In a horrible storm, Jonah admitted that he was probably the cause of it, so at Jonah's request they threw him overboard, and "the LORD had prepared a great fish to swallow Jonah" (Jonah 1:17).

Jonah reached Nineveh, preached the message of repentance, and—much to his disgust—the pagans repented. The book of Jonah was a sign that the Israelites were beginning to see that God loved all people, not just Israel.

355. water into wine

Jesus' first miracle, according to John's gospel, was at a wedding in the town of Cana, where the hosts ran out of wine. Jesus turned six large jars of water into wine—not just ordinary wine, but wine so good that someone said to the groom, "You have kept the good wine until now." And, says John, Jesus thus "manifested His glory; and His disciples believed in Him" (John 2:1–11). Like all of Jesus' miracles, this was not a divine power "showing off" but a man of compassion using His power to fill a human need.

356. walking on water

Jesus did walk on water on one occasion, according to Matthew 14:22–33. His disciples were in a boat on a storm-tossed lake, and when Jesus approached them they thought He was a ghost. Peter tried to walk toward his Master, and Jesus encouraged him. Peter lost faith and sank, but Jesus caught him. "Those who were in the boat came and worshiped Him, saying, 'Truly You are the Son of God.'" The miracle showed that the Son of God ruled over nature.

357. the hem of Jesus' robe

Jesus was known as a healer, and one woman had such faith in His power that He healed her without even trying to. A woman who had had "a flow of blood" for twelve years and had spent her income on doctors came up behind Jesus in a crowd and touched the hem of His garment. "And immediately her flow of blood stopped." Jesus asked, "Who touched Me?" and the disciples thought it a foolish question, with so many people crowding around. But the woman came forth, trembling, and explained what she had done. Jesus was moved: "Daughter, be of good cheer; your faith has made you well. Go in peace" (Luke 8:43–48).

358. calming the storm

Jesus and His disciples were in a boat when a fierce storm struck. Jesus had fallen asleep, and the disciples woke Him, pleading, "Teacher, do You not care that we are perishing?" Jesus spoke to the wind and sea and ordered, "Peace, be still!" and the storm subsided. The disciples were in awe, saying to one another, "Who can this be, that even the wind and the sea obey Him!" (Mark 4:35–41).

359. healing the man born blind

Jesus healed several cases of blindness. John 9 tells the story of a man born blind, a beggar. Jesus spit on the ground, made some mud with the saliva, and placed it on the man's eyes. He sent him to wash in a nearby pool, and he came back with his sight. The Jewish religious establishment, instead of praising the deed, asked the man to denounce the One who healed him! The man's reply: "One thing I know: that though I was blind, now I see" (v. 25).

360. blind Bartimaeus

The poor beggar Bartimaeus of Jericho knew that Jesus was passing through, and he continually called out, "Jesus, Son of David, have mercy on me!" Jesus was impressed with Bartimaeus's faith that his blindness could be cured. He did so, and Bartimaeus "received his sight and followed Jesus on the road" (Mark 10:46–52).

361. the daughter of Jairus

Jairus, head of a synagogue, begged Jesus to come and heal his daughter, who was at the point of death. When Jairus and Jesus arrived at the house, the child was already dead. Jesus saw the people weeping and said, "The child is not dead, but sleeping." They mocked Him, but Jesus took the child by the hand and said, "Little girl, I say to you, arise." She stood up and began walking. "And they were overcome with great amazement" (Mark 5:35–43).

362. feeding the five thousand

All four Gospels report the great miracle of Jesus feeding a crowd with only a small amount of food. After a full day of teaching and healing, Jesus told His disciples to feed the people. They replied that they only had five loaves of bread and two fish—and a crowd of five thousand. Jesus offered thanks over the food then broke the loaves apart, and they all ate and were satisfied (Luke 9:10–17). Skeptics like to explain away the event, saying the people probably had food with them and, under Jesus' influence, shared their food with others, turning the event into a large church supper. But taking the Gospels at face value, Jesus performed a rather amazing miracle—obviously not for show, but because, as His disciples had told Him, they were in a remote place and there was no other way to feed the people who had come to see the Christ.

363. the son of the widow of Nain

Jesus raised His dear friend Lazarus from the dead after being buried four days. On another occasion He encountered, in the town of Nain, a young man being carried out for burial. Jesus told the man's mother, a widow, "Do not weep." Jesus said to the dead son, "Young man, I say to you, arise." He stood up and began to speak. The people were astounded, shouting, "God has visited His people" (Luke 7:11–17).

364. the Roman centurion's servant

Since Romans were conquerors and Jews the conquered, the Jews had obvious reason to dislike Romans. As a rule, no Jew would enter a Roman's home. But on one occasion Jesus had a request to heal the servant of a Roman centurion. The centurion was a "God-fearer" (see 305 [proselytes]), not anti-Jew as most Romans were. He had such faith in Jesus' power that he requested that Jesus not even enter his home to perform the healing, but accomplish it from a distance. Jesus was touched by this, saying, "I have not found such great faith, not even in Israel!" (Matt. 8:10). And sure enough, the centurion's servant was made well.

365. the Transfiguration

For the Jews of Jesus' day, Moses symbolized the Law and Elijah symbolized the prophets—two of the most honored men in Jewish tradition. The Gospels record an amazing incident involving Jesus and these two long-dead men. Jesus took three of His disciples to a high mountain, and "He was transfigured before them. His clothes became shining, exceedingly white, like snow . . . Elijah appeared to them with Moses, and they were talking with Jesus . . . And a cloud came and overshadowed them; and a voice came out of the cloud, saying, 'This is My beloved Son. Hear Him!'" (Mark 9:2–7).

"Transfiguration" refers to the dramatic change in Jesus' appearance. The meaning of the event was God's approval of His Son. The presence of Moses and Elijah indicates that Jesus is the fulfillment of the Jewish tradition.

366. the raising of Lazarus

Besides His disciples, Jesus did have close friends, notably three residents of Bethany, Lazarus and his sisters, Martha and Mary. John 11 relates that the sisters, fearing for Lazarus's life, sent Jesus a message that "he whom You love is sick." Jesus delayed going to them, and by the time He arrived Lazarus had been dead and buried for four days. Jesus told Martha that Lazarus would rise again. Martha thought Jesus was talking about the future resurrection of the righteous, but Jesus replied, "I am the resurrection and the life. He who believes in Me, though he may die, he shall live" (v. 25). Later Jesus encountered Mary; she and her companions were weeping, and Jesus Himself was so moved that (in the Bible's shortest verse) "Jesus wept" (v. 35). Jesus went to the tomb, ordered the stone over the entrance rolled away, and called "Lazarus, come forth!" (v. 43). Lazarus did, and this, the most impressive of Jesus' miracles, led many Jews to put their faith in Him.

When the story was reported to the Jewish priests, they feared (correctly) that Jesus' following would increase. They decided not only that Jesus must be killed but Lazarus as well.

This is the high point in Jesus' ministry, the sign that He could not only heal the sick and revive those who had just died but also raise someone already buried. It is a sort of "preview" of what will happen to all believers.

367. Peter and the angel

As Jesus predicted, His apostles were persecuted, imprisoned, and even killed. Peter was thrown into prison by Herod, bound with chains with a soldier on each side. Peter was sleeping, but awakened to a glowing angel, who made Peter's chains fall off. Peter followed him out and went to a home where some fellow Christians were praying for him. When Peter knocked, the servant girl was hysterical at seeing him set free. Peter's miraculous deliverance had an unfortunate consequence for his guards: Herod had them executed (Acts 12).

368. the raising of Eutychus

Paul was a dynamic preacher of the gospel, but on one occasion he put someone to sleep. Acts 20 relates that during Paul's sermon a young man named Eutychus dozed off and fell from a third-story window. They found him dead, but Paul embraced the young man, saying, "Do not trouble yourselves, for his life is in him" (v. 10). He was alive, and Paul deeply impressed his listeners.

9

Some Other Highlights

369. the Old Testament Trinity

Genesis 18 relates that the Lord appeared to Abraham as he was sitting in his tent doorway. But "the Lord" appeared as three men. Abraham entertained them hospitably, and "He" (the Lord—but which of the three men was speaking?) predicted that when He came again later, Abraham's wife, Sarah, would have a child. Sarah, listening nearby, laughed, since she and Abraham were both old. But the prophecy came true, for she gave birth to Isaac.

This passage fascinates Bible readers, since it refers to "the Lord" and "He" but also insists that three men, not one, visited Abraham. Was one of the three men God in the flesh while the other two were angels? Some readers have suggested that this was the Trinity—what the New Testament refers to as God the Father, the Son, and the

Holy Spirit. So perhaps Abraham's visitors were a kind of "Old Testament Trinity."

370. the sacrifice of Isaac

This is one of the most touching stories in the Bible. Abraham finally had a son, Isaac, (as God promised) in his old age (a hundred years old, in fact). But, surprisingly, God later commanded Abraham to "take now your son, your only son Isaac, whom you love, and go to the land of Moriah, and offer him there as a burnt offering" (Gen. 22:2). Abraham, the role model of trust in God, obeyed. The story relates that the boy Isaac asked his father why there were fire and wood but no lamb for a sacrifice. Abraham answered, "God will provide." Abraham bound the boy and raised his knife to kill him, but was stopped by an angel, who said, "Do not lay your hand on the lad, or do anything to him; for now I know that you fear God" (v. 12). The angel said that because of Abraham's faith God would surely bless him.

Many ancient nations near Israel practiced child sacrifice. Israel always condemned it.

The near sacrifice of Isaac has been a favorite subject for artists.

371. Jacob and Esau

Here were two twins that were nothing alike. Jacob was a "household" type, while Esau was a hunter, a "woodsy" man. The two sons of Isaac (grandsons of the patriarch Abraham) were unlike even in appearance—Jacob was smooth-skinned, Esau was hairy. Jacob was the favorite of his mother, Rebecca, and with her he plotted to cheat Esau out of his inheritance as the firstborn. (Even though they were twins, Esau was technically the firstborn of the two.) Jacob covered his hands with goatskins and deceived the old man into giving him Esau's blessing and inheritance. Once pronounced, the blessing could not be revoked. Esau was furious when he found out, and Jacob wisely fled (Gen. 27–28). Years later, when Jacob eventually returned home, he expected the worst from Esau, but the two had a tearful and peaceful reunion.

Jacob and his twelve sons were the ancestors of the Israelites. Esau, also called Edom, was ancestor of the Edomites.

372. wrestling God

Jacob, grandson of Abraham, had a colorful life, and Genesis 32 tells of how he literally wrestled God, or God's angel. On the lam from his angry brother, Esau, Jacob met a man who wrestled with him till daybreak. The man ripped Jacob's hip out of its socket, then demanded to go, but Jacob replied, "I will not let You go unless You bless me!" (v. 26). The man (or angel) told Jacob that from then on his name would be "Israel," meaning "struggles with God" because Jacob had "struggled with God and with men, and . . . prevailed." The man (or angel) would not tell Jacob his own name, and Jacob—now renamed Israel—concluded he had seen God face-to-face.

See 274 (the Israelites).

373. the Ten Commandments

They are found in Exodus 20 and Deuteronomy 5 and have probably been the most-discussed moral commands in the world. Exodus records that God engraved them on stone tablets with His own finger and gave them to Moses. When Moses came down from Mount Sinai with the tablets, he found the Israelites in an idol-worshiping frenzy, and he angrily broke the tablets. Later God supplied a new set, which were placed inside the ark of the covenant.

The commandments can be summarized in this way: (1) Worship no other gods; (2) make no idols to worship; (3) do not take God's name in vain; (4) keep the Sabbath day holy; (5) honor father and mother; (6–10) do not murder, commit adultery, steal, bear false witness, or covet another's belongings. Though the Old Testament contains hundreds of other commandments from God, the Ten are the foundation of the rest.

The commandments are sometimes referred to as the *Decalogue,* meaning "the Ten Words."

374. the Shema

Every faithful Jew is expected to repeat the Shema, Deuteronomy 6:4, every day: "Hear, O Israel: The LORD our God, the LORD is one!" It is a central confession of the Jewish faith, a statement of belief in only one true God. The verse that follows it is also important: "You shall love the LORD your God with all your heart, with all your soul, and with all your strength." When someone asked Jesus what the greatest commandment was, He replied with that verse.

375. David and Goliath

The Bible's—and maybe the world's—most famous giant was a Philistine warrior. The hulk was over nine feet tall, and his spear shaft was like a weaver's rod (1 Sam. 17:7). He challenged Israel to send its best man out for a one-on-one showdown. No one accepted until the spunky shepherd boy David came forward. King Saul was impressed with his courage, and said to him, "Go, and the LORD be with you." David wore no armor, only his shepherd's bag, a sling, and "five smooth stones." Goliath was amazed and appalled that this was the best man Israel could send. But David, with one stone from his sling, felled the giant, then cut off Goliath's head with his own sword. The Philistines panicked and fled. This was the deed that set David on the road to fame.

This is one of the most appealing stories in the Bible, and the young boy David vs. the hulking Goliath has stirred the creative juices of thousands of authors, painters, and sculptors.

376. Solomon's sword

Solomon's name has become a synonym for "wise one." In 1 Kings 3 is the story of how the young king asked God for one gift, wisdom. God was so pleased that He blessed Solomon not only with wisdom but wealth as well. Solomon's wisdom was tested in the case of two prostitutes who both claimed that a certain baby was theirs. Solomon asked an aide to bring a sword and divide the child in half. The true mother intervened and insisted that the child be given to the other woman. Solomon knew that the true mother would do so to preserve her child's life, so he gave the child to the one who intervened. So the Israelites saw "that the wisdom of God was in him to administer justice" (v. 28).

377. the Shepherd Psalm

Psalm 23, which begins "The LORD is my shepherd," is the most quoted of all the Psalms. Tradition says its author was David, Israel's king, in his youth as a shepherd boy. It is a beautiful picture of God as protector and guide. It has been read, recited, set to music, and illustrated countless times.

378. the Penitential Psalms

Seven of the Psalms are deep expressions of repentance over sin—7; 32; 38; 51; 102; 130; and 143. All but two are attributed to King David. Psalm 51 is David's lament after being confronted with his adultery with Bathsheba. Psalm 102 bears the inscription "a prayer of an afflicted man" (NIV). The Penitentials have been very popular in Christian worship.

379. Psalm 51

This favorite psalm, one of the "Penitential Psalms" (see 378), is a heartfelt confession of sin. Tradition says it was composed by David after the prophet Nathan confronted him with his adultery with Bathsheba. The touching poem admits fault and begs for God's mercy. It contains the oft-quoted words "Wash me, and I shall be whiter than snow" (v. 7).

380. the acrostic Psalm

The longest chapter in the Bible, Psalm 119, is a long hymn of praise to God for giving His divine Law to man. The Psalm (with 176 verses) is an acrostic: The verses of each stanza begin with the same letter of the Hebrew alphabet. This was probably an aid to memorization.

381. the Babylonian captivity

After Nebuchadnezzar of Babylon sacked Jerusalem and destroyed the temple in 586 B.C., most of the Jews were carried to exile in Babylon. The years in Babylon are known as the Babylonian captivity. In 539 the Persians conquered Babylon and allowed the Jews to return to their homeland and rebuild their temple. Interestingly, some chose not to return.

382. Nebuchadnezzar's madness

The mighty king of Babylon is a prominent character in the book of Daniel. The man who had conquered Jerusalem and destroyed its temple finally did receive a divine punishment. While surveying his palace and congratulating himself on his achievements, the king heard a voice from heaven telling him it was all at an end. The king went and lived "with the beasts of the field," eating grass, with his hair growing long, "and his nails like birds' claws." Eventually the king came to his senses and returned to the throne, after admitting that God was truly God (Dan. 4:28–37). Several artists, notably William Blake, have portrayed the once mighty king down on all fours like a beast.

383. the call of Wisdom

Proverbs 8–9 presents Wisdom (always referred to as "she") calling to mankind. "Receive my instruction, and not silver . . for wisdom is better than rubies, and all the things one may desire cannot be compared with her" (8:10–11). According to 8:22, Wisdom was the first creation of God, made before the world began. The passage includes the most quoted verse from Proverbs, "The fear of the LORD is the beginning of wisdom" (9:10).

384. Ecclesiastes

This Old Testament book claims to be written by the "son of David, king in Jerusalem," and it is obviously referring to the wise king Solomon, who calls himself the "Teacher" (or "Preacher" in some translations). The Teacher looks at all the things that people pursue in life—power, wisdom, pleasure, wealth, work—and concludes that much of it is "Meaningless! Utterly meaningless! Everything is meaningless!" (Some translations have "Vanity of vanities, all is vanity.") Solomon, who had wealth, power, and wisdom, was obviously the right person to deal with this subject. The book is full of wise observations, such as 5:10, "He who loves silver will not be satisfied . . . this also is vanity." And 12:1 is often quoted: "Remember now your Creator in the days of your youth, before the difficult days come." The conclusion of this sometimes pessimistic book is sensible: "Fear God and keep his commandments, for this is the whole duty of man" (12:13 NIV).

Chapter 3, with its section beginning "To everything there is a season . . ." is often quoted.

385. Song of Solomon

It appears to be—and undoubtedly is—a set of love poems between a man and a woman. While it communicates the message that physical attraction is a fine and healthy thing, some readers wonder why the book is in the Bible. It does not mention God or anything spiritual. But centuries ago Jewish leaders decided that it had an allegorical meaning: The man in the poem represented God, the woman represented Israel, so the Song was a celebration of God's love for His chosen people. Later, when Christians accepted the Old Testament as Scripture, they decided the book had another meaning: The man represented Christ and the woman represented their church. Taken at face value, the Song reminds Christians that passion has its place in human life.

386. Isaiah (and Second Isaiah?)

This is one of the best-loved Old Testament books. The first Christians believed many of Isaiah's prophecies were fulfilled in the life of Jesus, notably the passages about Israel's "Suffering Servant" (see 387), an innocent one who suffers to bring salvation to his people. Isaiah is quoted more in the New Testament than any Old Testament book. Scholars believe that the book may have had more than one author. In fact, there is a noticeable change beginning with chapter 40, which seems to be written to people *after* the Babylonian conquest, while chapters 1–39 seem to be written by someone long *before* that event. Were there two Isaiahs? Evangelist D. L. Moody once stated that he thought this was unimportant, since he was often preaching to people who were not aware there was even *one* Isaiah.

387. the Suffering Servant

Several passages in Isaiah speak of a "servant of the Lord," a gentle, innocent man who endures suffering but is God's chosen one, the Messiah. The passages (42:1–4; 49:1–6; 50:4–9; 52:13–53:12) are often called the "Servant Songs" and the person they refer to is known as the "Suffering Servant." A good summary is Isaiah 53:4–5: "He has borne our griefs and carried our sorrows . . . He was wounded for our transgressions, He was bruised for our iniquities . . . and by His stripes we are healed."

The early Christians believed these passages applied to Jesus, Israel's Messiah who suffered greatly, the innocent man suffering for the guilty.

Handel, in his *Messiah,* included several passages from the Servant Songs.

388. born of a virgin

Isaiah prophesied the virgin birth with these words: "The virgin shall conceive and bear a Son, and shall call His name Immanuel" (Isa. 7:14). His words are repeated in Matthew 1:23, where it is connected with the miraculous conception of the child Jesus. Faith in Jesus involved accepting Him as the Son of God, God in the flesh—as the prophecy says, "God with us." The name occurs in many Christian writings, notably the hymn "O Come, O Come, Immanuel," popular at Christmastime.

389. valley of the dry bones

The prophet Ezekiel had several unusual visions, none more striking than that of a valley filled with dry bones. God asked him, "Can these bones live?" Ezekiel replied, "O Lord GOD, You know," and God commanded him to preach to them, saying, "O dry bones, hear the word of the LORD!" Ezekiel did so, and the bones reattached to one another and came to life. God told Ezekiel that the bones represented Israel, which thought itself spiritually dead. Yet God could and would put His Spirit in the people and return them to their homeland.

The story, found in Ezekiel 37:1–14, is the basis of the old spiritual, "Dem Bones, Dem Bones, Dem Dry Bones."

NEW TESTAMENT

390. the boy Jesus in the temple

We know nothing of Jesus' childhood except for the one incident reported in Luke 2:41–51, the twelve-year-old Jesus in the temple at Jerusalem. His family was there for the Passover Feast, and at age twelve a Jewish boy was considered a man. The family departed for home, found the boy had been left behind, then returned to Jerusalem to find Him among the religious teachers in the temple. "All who heard Him were astonished at His understanding and answers." Mary and Joseph scolded Him for remaining behind, and Jesus replied, "Why did you seek Me? Did you not know that I must be about My Father's business?" It is the first hint of the young Jesus' sense of His destiny and mission.

391. Jesus' family trees

Family trees were very important in the Bible, since the people of Israel were eager to prove that they could trace their ancestry all the way back to Abraham. Jesus was descended from Abraham, and His family tree appears in Matthew 1 and Luke 3. Matthew traces the family line of Joseph, Jesus' legal (but not biological) father, and he shows Joseph as a descendant of King David and, fourteen generations earlier, Abraham. Luke traces the family line even farther back—all the way to Adam.

392. Jesus' baptism

This act, performed by Jesus' kinsman John the Baptist, marked the beginning of Jesus' public life. All four Gospels report the event, and Matthew's gospel reports that John was reluctant to perform a baptism of repentance on Jesus, the sinless One. John said, "I need to be baptized by You, and are You coming to me?" Jesus replied, "Permit it to be so now, for thus it is fitting for us to fulfill all righteousness" (Matt. 3:15). When Jesus came up out of the water the Spirit descended on Him "like a dove" and a voice from heaven said, "This is My beloved Son, in whom I am well pleased." Jesus had received a divine and public approval of the ministry He was beginning.

Paintings of Jesus' baptism always show a dove (the Spirit) over His head. The baptism is the chief reason that the Holy Spirit is always symbolized by a dove.

393. the Sermon on the Mount

Found in Matthew 5–7, this is probably the most-quoted and quotable passage in the Bible. It takes its name from its opening verse: "Seeing the multitudes, He [Jesus] went up on a mountain." From there He delivered His most famous sermon. It includes the famous Beatitudes, the list of "blessings" on certain types of behavior. It includes the "salt of the earth" and "light of the world" passages, the words on committing murder and adultery in one's heart, a strict teaching on divorce, a new standard about loving one's enemies ("turn the other cheek"), the Lord's Prayer, some comforting words about not worrying, the memorable "seek and ye shall find" passage, and the parable of the wise man building his house upon a rock. Every verse in the Sermon on the Mount has been quoted, turned into hymns and poems, preached about, commented on, and discussed in a million Sunday school classes and Bible study groups.

Why? It is probably the best essence of Christian ethics found in the Bible. It's also incredibly hard to put into practice (particularly the parts about loving one's enemies and not resisting evil). But it is very direct, simple teaching, so basic that even small children can grasp it.

394. the Beatitudes

These are the best-known portion of Jesus' Sermon on the Mount, a pronouncement of blessings on certain categories of people. Found in Matthew 5 and Luke 6, they are blessings on the poor in spirit, those who mourn, the meek, those who hunger and thirst for righteousness, the merciful, the pure in heart, the peacemakers, and those who are persecuted for righteousness' sake. Jesus was setting forth the type of person who was part of "the kingdom of God."

The word *Beatitude* is not found in the Bible itself, but is based on the Latin word *beatitudo,* meaning "blessedness."

No portion of the Bible has been read, recited, discussed, commented on, or loved more than the Beatitudes.

395. the Lord's Prayer

It's the most repeated prayer in the world, and it's found in Matthew 6:9–13 and Luke 11:2–4. It is a simple, direct prayer to the Father, asking for daily necessities and forgiveness of sins. Luke 11 indicates that Jesus gave His disciples the prayer in response to the request "Lord, teach us to pray." Jesus intended it as a kind of model for prayer. It has been set to music countless times.

396. parables

Jesus used them frequently in His teaching, and many people's earliest memories of the Bible are the parables. Essentially they are comparisons—X is like Y—that illustrate some spiritual truth. Jesus had several "kingdom parables": "The kingdom of heaven is like a man who sowed good seed in his field . . . like a mustard seed . . . like yeast . . ." Using concrete, everyday images, Jesus' parables had a broad appeal. But they also puzzled people, even His own disciples, who often asked for interpretations.

Some of the best-known parts of the Bible are parables: the good Samaritan (Luke 10:25–37); the sower (Matt. 13:3–8); the workers in the vineyard (Matt. 20:1–16); the unjust judge (Luke 18:1–8); the Pharisee and the tax collector (Luke 18:9–14); the pearl of great price (Matt. 13:45–46); the prodigal son (Luke 15:11–32); and the rich fool (Luke 12:13–21).

John's gospel, unlike the other three, contains no parables.

397. the parable of the good Samaritan

Jesus' best-known parable was told following His command to "love your neighbor as yourself." A Jewish teacher asked

Him, "Who is my neighbor?" Jesus told the tale of a man who was beaten by robbers and left for dead. A priest and a Levite—representing the Jewish faith—passed by and did nothing, but a Samaritan (a people whom the Jews despised) stopped, bandaged the man, and carried him to an inn. Jesus then asked, "Which of these three do you think was a neighbor to the man?" The Jewish teacher could not bring himself to say "the Samaritan," so he replied, "He who showed mercy on him." Jesus replied, "Go and do likewise" (Luke 10:25–37).

The tale of compassion that moves beyond social prejudice is one of the most appealing stories in the Bible.

See 301 (Samaritans).

398. the seven woes

Jesus frequently criticized the Jewish religious establishment, particularly the Pharisees and the scribes (called in some translations "teachers of the law"). The most famous speech against them is in Matthew 23, the "seven woes," each beginning "Woe to you, scribes and Pharisees, hypocrites!" Jesus lambastes them for their fastidiousness about minor religious rules and enjoying the appearance of being religious but on the inside being full of hypocrisy. The speech ends with His lament, "O Jerusalem, Jerusalem, the one who kills the prophets and stones those who are sent to her!" (v. 37). It is one of the world's most eloquent sermons against religious hypocrisy.

399. the parable of the sheep and goats

Matthew's gospel relates this parable of the Last Judgment. Jesus depicted Himself as a shepherd separating a flock—sheep on one side, goats on the other (Matt. 25:31–46). He thanked the sheep (the righteous ones) for giving Him food, clothing, and hospitality. The sheep were surprised, asking when they ever did those things for Him. He replied, "Inasmuch as you did it to one of the least of these My brethren, you did it to Me." Then He said to the goats, "Depart from Me, you cursed, into the everlasting fire prepared for the devil and his angels . . . Inasmuch as you did not do it to one of the least of these, you did not do it to Me." The goats learned that loving God involves everyday acts of kindness to human beings.

400. the parable of the Pharisee and the tax collector

Jesus criticized the Pharisees, not for being righteous but for being proud and hypocritical. One of His best-known parables is found in Luke 18:10–14. Two men prayed in the temple. The Pharisee's prayer was self-congratulation: "God, I thank You that I am not like other men." The tax collector, aware of his sins (as well as being despised by most other Jews) could only say, "God, be merciful to me a sinner!" Jesus explained that the tax collector, not the Pharisee, was justified before God. "For everyone who exalts himself will be humbled, and he who humbles himself will be exalted."

401. the parable of Lazarus and the rich man

Luke's gospel is notable for its sympathy for the poor, and this is clear in 16:19–31, the story of a wealthy man and a beggar named Lazarus. Both died, and Lazarus was at Abraham's side (meaning heaven) while the rich man was tormented in hell. The rich man begged for relief, but Abraham reminded him that his earthly life was happy, while then the tables were turned and Lazarus was happy. The rich man begged that someone might warn his family of the danger of hell, but Abraham replied that they (the parable is obviously referring to the Jews) had the Torah and the Prophets to guide them—in fact, Abraham said, they would not change their ways even if someone rose from the dead. The parable was a slap at the Jewish religious establishment, which rejected Jesus, while "outsiders" (like Lazarus) had a home in heaven.

402. the parable of the prodigal son

Hardly anyone knows what *prodigal* means anymore (it refers to spending recklessly), but most people have heard of the prodigal son. Jesus' great parable of forgiveness is found in Luke 15:11–32, and could be more appropriately called "the forgiving father." One son asked his father for his share of the inheritance, squandered it quickly, realized he had been a fool, and shamefully returned home, where his father joyfully accepted him. The father's other son groused, for he had stayed home and lived rightly. But the father told him that he should rejoice that the wild-living son had returned home.

The parable mentions the father's order to "kill the fat-ted calf" for the homecoming party. Sitcoms and pop songs still make occasional reference to the "fatted calf."

The parable is a touching story of divine mercy. It is Jesus' reminder to people who have always lived moral lives that they ought to rejoice when sinners repent and turn to God.

403. a new commandment

"A new commandment I give to you, that you love one another; as I have loved you, that you also love one another." So Jesus said to His disciples in John 13:34. He gave this commandment after He had washed His disciples' feet, so when He commanded them to love "as I have loved you," He was speaking of an unselfish, giving, serving love.

Jesus spoke the commandment to the disciples just after Judas Iscariot the traitor had left the room.

404. the parable of the sower

Jesus' longest and most complex parable is a story of how people respond differently to the gospel. In the parable, a farmer sows seed, some of it falling on good ground, on rocky soil, among thorns, and along the path. Jesus explained the parable in this way: The seed is the Word of God. The seed on the path is eaten by birds—that is, Satan takes away what is sown. The seed on rocky soil grows but withers away—people receive the Word but it never takes root. The seed among thorns grew but was choked out—people receive the Word but worldly worries keep it from growing. The seed on good soil grew and produced "some thirtyfold, some sixty, and some a hundred" (Mark 4:3–9).

405. the parable of the unjust judge

Jesus prayed often and emphasized the importance of prayer. In the parable of the unjust judge, a judge "who did not fear God nor regard man" is pestered by a widow who begs him for justice. He refuses to hear her case, but eventually she wears him down, and he sees that she gets justice. Jesus tells the disciples that God, who is much better than this unrighteous judge, will certainly bring justice for His people. Jesus told them this parable to show them "that men always ought to pray and not lose heart" (Luke 18:1–8).

406. the lists of disciples

Matthew, Mark, Luke, and Acts (but not John, oddly enough) list Jesus' twelve disciples. Matthew's list runs as follows: Simon (also called Peter) and Andrew his brother, James the son of Zebedee, and John his brother, Philip, Bartholomew, Thomas, Matthew the tax collector, James the son of Alphaeus, Thaddaeus, Simon the Cananite, and Judas Iscariot, who betrayed him (Matt. 10:2–4). Peter, the most outspoken disciple in the Gospels, had some sort of prominence, and Jesus' inner circle also included James and John. Most of the other disciples (later called the apostles) play minor roles in the Gospels and Acts.

The list found in Acts 1:13 has one notable omission: Judas Iscariot by that time had killed himself.

The other lists are in Mark 3:16–19 and Luke 6:14–16.

407. the pearl of great price

Jesus told many parables comparing the kingdom of God to various things. In Matthew 13:45–46 He told of a pearl merchant who found one pearl so valuable that he sold all he had to buy it. Jesus was saying that finding the kingdom was the greatest thing that could happen to a person.

408. the widow's coins

Jesus valued heartfelt generosity. Once in the temple He saw rich people making a show of giving large amounts to the temple treasury. He saw a poor widow dropping in two copper coins and realized that, in proportion to what she had, she was giving generously. He told His disciples, "This poor widow has put in more than all those who have given to the treasury" (Mark 12:43).

409. the parable of the two houses

In Jesus' Sermon on the Mount He spoke of two responses to listening to His words: hearing and following, or hearing but not following. The one who follows Jesus' sayings is like one who builds his house on rock, able to withstand flood, storm, or any disaster. The one who does not follow His words is like he who built upon sand. When disasters came, the house fell, "and great was its fall" (Matt. 7:24–27).

410. Jesus and the children

Practically every children's Sunday school room in the world has had a picture of Jesus blessing the children in His arms. In an era when children were "seen but not heard," Jesus' compassion toward them was notable. People brought their children to Jesus for blessing, and when His disciples tried to shoo them away, Jesus said, "Let the little children come to Me, and do not forbid them; for of such is the kingdom of God . . . Whoever does not receive the kingdom of God as a little child will by no means enter it" (Mark 10:14–15). Jesus was referring to the qualities of trust and acceptance.

411. God and mammon

"You cannot serve God and mammon," Jesus said (Matt. 6:24). Many versions translate the Greek word *mammon* as "money," but it really means "material possessions" in general. Jesus said elsewhere that it is difficult for the rich to enter heaven (Mark 10:25). But people who "serve mammon" aren't necessarily rich—even a poor person can be a worshiper of material things. "You cannot serve God and mammon" was His way of saying that deep love for God and an obsession with possessions cannot exist together.

412. the eye of the needle

"It is easier for a camel to go through the eye of a needle than for a rich man to enter the kingdom of God" (Mark 10:25). When Jesus said this He knew His listeners were familiar with the bulk of the camel (as opposed to the smallness of a needle's eye). While Jesus made it clear that it *was* possible (but rare) for the wealthy to enter heaven, the New Testament consistently states that people in love with possessions cannot be in love with God.

413. the narrow gate

Jesus' great Sermon on the Mount includes His words about the way to eternal life: "Enter by the narrow gate; for wide is the gate and broad is the way that leads to destruction, and there are many who go in by it. Because narrow is the gate and difficult is the way which leads to life, and there are few who find it" (Matt. 7:13–14).

414. the parable of the lost sheep

Jesus taught the love of God, but He also taught that hell was real. Even so, He made it clear that God desired that everyone would come to Him. Jesus told the parable of a shepherd who had one hundred sheep, one of which had strayed into the mountains. The shepherd left the ninety-nine to seek out the stray. "Even so it is not the will of your Father who is in heaven that one of these little ones should perish" (Matt. 18:10–14).

415. the parable of the talents

Life is precious, not something to be wasted. Jesus told the story of a man who goes on a journey and gives each of his servants some money (a "talent" was a unit of money in those days). The servant given five talents managed to make another five, and the servant with two talents also doubled his amount. But the servant given one talent buried it in the ground. When the master returned, he praised the first two servants for being productive, but condemned the one who buried the money in the ground. Jesus' point was that those who are wise and responsible will be rewarded by God. (See Matt. 25:14–30.)

416. consider the lilies

Jesus, like any wise man, knew that anxiety could sap the joy from a person's life. He spoke poetically about God's care for our needs, and the foolishness of worrying: "Consider the lilies, how they grow: they neither toil nor spin; and yet I say to you, even Solomon in all his glory was not arrayed like one of these. If then God so clothes the grass, which today is in the field and tomorrow is thrown into the oven, how much more will He clothe you, O you of little faith?" (Luke 12:27–28).

417. the golden rule

"Do to others what you would have them do to you, for this sums up the Law and the Prophets" (Matt. 7:12 NIV). This is one of Jesus' best-known teachings, one of many found in the Sermon on the Mount (Matt. 5–7). The name for it, "the golden rule," is not found in the Bible but is centuries old.

418. the Greatest Commandments

The Jews of the New Testament era had many rules to follow—not only the ones in the Torah (the first five books of the Bible), but many other additional rules that the rabbis had added over the centuries. One of the Pharisees, who prided themselves on following rules to the letter, questioned Jesus: "'Teacher, which is the great commandment in the law?' Jesus said to him, '"You shall love the LORD your God with all your heart, with all your soul, and with all your mind." This is the first and great commandment. And the second is like it: "You shall love your neighbor as yourself." On these two commandments hang all the Law and the Prophets'" (Matt. 22:34–40). Both commandments are from the Torah—the first from Deuteronomy 6:5, the second from Leviticus 19:18. Jesus was saying that love of God and love of one's fellow man are the goal that all the other rules aim toward.

419. cleansing the temple

Jesus angry and wielding a whip? On one occasion, yes. All four Gospels relate that Jesus entered the Jerusalem temple and drove out the sellers and money changers. He quoted Isaiah 56:7, "Is it not written, 'My house shall be called a house of prayer for all nations'? But you have made it a 'den of thieves'" (Mark 11:17). He was angered that a place for worshiping God seemed more like a marketplace. Merchants sold the wine, oil, and animals used in the sacrifices. The money changers also made a nice profit. As expected, Jesus' violent act angered the Jewish religious establishment, who made money off the system. So, "the scribes and chief priests heard it and sought how they might destroy Him" (Mark 11:18).

The cleansing is a dramatic incident, one that reminds us that Jesus could be forceful as well as gentle.

420. the anointing at Bethany

Washing the feet of one's guests was a normal custom in the dusty lands of the Bible. Ordinarily a servant did the task, but the Gospels record that a woman bathed Jesus' feet herself—not with water, but with expensive perfume and with her own tears. The woman was known as being immoral, but Jesus was impressed with her devotion and told her her sins were forgiven. The disciple Judas Iscariot criticized the "waste" of the perfume, saying the money for it could have aided the poor. But Jesus commended her generous act (John 12:1–8; Luke 7:36–50).

421. the Last Supper

Before His arrest and crucifixion, Jesus shared a Passover meal with His disciples, a scene that artists have been painting for centuries. The meal, like most Jewish meals, included wine and bread. Knowing what was about to happen, Jesus took the bread and told His disciples, "This is My body which is given for you; do this in remembrance of

Me." Then He took the wine and said, "This cup is the new covenant in My blood, which is shed for you" (Luke 22:19–20). At that moment the disciples probably did not know the significance of what He said. Afterward, Jesus went with the disciples (except Judas, the betrayer) to the Garden of Gethsemane, where He prayed to be spared death, but was arrested after Judas betrayed Him to the Jewish authorities.

Most Christians celebrate holy Communion (or Eucharist), which is a reminder of Jesus' Last Supper. Christians have argued over whether the wine and bread are really the blood and body of Christ (which Catholics believe), but all agree that Communion is a reminder that Christ gave up His life as the ultimate sacrifice for human sin. It is one of the key incidents in Jesus' life, and Acts and the Epistles affirm that the early Christians took care to celebrate the Lord's Supper regularly.

422. Jesus' trial before Herod

Luke's gospel records that Jesus was not only tried before the Roman governor Pilate but also before Herod, who had power over Jesus' homeland, Galilee. Herod was pleased, since he'd heard many things about Jesus and hoped He would perform a miracle. Jesus would say nothing at all to the decadent ruler, and Herod and his soldiers mocked Jesus, dressing Him in a royal robe before they sent Him back to Pilate (Luke 23:6–12).

This was the same Herod who had executed John the Baptist.

423. crown of thorns

The Gospels state that it was Jesus' fellow Jews who brought about His crucifixion. The Romans, who governed the area, only carried out the sentence. But the Romans come across as cruel and barbarous also. The Roman soldiers despised the Jews, and they enjoyed making sport of their captive, the "King of the Jews." They put a crown of thorns on His head and a reed in His hand (a mock crown and scepter), kneeling and saying, "Hail, King of the Jews!" They spat on Him and beat Him with the reed. Before He was even crucified, He was already humiliated and bleeding.

Many artists have painted *The Mocking of Christ*.

424. scourging / flogging

This punishment involved a rod or whip, applied to the victim's bare back while he was tied to a stake. The Romans used whips studded with jagged metal or bone. Loss of blood meant that scourging could be fatal. Jesus was scourged before being crucified, which explains why His death on the cross came relatively fast (John 19:33).

Jesus predicted that His followers would also be scourged, and Acts reports that this was so (Acts 5:40; 16:23). Paul was flogged, though on one occasion he was saved from flogging by mentioning he was a Roman citizen and not subject to this brutal punishment (Acts 22:25).

425. the Crucifixion

This was a horrible punishment, one the Romans used to keep their conquered people in line. The convicted criminal carried the heavy wooden crosspiece (for his arms) to the site, where his wrists (not his hands) were nailed to the wood. This piece was raised by ropes to the vertical wooden piece already in the ground. The pain was excruciating, especially since it often took many hours, even days, to die. Crosses were placed in highly visible spots, usually along well-traveled roads, so people could see what happened to criminals convicted by Rome. Interestingly, the four Gospels do not give many details of Jesus' crucifixion. They probably assumed their readers would know how brutal a death it was.

The Romans normally crucified men nude—but they made an exception for the Jews, allowing them to wear a loincloth.

426. the seven words of Christ on the cross

All four Gospels report Jesus' crucifixion, and each provides details the others leave out. Drawing from all four Gospels, Jesus' words while on the cross were: (1) "Eli, Eli, lama sabachthani?" (meaning, "My God, my God, why have You forsaken Me?"). (2) "Father, forgive them, for they do not know what they do." (3) To the thief: "Assuredly, I say to you, today you will be with Me in Paradise." (4) "Father, into Your hands I commit My spirit." (5) "I thirst." (6) "It is finished." (7) To Mary and the beloved disciple: "Woman, behold your son. Behold your mother."

427. the resurrection of Jesus

This is *the* key event in the New Testament, as important for the Christians as the deliverance from Egypt was for the Jews. All four Gospels report that the body of Jesus, crucified on a Friday and placed in a tomb, was not in the tomb on the following Sunday. The Gospels do not explain how the event occurred, only that it did, and that many people saw the risen Jesus. When Mary Magdalene and another woman went to the tomb on the Sunday morning, an angel at the empty tomb told them, "He is not here, but is risen!" Jesus' body was somehow changed—He was like Himself enough to be recognized, yet changed enough that two of His disciples did not immediately know Him (Luke 24:13–27). Some of the disciples thought He was only a phantom, but clearly He had a body of flesh: He told them, "Handle Me and see, for a spirit does not have flesh and bones as you see I have" (Luke 24:39). He also ate some food to show He was truly alive, not just a ghost. After some days He blessed His disciples and ascended into heaven (see 627 [Ascension]).

The New Testament never tires of speaking of the risen Jesus. While Jesus was admired as a teacher, healer, and miracle worker, the key event was that after dying a horrible death on the cross, God raised Him from the dead. Had the disciples not sincerely believed that their dead Master had been raised up by God, Christianity would not have spread across the globe.

428. the Great Commission

Must Christians evangelize? Yes, according to Matthew 28:19–20. Jesus' last words to His disciples were: "Go therefore and make disciples of all the nations, baptizing them in the name of the Father and of the Son and of the Holy Spirit, teaching them to observe all things that I have commanded you; and lo, I am with you always, even to the end of the age." To this day, Christian baptisms are done with the "Father, Son, Spirit" formula.

429. the council of Jerusalem

To circumcise or not to circumcise? That was the question confronting the early Christians. Most of them were Jews, so they followed Jewish law in regard to circumcision (performed on all male infants) and dietary laws (the law of kosher). But Paul and other apostles had begun to spread Christianity to non-Jews. According to Acts 15, some Jewish Christians insisted that circumcision was required in order to be a Christian. At an important Christian gathering in Jerusalem, the apostle Peter told the assembly that conversion to Christianity was a spiritual matter, so circumcision must not be required. Paul backed him up in this, and the council drafted a letter to non-Jewish Christians, telling them to avoid immorality but making no mention of mandatory circumcision.

Something important was at stake: Was Christianity just an offshoot of the Jews' religion, or was it (as Paul and Peter believed) a universal faith, a spiritual faith that could not be confined by the old requirements of the Jews?

A practical matter: Adult men who were drawn to Christianity balked at the prospect of undergoing an extremely painful procedure—a procedure that they saw as "a Jewish thing," having nothing to do with faith in Christ. Most non-Jews thought circumcision was a silly practice, a sort of tribal relic that the Jews held to. The council of Jerusalem was wise in opting not to require circumcision.

See 118 (circumcision).

430. the Ephesian farewell

The early Christians were certainly not uptight or unemotional. Acts 20 records Paul's farewell to his Christian friends in Ephesus. After addressing them, Paul knelt with them and prayed. "Then they all wept freely, and fell on Paul's neck and kissed him, sorrowing most of all . . . that they would see his face no more" (vv. 17–38).

431. Paul's Macedonian vision

Paul and the other apostles had spread the gospel through much of the Near East. Acts 16:6–10 tells how they came to take the faith into Europe. In the town of Troas, Paul had a vision of a man of Macedonia standing and begging, "Come over to Macedonia and help us." Paul and his companions responded to this divine vision.

Christian missionaries through the centuries love repeating this story, picturing people around the world saying, "Come over and help us."

432. "Vengeance is Mine, I will repay"

The New Testament faith is one of forgiveness and mercy—not one of revenge. Paul, in Romans 12:19, quotes a verse based on Deuteronomy 32:35: "'Vengeance is Mine, I will repay,' says the Lord." Paul continues this line of thought by saying, "Do not be overcome by evil, but overcome evil with good." It is a good summation of Christian ethics.

433. "You are God's temple"

The early Christians set high standards for sexual morality—a notable contrast to the morals of nonbelievers. In 1 Corinthians, Paul stressed that a Christian's body is not just his own possession, but also "the temple of God," in which dwells the Holy Spirit. Paul advised the Corinthian Christians to "flee sexual immorality. Every sin that a man does is outside the body, but he who commits sexual immorality sins against his own body. Or do you not know that your body is the temple of the Holy Spirit? . . . Therefore glorify God in your body" (6:18–20).

434. Paul on husbands and wives

Feminists have a low opinion of the apostle Paul's teachings about the roles of husbands and wives. They find Ephesians 5:22 particularly offensive: "Wives, submit to your own husbands, as to the Lord." In fact, Paul had no desire to see husbands dominate or abuse their wives. He emphasized that husbands must love their wives just as Christ loves His people, and that they must not be harsh with their wives

(Col. 3:19). Paul saw marriage as mutual responsibility, with both parties belonging to each other (1 Cor. 7:3–4). Paul saw the husband as the "head of his household," but also saw the husband as responsible to a higher authority, Christ.

435. Paul's arrest

Paul and the other apostles made many Jewish converts to Christianity, but other Jews opposed them, sometimes violently. On more than one occasion Paul was beaten, stoned, and imprisoned. But his most dramatic confrontation with the Jews came when they accused him (falsely) of taking a Gentile into the temple area—an offense worthy of death. Had the Roman military commander not intervened, Paul would have been killed by the mob. While Paul was in Roman custody, Paul's nephew told the commander that the Jews had plotted to kill Paul. The commander wisely chose to keep Paul out of the Jewish courts and sent him to the Roman governor Felix (Acts 21:26–23:24).

436. Paul's shipwreck

Paul the Apostle had a life with many interesting scrapes and escapes, and Acts 27 tells of a dramatic storm and shipwreck. The storm raged for days, and almost everything was thrown overboard. The crew was about to despair, but Paul (on his way to trial in Rome) announced that an angel had assured him that he would reach Rome, and though the ship would be lost, no one would die. The ship ran aground on Malta, and the soldiers on board planned to kill the prisoners, fearing they would try to escape. But a Roman centurion who apparently liked Paul kept the soldiers from killing anyone.

437. the Love Chapter

Paul's great chapter of the nature of love is found in 1 Corinthians 13. It follows a discussion of the various "spiritual gifts" that Christians have. Paul says that love—not romantic love, but the more durable and unselfish *agape* love—is greater than possessing any other "spiritual gift." Paul says that if a person is not loving, other good qualities mean nothing. The chapter is quoted often: "Love is patient . . . kind . . not self-seeking . . . always protects, always trusts, always hopes . . ." It has probably been read at weddings more than any other part of the Bible.

438. the whole armor of God

In Ephesians 6:10–18, Paul speaks of the "spiritual armor" that Christians wear to face the powers of evil. The "whole armor of God" includes the belt of truth, breastplate of righteousness, shoes of the gospel of peace, shield of faith, helmet of salvation, and sword of the Spirit.

Christian art often pictures the apostle Paul with a sword, which is based on the "sword of the Spirit" mentioned in this passage.

439. the Pastoral Letters

First Timothy, 2 Timothy, and Titus are called the "Pastorals" because their author, the apostle Paul, was giving advice to two pastors, Timothy and Titus. Timothy was fairly young, and Paul took a fatherly interest in the man he called "my true son in the faith." Paul set high moral and spiritual standards for ministers and other church officials. The three letters are interesting for their advice (still useful) on the Christian ministry, and for the light they shed on how an institutional church was developing.

One interesting note: The Pastorals do *not* teach that ministers must be unmarried and celibate.

440. Paul on the Resurrection

The Bible's key chapter of the eternal fate of believers is 1 Corinthians 15. Paul explains that just as Christ was raised from the dead and existed in a new "spiritual body," so the same end awaits believers. As children of Adam we have earthly bodies, and as (spiritual) children of Christ we have spiritual bodies that will never perish. Paul speaks eloquently of the great resurrection of God's people: "The trumpet will sound, and the dead will be raised incorruptible, and we shall be changed" (v. 52).

441. "a thief in the night"

More than once the New Testament uses this expression to refer to the return of Jesus to earth. The idea is that it will catch people unaware, thus the faithful must be alert at all times. According to Paul, "The day of the Lord so comes as a thief in the night" (1 Thess. 5:2). Peter elaborates on this return: "The day of the Lord will come as a thief in the night, in which the heavens will pass away with a great noise, and the elements will melt with fervent heat" (2 Peter 3:10).

442. the epistle to the Hebrews

It is the only New Testament epistle that is anonymous, which is just as well, since its message is more important than its author. Jesus is seen as not only God's Son but also the Great High Priest, mediator between sinful man and God. He was truly divine, but also fully human, and so sympathetic to our own human weakness. He was the ultimate Priest, and also the ultimate sacrifice for man's sin.

Not only is its author unknown, but its recipients as well. It was probably a widely circulated letter to Christians everywhere. No doubt its title "Hebrews" referred to the many ways the epistle looks at the Hebrew priesthood and sacrifices.

The epistle is most noted for its "faith hall of fame" (see 443) in chapter 11.

Notable quote: "Jesus Christ is the same yesterday, today, and forever" (13:8).

443. the "faith hall of fame"

Hebrews 11 looks at key figures from the Old Testament, considering how each one was an example of faith in God. It begins with Abel and continues on through the prophets.

Particular attention is paid to Abraham and Moses (not surprisingly, since they are the two most important figures in Jewish tradition). The chapter mentions that many faithful people have suffered persecution and martyrdom, so much so that the world was not worthy of them. Yet, it continues, these faithful ones were missing something: the fuller revelation through Christ.

444. Apocalypse

This is another name for the book of Revelation. The name (from the Greek word *apokalupsis*) means "revealing" or "unveiling." Bible scholars use the word *Apocalypse* to refer to a writing that (like Revelation) reveals dramatic events at the end of the world, often in the form of symbolic visions. There were several Apocalypses written by the early Christians, but the church finally decided that Revelation, written by John, was the only one that was truly inspired and sacred.

10

Notable People, Alphabetically

445. Aaron

Moses' elder brother was at his side during his many confrontations with Egypt's pharaoh in Exodus. The staff Aaron carried was miraculously turned into a serpent, and when Egyptian magicians duplicated the miracle, Aaron's serpent devoured theirs (Ex. 7). Aaron was Israel's first high priest and ancestor of its later priests. One blot on his character: While Moses was on Sinai receiving the Ten Commandments from God, Aaron aided the Israelites in making a golden calf idol to worship (Ex. 32). Later, Aaron and his sister, Miriam, angered God by their jealousy of Moses (Num. 12). Like Moses, Aaron was denied the privilege of entering the promised land with the Israelites.

446. Abraham

His name Abram (meaning "exalted father") was changed by God to Abraham (meaning "father of a multitude"). God called Abram from his pagan homeland of Ur to live in Canaan, where, God promised, his many descendants would prosper if they would serve the one true God. Abraham was the physical and spiritual ancestor of the Israelites (and, later, the Christians looked to him as a spiritual role model). Abraham's story is told in Genesis 12–25, and several of the key events are covered elsewhere in this book. He and his beloved wife, Sarah, were old and childless, leading him to doubt God's promise of many descendants. But three heavenly visitors told him that, miraculously, Sarah would give birth. She bore Isaac, whom God later ordered Abraham to sacrifice (see 370 [the sacrifice of Isaac]). With Abraham, God mandated the ritual of circumcision, which Jews still observe.

447. Adam and Eve

The first man's name means, in Hebrew, "from the ground," which is (according to Gen. 2:7) what God made Adam from. He was from the earth, but also made in God's image, unlike the animals. Adam was given the task of tending the Garden of Eden, and he named the animals, his only companions. But God saw that he needed a more suitable companion, so He put Adam into a deep sleep, took one of his ribs, and fashioned the first woman, Eve. The two lived in the Garden naked "and were not ashamed" (Gen. 2:25). God had given them only one rule: Do not eat the fruit of the Tree of Knowledge of Good and Evil. Genesis 3 is the story of the wily serpent who tempted Eve (who then tempted Adam) to eat the fruit, saying that God had imposed the rule to withhold something from the two. The disobedience is known as the fall of man (see 232). Man and wife were suddenly ashamed to be naked. They covered themselves with fig leaves and hid from God. He punished them by banishment from the Garden. He punished Adam by making him sweat to earn his living. He punished Eve with the pains of childbirth and the domination of her husband. The pair's first child was Cain, who later murdered the younger son, Abel.

Presumably Adam and Eve would have lived forever had they not disobeyed God. As it was, they did die, as He promised, but Adam lived to be 930 and had many children.

The New Testament authors saw Adam as the one who brought the curse of disobedience and sin on his descendants. The "old Adam" disobeyed, but the spiritual "new Adam" (Christ) was totally obedient to God. Adam's sin is "undone" by the perfect Christ (Rom. 5; 1 Cor. 15:20–22).

The Hebrew word *adam* is used many times in the Old Testament to mean simply "mankind."

448. Amos

Amos is often called the "prophet of justice." In his brief book he condemns the people of Israel for living selfishly and oppressing the poor. He rails against practicing religious rituals while living immorally. Like other prophets, he predicted the "day of the LORD," when God would judge

Israel's sins. Amos's most-quoted verse is 5:24, "Let justice run down like water, and righteousness like a mighty stream."

449. Barnabas

He was a fellow missionary with the apostle Paul. He was extremely generous, for he sold his property and gave it to the apostles in Jerusalem (Acts 4:36–37), and he encouraged the doubtful Christians to accept Paul into the fellowship (Acts 9:26–29). His name was Joseph, but he was renamed Barnabas, which means "Son of Encouragement" (Acts 4:36). In one town Barnabas and Paul were mistaken for the gods Zeus and Hermes because they had worked miracles (Acts 14:8–20). The two men parted company over a dispute, and Paul's new missionary partner was Silas (Acts 15:36–41). Paul mentioned Barnabas in several of his letters.

450. Caleb

His name means "dog," and he is represented as a loyal character. He was one of twelve spies Moses sent ahead of the Israelites to give a report on the land of Canaan. Caleb gave a glowing report of the land and encouraged the people to press on and settle there. But the other spies were pessimists and said the Canaanites were giant warriors, "and we were like grasshoppers" (Num. 13:33). The gloomy report almost led to a rebellion against Moses. God promised that Caleb, but not the pessimistic spies, would settle in the land while the others would die.

451. Claudius

The fourth Roman emperor, who ruled from A.D. 41 to 54 is mentioned twice in Acts, which states that he had expelled the Jews from Rome (Acts 18:2). This expulsion resulted in Paul meeting his dear friends Priscilla and Aquila (see 497) in Corinth.

452. Cornelius

One of the most appealing characters in the New Testament is Cornelius, a Roman centurion. Acts 10:2 describes him as "one who feared God," which meant he practiced a Jewish spirituality, including prayer and aiding the poor. He is also described as being visited by an angel, who linked him up with the apostle Peter. Peter had a curious vision of a large sheet holding nonkosher animals, with a voice telling him, "Rise, Peter; kill and eat." Peter, raised as a Jew, replied that he couldn't eat creatures that were "unclean" according to Jewish law. The voice told him, "What God has cleansed you must not call common." Peter's vision was a turning point in Christianity: Peter is being told to take the Christian faith to non-Jews. He met with Cornelius, even though Jewish custom required him to avoid the homes of non-Jews. Cornelius's household was converted to Christianity. Peter's fellow Christians called Peter on the carpet for hobnobbing with non-Jews, but Peter explained his vision, and the other Christians rejoiced that God had included non-Jews in His plan of salvation.

See 429 (council of Jerusalem).

453. David

His name means "beloved," and the Bible speaks of him as "a man after [God's] own heart" (1 Sam. 13:14). David, Israel's great king, psalm writer, and military leader, was also an adulterer, overly indulgent father, and a failure in several other ways. His story is the fullest biography of anyone in the Old Testament, and the Bible shows him (as it shows all its heroes) "warts and all." David the shepherd boy, harpist, slayer of Goliath, bosom friend of Jonathan, loyal servant (and prey) of paranoid King Saul, husband of many wives, military man—David was so many things (most of them covered elsewhere in this book). Despite his flaws, Israel remembered him as an ideal king, an emotional man so God-obsessed that he danced publicly when the ark of the covenant was brought into Jerusalem. Israel had reasons to regret it had ever asked God for a king, but David was, in the final analysis, a *good* king, loyal almost always to God and people near him.

The books of 1 and 2 Samuel are somewhat misnamed, since David (not Samuel) is the chief character.

David's birth in Bethlehem led to the idea that Israel's spiritual King, the Messiah, would be born in Bethlehem. It was, of course, Jesus' birthplace.

454. the disciple Jesus loved

John's gospel refers several times to "the disciple whom Jesus loved," not mentioning him by name. At the Last Supper this disciple was leaning on Jesus' chest, and while He was on the cross Jesus gave His mother, Mary, into the care of this disciple. Along with Peter, he was the first of the disciples to find Jesus' empty tomb.

At the end of the Gospel the author writes, "This is the disciple who testifies of these things, and wrote these things" (21:24). In other words, John himself was the "disciple whom Jesus loved" (John 13:23; 19:26; 20:2; 21:20).

455. Elijah

Was Israel's God the LORD of history and all the universe— or just another fertility god? Israel's prophets constantly preached against their people's idol worship. The Canaanite fertility god Baal (see 225) was one of many false gods the Israelites worshiped. The great prophet Elijah struggled against a formidable opponent, Queen Jezebel, who tried to make Baal the national god. Elijah challenged 450 prophets of Baal to a showdown on Mount Carmel (1 Kings 18). There the frenzied Baal prophets had no success in calling down Baal to devour the animals they sacrificed, but Elijah's God sent down fire (possibly lightning) to consume the sacrifice. When the people saw that God was the true God, "they fell on their faces; and they said, 'The LORD, He is God!'" It is one of the most dramatic stories in the Bible. Unfortunately, it made Jezebel determined to kill Elijah, so he fled to the desert, where God comforted him and reminded him that there were other godly people in Israel.

Elijah had several confrontations with Jezebel's wicked husband, King Ahab (see 238 [Naboth's vineyard]). He predicted doom for both Jezebel and Ahab, prophecies that came true. Elijah's successor, Elisha, saw his master taken to heaven in a fiery chariot (2 Kings 2). Both prophets worked many miracles, including bringing people back from the dead.

Elijah became a symbol of Israel's prophets, and since he did not die but was taken to heaven, people began to believe that he (or someone like him) would some day return to turn the people back to God. The prophet Malachi predicted that God would send Elijah before the "day of the Lord" to prepare the people. Jesus said that John the Baptist indeed was (spiritually speaking) Elijah returned (Matt. 11:14).

456. Elisha

Very much Israel's "miracle man," the prophet Elisha performed more wonders than anyone until Jesus, centuries later. He was the successor to the great prophet Elijah, whom he saw taken into heaven in a fiery chariot (see 349 [chariots of fire]).

Elisha's miracles could have good or bad effects. He made bad water drinkable by throwing salt into it, but immediately afterward he punished some teens who poked fun at his baldness by having two bears maul them (2 Kings 2:19–25). The son of a woman who showed hospitality to Elisha died suddenly. Elisha brought the dead boy to life by lying on him and breathing into him. Elisha also made some poison stew edible and, in another food miracle, used a few loaves of bread to feed a hundred men. He cured the Syrian soldier Naaman of leprosy, made an ax head float to the surface of a river, and blinded Aramean troops that pursued him. Elisha's miracle-working power continued even after his death. When a dead man's body fell into Elisha's tomb and touched his bones, the dead man came to life (2 Kings 13:20–21).

Alert Bible readers have observed that some of Elisha's miracles—healing the sick, raising the dead, multiplying food to feed a crowd—were also done by Jesus.

457. the Ethiopian eunuch

There was an apostle named Philip, but more important in the book of Acts is Philip the deacon, a noted evangelist and healer. Acts 8:26–40 tells of his meeting a eunuch in the service of the queen of Ethiopia. (Eunuch might indicate a court official, not necessarily a castrated man.) Philip finds the man in a chariot, reading a scroll of the prophet Isaiah. Philip, at the eunuch's request, explains the passage from Isaiah as a prophecy of Jesus. He presents the gospel to the eunuch, who asks to be baptized nearby. Afterward the eunuch "went on his way rejoicing."

The story shows how the faith was spreading to people of far-flung nations.

458. Ezra

The book of Ezra tells some of the history of the Jews after Cyrus, the Persian ruler, released them from their exile in Babylon. He allowed them to return to their homeland and gave them back the temple articles that the Babylonians had plundered. Eventually the temple was rebuilt and rededicated. Ezra, a priest, returned with a group to Jerusalem in 458 B.C., and "Ezra had prepared his heart to seek the Law of the LORD, and to do it, and to teach statutes and ordinances in Israel" (7:10). Ezra is referred to as both "priest" and "teacher," and clearly is the most dedicated religious leader in the group of resettlers. In chapter 10 he leads the people in confessing their sins.

Parts of the book are written in the first person, meaning that Ezra wrote parts of the book that bear his name. Ezra is also a prominent character in the book of Nehemiah (see 490).

459. Felix and Festus

Felix was governor of Judea after Pilate, and the apostle Paul was brought before him for trial. Paul defended himself and his faith eloquently, and Felix thought enough of Paul to allow him to have visitors. But Felix was notoriously corrupt, and he hesitated to free or condemn Paul, hoping someone would offer him a bribe to release Paul. Felix's successor, Festus, was more honorable. He believed Paul was a good man, but as Paul spoke about his faith, Festus responded, "Paul, you are beside yourself! Much learning is driving you mad!" (Acts 26:24). Had Paul not insisted on having a trial in Rome (his right as a Roman citizen), Festus would have released him.

460. Gamaliel

Tolerance and *diversity* weren't highly valued in the ancient world. Most people believed their god (or gods) was the true one, and everyone else's was not. The Jews were intolerant, but so were most other people in those days. It was no surprise to the first Christians that the Jews (and most of the first Christians had been Jews themselves) persecuted them for their religion. Acts 5 describes how the apostle Peter and other apostles were dragged in before the Jewish leaders and told to stop preaching the new faith. Peter's famous reply was, "We ought to obey God rather than men" (v. 29). One of the Jewish leaders was the respected Gamaliel. The wise Gamaliel advised the other Jewish leaders to leave the Christians alone, "for if this plan or this work is of men, it will come to nothing; but if it is of God, you cannot overthrow it" (vv. 38–39). His speech had an effect—sort of. The Jewish leaders released the Christians . . . after having them flogged.

The apostle Paul had been trained in the Jewish traditions under Gamaliel.

461. Habakkuk

Habakkuk's book of prophecy is a kind of dialogue between himself and God. He asks that age-old question, Why do the wicked prosper? Habakkuk knew that the leaders in Judah were selfish and oppressive, but he marveled that God would use the people of an even crueler nation, the Babylonians, to punish Judah. God's reply is that Babylon will, in time, itself be punished. A phrase the apostle Paul used in Romans 1:17 was quoted from Habakkuk: "The just shall live by his faith" (Hab. 2:4).

462. Hezekiah

The righteous king's reign is described in 2 Kings 18–20. He worshiped God alone and did his best to prohibit idol worship. He also rebelled against Assyria, which led to Jerusalem being threatened by the mighty king Sennacherib. The prophet Isaiah told Hezekiah that God would deliver them from the brutal Assyrians. The angel of the Lord struck down 185,000 Assyrian soldiers and Sennacherib returned home—to be murdered by his own sons.

Deathly ill, Hezekiah was told by Isaiah that he would soon die. Hezekiah prayed sincerely, and God relented, allowing him to live another fifteen years.

Later, Hezekiah showed ambassadors from Babylon his royal treasures. Isaiah then predicted that the Babylonians would some day carry away all those treasures, along with Hezekiah's descendants. The prophecy was fulfilled when Babylonians sacked the country in 586 B.C.

463. Hosea

One of Israel's prophets, Hosea had a home life that illustrated the relationship of God and Israel. He married (at God's command) a promiscuous woman (with the unlikely name of Gomer) and was told by God to give his children names symbolizing Israel's religious unfaithfulness. Hosea, like God Himself, is willing to show love to the unfaithful. Hosea's book contains some often-quoted passages, notably "I desire mercy and not sacrifice" and "They sow the wind, and reap the whirlwind" (6:6; 8:7). Hosea is quoted several times in the New Testament.

464. Ichabod

The most famous Ichabod is the gangly schoolmaster Ichabod Crane in Washington Irving's story "The Legend of Sleepy Hollow." Irving probably picked the name because it sounds absurd, and also because he knew the name's Hebrew meaning, "no glory." The Ichabod in the Bible was the grandson of the priest Eli. The Philistines had captured the ark of the covenant from Israel, and Eli was so appalled he literally fell over and died. His daughter-in-law named her newborn Ichabod because the glory (of God, connected with the ark) had departed from Israel (1 Sam. 4:19–22).

465. Ishmael

He was the son of Abraham and his concubine Hagar. After Ishmael was born, Abraham's wife, Sarai, drove mother and child away, and an angel saved them from perishing (Gen. 16). The nation of Israel was descended from Abraham's son Isaac, but Genesis records that a great nation was descended from Ishmael also.

Arabs trace their ancestry to Ishmael, called *Ismail* in the Koran, the holy book of the Muslims. The Koran, in contrast with the Bible, says that Ismail, not Isaac, was the favorite son of Abraham.

466. James, brother of Jesus

The Gospels mention several brothers of Jesus: James, Simon, Joses, and Judas (Matt. 13:55; Mark 6:3). John 7:5

indicates that the brothers did not accept Jesus' divine authority in His lifetime. But 1 Corinthians 15:7 states that James was privileged to see the risen Jesus. Later on James became a leader of the Christians in Jerusalem, and Acts 15 shows him presiding over the council that debated the issue of Gentiles becoming Christians. Paul referred to James as an apostle even though he was not one of the original twelve (Gal. 1:19).

James is a common name in the New Testament. Tradition says that James the brother of Jesus was the one who wrote the epistle of James, though we can't be certain.

467. James the apostle

Brothers James and John were two of Jesus' twelve disciples, both fishermen, and both part of Jesus' "inner circle" that also included Peter. James and John asked Jesus that they be given special positions in the kingdom of God, and Jesus replied that they should desire to serve, not to dominate, for Jesus Himself came as a servant (Mark 10:35–41). James, John, and Peter were present with Jesus at the glorious Transfiguration (Mark 9).

James became the first disciple to die for his faith. In the persecution of Christians under Herod Antipas, James was put to death with the sword (Acts 12:2).

468. Jeremiah

Jeremiah is known as the "weeping prophet" because he wrote the sad book of Lamentations, and his own book of prophecy shows his deep sensitivity to his nation's forsaking

God. His book is summarized in 9:1: "Oh, that my head were waters, and my eyes a fountain of tears, that I might weep day and night . . . !" Jeremiah sent a scroll with his warnings of repentance to the king, Jehoiakim. The king thought so little of Jeremiah's preaching that as his scribe read Jeremiah's scroll, the king cut off each section with his knife and threw it on the fire (36:20–26). After the Babylonians conquered his country in 586 B.C., Jeremiah was one of the group that sought refuge in Egypt.

469. Jephthah

He was one of Israel's judges (see 281), delivering Israel from the Philistines and Ammonites. Jephthah's most famous act was a rather tragic vow he made: He promised God that if he won a victory over the Ammonites he would sacrifice as a burnt offering whoever came out of his door when he returned home. That turned out to be his daughter, his only child, who came out dancing to the sound of tambourines. He was grief-stricken over his vow. The poor daughter requested two months' time "to wander on the mountains and bewail my virginity, my friends and I" (Judg. 11:29–40). He granted the request but kept his vow. Child sacrifice was common among Israel's neighbors but abhorred by the Israelites, which makes the story all the more tragic.

470. Job

The book of Job is a profound consideration of the question "Why do good people suffer?" Job, who was wealthy and also perfectly righteous, was tested when God allowed Satan to afflict Job with all kinds of troubles. (Satan in the book of Job is more of a tester than a tempter.) His children and wealth were taken, his skin was afflicted with boils, and his wife urged him to "curse God and die!" Job's reply: "Shall we indeed accept good from God, and shall we not accept adversity?" (2:9–10).

Another test came in the form of his three friends. They came to give comfort, but the more they talked, the more certain they were that if Job was suffering, he must have brought it on himself. They were determined to find some logic and purpose in all the suffering, but Job continued to insist that he had done nothing wrong. The speeches of Job and the three friends on the subject of God's justice are priceless.

Finally, God Himself appeared "out of the whirlwind." God never answered the puzzle of why good people suffer. God spoke of how amazing and complex His universe is, and Job, confronted with his awesome Creator, knew that there was no answer to the painful question. At the book's end, God restored Job's fortunes and scolded the three friends for speaking about things too deep for them.

471. Joel

The prophet Joel's book was quoted many times in the New Testament, particularly 2:28–32, a prediction of the Holy Spirit being poured out on mankind. Peter, in the book of Acts, quotes this prophecy on the day of Pentecost (see 628). Joel had a curious vision of an army of locusts plaguing the land. Joel 3:14 is often quoted: "Multitudes, multitudes in the valley of decision!"

472. John the Apostle

The brother of James and one of Jesus' disciples, John wrote a sizable part of the New Testament: the gospel of John, three epistles (1, 2, and 3 John), and Revelation (though it is possible that Revelation was written by some other John). He and James were fishermen, the sons of Zebedee, and Jesus called them as disciples while they were working (Matt. 4:21–22). Along with Peter and James, John was part of an "inner circle" of the disciples, privileged to be with Jesus at His transfiguration (Matt. 17), the raising of a dead child (Mark 5), and the agony in Gethsemane (Mark 14:32–42). Jesus referred to James and John as the "Sons of Thunder" (Mark 3:17), a name evident in Luke 9:51–56, where the brothers suggested to Jesus that they call down fire from heaven on a village that snubbed them. On one occasion the two brothers asked Jesus for privileged places when He went to glory. Jesus informed them that they should not seek status but seek to be servants like Himself (Mark 10:35–45).

In Acts, John and Peter heal a crippled beggar, a deed that leads to trouble with the Jewish authorities. Acts 3–4 describes the encounter, including the apostles' reply to their accusers: "Whether it is right in the sight of God to listen to you more than to God, you judge" (4:19). Later, Peter and John preached to the Samaritans (Acts 8:17–25).

The apostle may or may not be the author of Revelation. (John was a common name in those days.) Tradition says

John lived to an old age and was the only apostle not to be martyred.

473. John the Baptist

John was the kinsman and forerunner of Jesus Christ, and one of the Bible's most interesting characters. John's birth was, like Jesus', announced by the angel Gabriel, and he was born to the elderly couple Zechariah and Elizabeth. Gabriel foretold that the child would act "in the spirit and power of Elijah . . to make ready a people prepared for the Lord" (Luke 1:17). At the beginning of Jesus' ministry, John was living in the wilds, wearing his distinctive garb, a rough camel hair tunic and leather belt, living on locusts and wild honey. The people saw him as God's prophet, calling them to repentance and baptizing them in water as a symbol of spiritual renewal. Luke described him (in the prophet Isaiah's words) as a "voice of one crying in the wilderness: 'Prepare the way of the LORD'" (Luke 3:4). Some people thought John was the long-awaited Messiah of the Jews. But John insisted that there was a "greater one" coming soon. John baptized with water, but the "greater one" would baptize with the Holy Spirit. That greater One, Jesus, showed up to be baptized (see 392 [Jesus' baptism]), and this marked the beginning of Jesus' public life. John preached against the immorality of the ruler Herod Antipas, and this resulted in John's death by beheading (see 272 [Salome]), a tragic but perhaps fitting end to his colorful life.

Jesus thought highly of His great predecessor and told His disciples that John was (in a figurative sense) the prophet Elijah, sent to preach repentance. Jesus told them, "Among those born of women there has not risen one greater than John the Baptist" (Matt. 11:11). Most Jews believed that after the Old Testament period there were no more prophets, but John impressed many as God's true prophet, and Jesus confirmed that he was one (Luke 7:26).

John is shown in artwork as a sort of thin, rough-looking man in his camel tunic (exactly the sort of desert prophet living on a meager diet that the Bible describes). He is often shown holding a lamb, which refers to his identifying Jesus as "the Lamb of God who takes away the sin of the world" (John 1:29).

474. Jonathan

One of the Bible's closest friendships was between Jonathan, son of Israel's king Saul, and the shepherd boy David, who later became king himself. Both David and Jonathan were gutsy soldiers, and some serious male bonding took place between the two. According to 1 Samuel 18:1, "the soul of Jonathan was knit to the soul of David, and Jonathan loved him as his own soul." The friendship went well beyond being just "buddies." Jonathan's father, Saul, had many excellent qualities, but he was moody and sometimes paranoid, and he resented David's increasing popularity with the people. He ordered Jonathan to kill David, but Jonathan would not. Jonathan walked a thin line, trying to be a good son, but also devoted to his best friend.

Saul and Jonathan both died while fighting the Philistines. David's famous lament for both is in 2 Samuel

1:19–27. It contains the famous line "How the mighty have fallen!" but also contains the interesting line "I am distressed for you, my brother Jonathan; you have been very pleasant to me; your love to me was wonderful, surpassing the love of women" (v. 26). Some have wondered, Was there a sexual element in the friendship? Certainly David, who had several wives and numerous children, proved that he was fond of female company, and Jonathan himself fathered children. It is probably best to assume that the two men had a friendship of such depth that most people can hardly comprehend it.

475. Joshua

After Moses died, the Israelites' leader was Joshua, the main character in the book that bears his name. The book is the story of the Israelites' taking possession of the promised land, Canaan. It includes several colorful stories, such as crossing the Jordan River on dry land (chap. 3), the miraculous fall of the walls of Jericho (chap. 6), and the sun standing still during a battle (chap. 10). An oft-quoted verse from the book is 24:15, where Joshua tells the people, "Choose for yourselves this day whom you will serve . . . As for me and my house, we will serve the LORD." Joshua was reminding the people that they could not let their religion be corrupted by the Canaanites' pagan worship.

Joshua's name means, in Hebrew, "salvation." The Greek form of the name Joshua is Jesus.

476. Joseph, Jacob's son

Genesis 37–50 tells the saga of Joseph, the eleventh and favorite son of Jacob. Jacob doted on the boy and gave him a lovely "coat of many colors." The older brothers were jealous, particularly when Joseph reported his dreams of his brothers and parents bowing down and honoring him. The brothers sold him into slavery in Egypt, where he served an official named Potiphar. The randy wife of Potiphar tried to seduce Joseph, who refused her; she cried "Rape!" and Joseph was thrown into prison, where he interpreted the dreams of two other prisoners. One of them, a servant of Pharaoh, told him that Joseph could interpret his troubling dreams. Joseph did so, predicting a famine. The grateful pharaoh made him Egypt's prime minister, in charge of planning for the famine. The rest of Genesis tells of his brothers' journey to Egypt in search of food. They failed to recognize the brother they wronged, but eventually he and they were reconciled, and the elderly father Jacob came to Egypt to see his lost son.

Joseph's story is one of the Bible's masterpieces, full of drama and sentiment. Joseph is a role model of a young man keeping his courage and morals in adversity.

477. Joseph, husband of Mary

Joseph was descended from King David, and his hometown was (like David's) Bethlehem. He lived in Nazareth, but returned to Bethlehem for the Roman census. According to Matthew's gospel, Joseph was engaged to Mary, but she became pregnant (by the Holy Spirit). Joseph, "a just man," did not want to disgrace her, so he opted to divorce her quietly. But a dream told Joseph to go ahead and marry Mary, who had conceived miraculously. Later, when wicked King Herod ordered the death of all male infants in Bethlehem, another dream warned Joseph to flee with the family into Egypt. A later dream told him to return to Israel and live in Nazareth.

Jesus was referred to as "the carpenter's son," and Jesus Himself followed the same trade. More than once Jesus is called "Joseph's son," although Luke mentions that Jesus was the son of Joseph "as was supposed." Legally, not biologically, Jesus was Joseph's son.

Joseph is not mentioned again after he and Mary take Jesus to Jerusalem when Jesus is twelve years old. We can assume that he died before Jesus reached adulthood.

Artists have given us many pictures of Joseph, particularly in the many Nativity scenes. Joseph is almost always shown as a man much older than Mary. The Bible gives no data on his age. According to Catholic tradition, Mary was not only a virgin when Jesus was born but *remained* a virgin throughout her life. So, since the Gospels mention Jesus as having "brothers," Catholic tradition says that these must have been Joseph's children from an earlier marriage. It is probably for this reason that he is shown as older than Mary.

Joseph has long been the patron saint of carpenters.

478. Joseph of Arimathea

Joseph was a wealthy Jew, a member of the Sanhedrin, the Jewish ruling council. The Gospels describe him as a good man, one who was "waiting for the kingdom of God." He was a follower of Jesus, "but secretly, for fear of the Jews" (John 19:38). With the Roman governor Pilate's permission, he took the body of the crucified Jesus and buried it in his own tomb.

The New Testament says nothing else about Joseph. According to legends, Joseph possessed the Grail, the cup Jesus had used in the Last Supper. The legends say that Joseph used the cup to catch blood that trickled from the crucified Jesus, and tales developed around the magical properties of the Grail. English legends say that Joseph brought the Grail to England, and that in time it was lost. King Arthur and the Knights of the Round Table made it their quest to find the Grail.

Joseph has been portrayed in many artworks, standing by the cross of Jesus and catching the blood in the cup.

See 775 (the Holy Grail).

479. Josiah

Israel and Judah had some notoriously wicked kings, but Josiah stands out as a saint and a reformer. When he was twenty-six Josiah learned that the priest Hilkiah had found the Book of the Law in the temple. (Probably this was the book of Deuteronomy.) When the king heard the book read aloud, he was grieved that the nation had departed so far from God's standards. He renewed the covenant with God, then launched a systematic removal of all pagan worship. He defiled the pagan worship sites, including Ben-Hinnom, where children had been sacrificed. All the places dedicated to fertility gods like Asherah, Baal, and others were demolished. For the first time in centuries the people celebrated Passover. "Now before him there was no king like him, who turned to the LORD with all his heart" (2 Kings 23:25). Alas, the saintly man was killed in battle by Egyptian forces.

480. Levi / Matthew

All four Gospels name Matthew as one of Jesus' disciples, and his name has been attached to the first Gospel. Mark and Luke report that Jesus called a tax collector named Levi to be His disciple, whereas Matthew names that tax collector as Matthew. Double names were fairly common among the Jews, so probably Matthew and Levi were indeed the same man.

Tax collectors, since they were in cahoots with the hated Roman government, were not popular. Matthew, Mark, and Luke all report that Jesus was criticized for hobnobbing with a tax collector. Jesus' reply: "I did not come to call the righteous, but sinners" (Matt. 9:13). It is a mark of Jesus' compassion for outcasts that He included a tax collector among His disciples.

481. Lot and his wife

Lot, the nephew of Abraham, was the only resident (along with his family) of the sinful city of Sodom that God chose to save. Genesis 19 tells the pathetic tale of two divine visitors (who were almost raped by the men of Sodom) who urged Lot to flee the doomed city. They fled; God rained down fire on Sodom. The angels had told the family not to look back, but Lot's wife did, and she became a pillar of salt. (Jesus said, "Remember Lot's wife!" a warning not to look back on one's past.)

Part two of Lot's story is bizarre. He and his two daughters lived in a cave and there were no men nearby. The women got their father drunk, seduced him, and each bore a child. The two children become the ancestors of two hostile neighboring nations, the Moabites and the Ammonites.

482. Luke

He was the author of both Luke and Acts, making him the first historian of Christianity. We know little about Luke except that he traveled for a while with the apostle Paul, who referred to him as "the beloved physician" (Col. 4:14). Tradition says he was a Gentile, not a Jew, which means he was the only Gentile author of any part of the Bible. Luke's gospel is similar to Matthew's and Mark's, but he includes several stories not found elsewhere, notably the events relating to the birth of John the Baptist, the angels' appearance to the shepherds, and several favorite parables, including the prodigal son.

483. Malachi

The last book of the Old Testament deals with religious problems of the fifth century B.C. But chapters 3 and 4 contain some prophecies that Christians believe were fulfilled in the New Testament. A "Sun of Righteousness shall arise with healing in His wings" (4:2). Christians believe this was fulfilled in the life of Jesus. Malachi predicts a "Messenger of the covenant" (3:1) who will purify the people, and 4:5–6 predicts a reappearing of the prophet Elijah before "the great and dreadful day of the LORD." The early Christians believed these verses referred to John the Baptist, the forerunner of Jesus.

484. Mark

"John, also called Mark" is mentioned several times in the New Testament. Tradition says he was author of the second (and shortest) Gospel and a companion of the apostle Peter, who would have been his chief source of information about Jesus. Acts 12 mentions Peter in the house of Mark's mother, where a Christian fellowship met. Mark later accompanied Paul and Barnabas as an "assistant" in their missionary work (Acts 13:5). Something he did displeased Paul (we don't know what), and Paul refused to take him on a later missionary journey (Acts 15:37). Later he and Paul reconciled. His closeness to Peter is obvious when Peter referred to him as "Mark my son" (1 Peter 5:13).

485. Matthias

Mentioned only in Acts 1:23–26, he was Judas Iscariot's replacement among the twelve apostles. Judas, after betraying Jesus, killed himself. The apostles apparently felt the need to maintain the number twelve.

486. Melchizedek

This mysterious character appears briefly in Genesis, where he blesses Abraham, ancestor of the Israelites. "Melchizedek king of Salem brought out bread and wine; he was the priest of God Most High" (Gen. 14:18). The combination of king and priest in one man was a rarity. He is not mentioned again until Psalm 110:4, "The LORD has sworn and will not relent, 'You are a priest forever according to the order of Melchizedek.'" Apparently a tradition had developed that the mysterious Melchizedek was a sort of eternal priest, unlike the priests of Israel who died and were replaced.

The early Christians took Psalm 110 as a sort of prophecy of Christ, who would be an eternal Priest (like Melchizedek), mediating between man and God forever. The letter to the Hebrews quotes the psalm and observes that the old system of priests from the tribe of Levi, along with the gory system of sacrifices, is no longer needed. Jesus Christ is now the eternal Priest, and also the eternal sacrifice for human sin. Like Melchizedek, Christ is both a Priest and a King (the "King of kings," as the book of Revelation calls Him).

487. Methuselah

"Old as Methuselah" is a phrase still in use. According to Genesis 5, Methuselah lived 969 years—but a close second was Jared at 962. All the life spans reported in Genesis 5 are, to put it mildly, amazing.

488. Micah

The prophet Micah is most noted for his prophecy of a great ruler being born in the small town of Bethlehem (5:2). The early Christians believed, of course, that this ruler was Jesus. Micah's most-quoted words are in 6:8, "He has shown you, O man, what is good; and what does the LORD require of you but to do justly, to love mercy, and to walk humbly with your God?"

489. Moses

Moses is the most important character in the Old Testament, the deliverer of the Israelites from Egypt and the man who communicated God's divine law to the people. His story is told from Exodus through Deuteronomy (and Genesis through Deuteronomy are traditionally called the "books of Moses"). Exodus relates that the Egyptian pharaoh chose to exterminate all the children of the Israelite slaves living in Egypt. Moses' mother and sister placed the infant in a basket in a river, where Pharaoh's daughter found him and raised him in Egypt's court. Moses could have led a royal life, but after killing an Egyptian official for abusing a Hebrew slave, Moses fled. He encountered God in the famous burning bush story (see 341). With his brother Aaron he confronted the pharaoh, demanding that he free the slaves to go to their homeland of Israel. It took ten horrible plagues from God to convince the pharaoh, and when the Israelites departed, Pharaoh changed his mind, pursued them, and his troops were drowned in the sea the Israelites had just crossed.

Key incidents in Moses' life are covered elsewhere in this book. One tragedy of Moses' life was that he once disobeyed God (see Num. 20:1–13) and God then refused to allow him to enter the land of Canaan, the goal of his leading the Israelites out of Egypt.

490. Nehemiah

He was a cupbearer (meaning a chief aide) to the king of Persia, who gave him permission to return home to Jerusalem and supervise the rebuilding of the city walls. (The city had been a shambles since the Babylonians sacked it and sent the Jews into exile years earlier.) Chapter 8 relates that Ezra the priest and scribe (the same one as in the book of Ezra) read aloud the Book of the Law of Moses from daybreak until noon while the people listened attentively. The people were shamed into weeping, but Nehemiah told them to rejoice, for the worship of Israel was being renewed. Later the people confessed their sins.

Most of the book is told in the first person, suggesting that Nehemiah himself was the author.

Many people find the books of Ezra and Nehemiah dull reading, but they shed light on how the Jews reestablished the worship of God when they returned from exile in Babylon. A dramatic change had taken place in Jewish spiritual life: Instead of God speaking directly to men, or speaking through the prophets, God spoke through the written law revealed to Moses centuries earlier. As Ezra read the text publicly, the *Word* of God took the place of the *acts* of God. Ezra and Nehemiah were good men, but they were not prophets, not men in direct communication with God.

491. Nicodemus

This member of the Jewish ruling council was interested in Jesus, but chose to meet Him at night (suggesting he didn't want the other council members to know). Chapter 3 of John records the meeting, which includes Jesus' famous words on being "born again" (see 669). He also told Nicodemus, "God so loved the world that He gave His only begotten Son, that whoever believes in Him should not perish but have everlasting life" (v. 16). Later, when the Jewish council was discussing how Jesus' followers were accursed, Nicodemus asked if they were willing to condemn Jesus without hearing Him. When Joseph of Arimathea went to take Jesus' body away for burial, Nicodemus accompanied him and helped embalm the body (John 19:39–40).

492. Nimrod

The name refers to any daring or outstanding hunter, based on Genesis 10:8–9: "Nimrod . . . began to be a mighty one on the earth. He was a mighty hunter before the LORD." He was a great builder, establishing both Babylon and Assyria, which became mighty empires.

493. Paul

The great apostle began as a persecutor of Christians but after a dramatic conversion experience became the most famous preacher of the gospel. Paul is the author of a large chunk of the New Testament: Romans, 1 and 2 Corinthians,

Galatians, Ephesians, Philippians, Colossians, 1 and 2 Thessalonians, 1 and 2 Timothy, Titus, and Philemon. All these epistles are earlier than any other parts of the New Testament, and probably 1 and 2 Thessalonians are earliest of all.

Paul was a Roman citizen, and like many Jews with Roman citizenship, he had two names, Saul (his Jewish name) and Paul. Since he was called to be "apostle to the Gentiles," he went by the name of Paul. The many important events in his life are covered elsewhere in this book. Much of the book of Acts is the story of Paul.

494. Peter

His original name was Simon, and he was Jesus' most outspoken disciple. He and his brother Andrew were fishermen, whom Jesus called to be "fishers of men." Jesus nicknamed him "Cephas" or "Peter" (from Greek *petros*, "rock"). He was the first of the disciples to state that he believed their Master was "the Christ, the Son of the living God" (Matt. 16). With James and John, Peter was one of Jesus' "inner circle" of disciples, present at His transfiguration (see 365) and His agony in Gethsemane (see 918). After the Last Supper, Jesus predicted Peter would deny Him three times before the rooster crowed. After Jesus' arrest, Peter did indeed deny knowing Him, afterward weeping bitterly (Matt. 26:69–75). But after the Resurrection, he became a bold spokesman for his risen Lord, notable in his stirring sermon at Pentecost (Acts 2). He is a key figure in Acts, persecuted for preaching the faith but continuing on boldly. Peter was also the author of two New Testament epistles.

Tradition says Peter was the first bishop of Rome (which is why Catholics regard him as the first pope). He was, probably, martyred in the persecution under Emperor Nero. Tradition says he believed he was not worthy to die in the same way as Christ did, so he was crucified upside down.

495. Philemon and Onesimus

Paul's letter to Philemon is a very personal letter on a personal matter. Philemon was a Christian friend of Paul's, and his slave Onesimus had run away to Rome, where he encountered the imprisoned Paul. Onesimus was also a Christian, and Paul sent him back to his master, bearing the letter. Paul urged Philemon not to be harsh to the runaway but to accept him warmly, "no longer as a slave but . . . a beloved brother" (v. 16), since both were Christians, serving the same Master, Christ.

496. Pilate

Pontius Pilate was the Roman Empire's "procurator" (governor) in Jerusalem at the time of Jesus' crucifixion. Like most Roman officials, Pilate despised the Jews, which is evident in Jesus' trial, where Pilate considered the whole matter a "Jewish thing," a religious question that should be no concern of his. He clearly did not consider Jesus a political threat to Rome and would have released Him, but the Jews insisted (falsely) that Jesus was intending to set Himself up as "King of the Jews." Pilate was amazed at Jesus' passivity during the trial, and probably even more amazed that the Jews begged for the release of Barabbas, a political revolutionary who really *was* a threat to Rome. Pilate gave in to the Jews' pleas but literally washed his hands of responsibility for Jesus' death (Matt. 27:19–24).

John's gospel records an interesting moment in Jesus' trial before Pilate. Jesus said to him, "Everyone who is of the truth hears My voice." Pilate's famous (and cynical) reply was "What is truth?" (John 18:37–38).

497. Priscilla and Aquila

This was the original Christian missionary couple, close friends of Paul mentioned in Acts and Romans. Like Paul, they were tentmakers by trade. Paul mentions them being in Corinth, Rome, and Ephesus, so apparently they were as widely traveled as he was. (Aquila was the husband, by the way.)

498. the rich young ruler

The New Testament makes it clear that most wealthy people rejected Christ's teaching. Mark 10 tells of a rich man who sincerely asked Jesus how to obtain eternal life. Jesus reminded him of the Jewish moral laws, which the young man said he had followed. Jesus told him to go and sell all he had and give the money to the poor. At this the man's face fell. He went away sad, because he had great wealth. Jesus told His disciples, "It is easier for a camel to go through the eye of a needle than for a rich man to enter the kingdom of God" (v. 25).

499. Samson

The Hebrew strongman is one of the more interesting Bible characters, maybe because his story involves violence, lust, betrayal, and revenge. His story is told in Judges 13–16. Samson was one of Israel's "judges"—not a judge in the modern sense, but more like a military leader. Israel was constantly plagued by the pagan Philistines. Samson was born to a woman who had been barren, and an angel told his parents to dedicate the child to God (see 284 [Nazirites]). In spite of being dedicated to God, Samson did some questionable acts. Instead of choosing an Israelite wife, he picked a Philistine woman. On the way to meet her, he ripped apart a lion with his bare hands and, much later, found that bees had made a honeycomb in the carcass. At his wedding feast he posed a riddle to the Philistines: "Out of the eater came something to eat, and out of the strong came something sweet." (The answer: honey from a lion.) The Philistines got Samson's bride to wheedle the answer out of him. Samson was so angry when the Philistines revealed the answer that he struck down thirty men. Later Samson burned the Philistines' fields by tying torches to foxes' tails.

But the best-known part of the Samson story concerns the woman Delilah. The Philistines used her to find out the secret of Samson's strength. She inquired several times, each time Samson lied to her. Finally, he told the truth: If his long locks were shaved (breaking his Nazirite vow), his strength would be gone. Asleep in Delilah's lap, Samson got his first haircut, and his strength departed. The Philistines bound him, blinded him, and forced him to work as a slave.

When his hair grew back, his strength returned, unknown to the Philistines. They dragged him to their temple for "entertainment." Mighty Samson pushed apart the main pillars of the temple, literally bringing the house down. He himself was killed but, as Judges 16:30 puts it, he killed many more when he died than while he lived.

500. Samuel

Samuel was Israel's judge and prophet, a faithful man who had been dedicated to the Lord's service since his birth. While still a child he heard the Lord's voice calling to him at night (1 Sam. 3). Samuel was a respected leader, but the Israelites demanded a king to lead them more effectively, and in 1 Samuel 8 the prophet told them what oppression a king would bring upon them. Even so, he anointed the handsome Saul as Israel's first king. Saul was bold but impulsive, and Samuel learned that God had another man, the shepherd boy David, in line as the next king. Samuel anointed David, who soon proved himself by killing the giant Goliath. Samuel wept for the disappointing Saul. After Samuel's death, he and Saul met once more: Saul had a sorceress bring Samuel's ghost from the underworld. The ghost predicted defeat and death for the king, which occurred the next day (1 Sam. 28).

501. Saul

Before Israel had a king the nation was (in theory) a *theocracy*—that is, ruled by no one but God. The prophet Samuel tried to discourage the people from having a king, but he relented and anointed as king the tall, handsome Saul. The king's key problem, politically, was constant war with the Philistines. He also battled what we would today call depression, experiencing deep gloom, soothed somewhat by his servant David's harp-playing. David, who slew the giant Goliath with only a stone, gained in popularity, and much of the book of 1 Samuel is the story of the jealous Saul alternately loving and trying to destroy the loyal David. Samuel learned that God had rejected Saul as king and intended David to replace him. Saul learned from the ghost of the dead Samuel that he would die in battle with the Philistines the following day, and David would become king. Seeing the battle going against him, Saul committed suicide. David lamented the loss of the king and the king's son, David's beloved friend Jonathan.

Saul was also the original name of Paul the Apostle.

502. Silas

Silas was a missionary partner with Paul. The most notorious incident in their travels involved an exorcism performed on a fortune-telling slave girl who made money for her owners. With her occult powers gone, the owners were furious, and Paul and Silas were beaten and jailed. They were fastened in stocks, but an earthquake occurred, and the jailer, assuming all the prisoners had fled, was about to kill himself when Paul and Silas stopped him. The event resulted in the conversion of the jailer and his whole family (Acts 16:16–39). Silas, like Paul, was a Roman citizen, a considerable privilege.

Paul's two letters to the Thessalonians each are labeled as being from "Paul, Silas, and Timothy." Peter, in 1 Peter 5:12, referred to Silas as "our faithful brother."

503. Solomon

The popular King David had numerous children, but the one who followed him on the throne was Solomon, son of David and Bathsheba. Solomon ruled Israel at its political and commercial peak, and his numerous political marriages aided him in his lavish building ventures, notably the Lord's temple and his own palace in Jerusalem. He gained a reputation as a wise judge and a keeper of an impressive court. The queen of Sheba journeyed far to meet the wise wonder.

In his younger days Solomon was a devoted follower of God, and his prayer at the dedication of the temple (1 Kings 8) is touching. But his many wives and concubines worshiped idols, and in his old age Jerusalem was not only the site of the Lord's temple but also of the many shrines he had set up for his wives' gods. As a punishment for Solomon's straying from the right path, God promised that the kingdom would be split in two after Solomon's death. This occurred in the reign of Solomon's son Rehoboam.

504. Stephen

He was the first martyr for Christianity, and his story appears in Acts 6–7. "Stephen, a man full of God's grace and power, did great wonders and miraculous signs among the people" (6:8 NIV). But some Jews accused him of blasphemy and dragged him before the Jewish council, the Sanhedrin. Stephen gave an eloquent defense of Christianity, seeing it as the fulfillment of Judaism. But the Sanhedrin were furious, and they dragged him outside Jerusalem and stoned him to death. While they were stoning him, Stephen prayed, "Lord Jesus, receive my spirit." A witness to the stoning was Paul, who approved of it. After his conversion to Christianity, he admitted he had been a part of the tragedy.

505. Theophilus

"One who loves God" is the meaning of *Theophilus*. Luke's gospel and the book of Acts are both addressed to *Theophilus*. This may have been the man's name, or it may be a way of saying Luke and Acts are for any readers who love God. Since Luke 1:3 calls him "most excellent Theophilus," it is likely he was a Roman government official.

506. the thief on the cross

Jesus was not crucified alone, but between two robbers. One of the robbers (like the crowd of onlookers) mocked Him: "If You are the Christ, save Yourself and us." But the other criminal reminded the first that they were being justly punished, while Jesus was innocent. Then he said to Jesus, "Lord, remember me when You come into Your kingdom." Jesus replied, "Today you will be with Me in Paradise" (Luke 23:39–44). The story of the repentant thief and his "last-minute conversion" is one of the most touching in the whole Bible.

507. wise men / Magi

What would the Christmas story be without the wise men? According to Matthew's gospel, the wise men (also called "magi") journeyed from the East and asked the Jewish king, Herod, "Where is He who has been born King of the Jews? For we have seen His star in the east and have come to worship Him" (2:2). This rattled the paranoid Herod, who considered himself the king of the Jews. Herod's court scholars told him the Christ (or Messiah) would be born in Bethlehem. The wise men journeyed to Bethlehem, found Jesus' family, and presented the baby with gold, frankincense, and myrrh. A dream warned them to return to their country without reporting back to Herod.

Were there *three* wise men? The Bible doesn't say so. The tradition of three developed because the Gospel mentions three gifts. We have no idea how many there were. There is also no basis for the tradition that the wise men were three kings.

Matthew refers to them as "magi," which means they practiced astrology and other magic arts. Since they came from "the East," their homeland was probably Persia or Arabia.

See 856 (Nativity); 234 (Herod the Great); 617 (Christmas).

508. Zacchaeus

"Zacchaeus was a wee little man, a wee little man was he." The children's song refers to the hated Jewish tax collector Zacchaeus, who lived in Jericho, where Jesus was passing through. Being a short man, he could not see Jesus through the crowd, so he climbed a sycamore tree. Jesus saw him and said, "Zacchaeus, make haste and come down, for today I must stay at your house" (Luke 19:5). People muttered about Jesus' socializing with a despised tax collector, but Zacchaeus was so touched by Jesus' kindness that he promised to pay back (with interest!) anyone he had cheated (Luke 19).

See 298 (publicans).

509. Zechariah

Zechariah (Hebrew for "the Lord remembers") is the name of one of the books of the Prophets. It is the most common name in the Bible: At least thirty-three men in the Bible are named Zechariah.

Notable Women

510. Abigail, the fool's wife

Sometimes attractive and intelligent women marry surly, stupid men. One of these was Abigail, wife of Nabal (whose name means "fool"). Nabal treated David's servants with amazing surliness, and Abigail (seeing that David was a rising star in Israel) tried to make amends by sending David gifts. When Abigail told Nabal later that she had made friends with David, Nabal "became like a stone." Ten days later he died, and David hastily asked Abigail to marry him (2 Sam. 25). She acted wisely, for David later became king.

511. Abishag

When King David grew old he could not keep warm. Abishag, a young woman, was brought in as a sort of "bed warmer"—but with no sex involved (1 Kings 1). The name Abishag passed into the language as referring to a woman who marries a much older man.

512. Cain's wife

According to Genesis 4:17, Cain had a wife. But Genesis makes it clear that the only human beings then in existence were Adam, Eve, and their son Cain (who killed the other son, Abel). So where did Cain find a wife? The Bible scholars enjoy squabbling over this, but the correct answer is "Who knows?"

513. Deborah

Her name is Hebrew for "bee," and she was Israel's only female judge, and also a prophetess. Judges 4:5 says she "held court under the Palm of Deborah . . . and the Israelites came to her to have their disputes decided" (NIV).

But like the other "judges," she was primarily a military deliverer. Her partner in getting the Canaanites off Israel's back was military man Barak, but the real star of the Deborah-Barak story is a woman named Jael. She lured Sisera, the enemy leader, to her tent, tucked him in for a nap, then while he was sleeping drove a tent peg through his head.

514. Elizabeth

She was a relative of the Virgin Mary and the wife of Zechariah, a priest. Both she and her husband were "righteous before God," but they had remained childless and were both old. The angel Gabriel announced to Zechariah that they would have a child who would "be filled with the Holy Spirit, even from his mother's womb." The aged Elizabeth gave birth to John the Baptist, the wilderness prophet whose ministry paved the way for Jesus (Luke 1).

515. Esther

One of the two books of the Bible that doesn't mention God (Song of Solomon is the other). It takes place in Persia, where many of the Jews lived in exile. The Persian ruler took a beautiful Jewish wife, Esther, who used her influence to save the Jews from a plot by the evil prime minister, Haman. He was eventually executed, and the Jews were allowed to destroy the ones who would have exterminated them. The Jewish holiday of Purim commemorates the events.

The Apocrypha contains a second—and longer—version of Esther, which refers to God and prayer.

516. Lydia

One of the most appealing women in the New Testament was Lydia, a businesswoman. Paul met her in Philippi, where she was a merchant in purple cloth (made from seashells in those days of "all-natural" dyes). Lydia met Paul, and "the Lord opened her heart to heed the things spoken by Paul." She and her household were baptized, and she invited Paul and his fellow missionaries to stay in her home (Acts 16:11–15).

517. Martha and Mary

These two sisters were kind enough to open their home to Jesus as He and His disciples traveled. Luke 10 relates that Mary sat at Jesus' feet while He taught, but Martha, the conscientious hostess, was distracted by all the preparations that had to be made. Martha went to Jesus and requested that He tell Mary to help. Jesus replied that Mary had chosen what was better. The lesson is that being a dutiful host is less important than listening to the word of God.

John 11 relates that Jesus became dear friends with Mary, Martha, and their brother, Lazarus. The two sisters play important roles in the story of Jesus raising Lazarus from the dead (see 366).

In their house Mary took a bottle of expensive perfume and anointed Jesus' feet with it. Judas Iscariot criticized this "waste," saying the perfume could have been sold and the money donated to the poor. Jesus scolded Judas and said, "The poor you have with you always, but Me you do not have always" (John 12:8).

518. Mary, mother of Jesus

Jesus' mother is one of the best-known Bible characters, even though the Bible mentions her only a few times. She was engaged to Joseph, but while still a virgin she learned from the angel Gabriel that she would bear God's Son. She and Joseph went to Bethlehem for a census, and while there she bore Jesus in a stable, where they were visited by shepherds and the magi. Later she and Joseph presented the infant in the Jerusalem temple, where Simeon and Anna blessed Him. At age twelve Jesus went again with them to the temple, where they found Him conversing wisely with the Jewish teachers. Luke's gospel says that "His mother kept all these things in her heart" (Luke 2:51). Mary is mentioned only a few times in Jesus' adult life. She was present at Cana when He turned water into wine (John 2:3). Matthew 12:46–50 reports that while Jesus was talking to the crowd, His mother and brothers stood outside, wanting to speak to Him, and Jesus responded "'Who is My mother and who are My brothers?' And He stretched out His hand toward His disciples and said, 'Here are My mother and My brothers! For whoever does the will of My Father in heaven is My brother and sister and mother.'"

Mary was present at Jesus' crucifixion, and though in agony He spoke tenderly to her: "When Jesus therefore saw His mother, and the disciple whom He loved standing by, He said to His mother, 'Woman, behold your son!'" (John

19:26). The last mention of Mary in the Bible is Acts 1:14: "These [the disciples] all continued with one accord in prayer and supplication, with the women and Mary the mother of Jesus, and with His brothers."

How did she become so important in Catholic worship? By A.D. 300 she was being referred to as "Mother of God," and later the church decreed that she, like Jesus, was sinless and that instead of dying she was taken bodily into heaven. The Protestants broke with the Catholic tradition in regard to honoring Mary.

See 477 (Joseph).

519. Mary Magdalene

One of the most appealing women in the Bible, Mary was a prominent character in *Jesus Christ Superstar*. In the Bible she is described as one of Jesus' many devoted women followers, someone from whom He had exorcised seven demons (Luke 8:2). According to tradition (but not the Bible itself) she was a reformed prostitute. She followed the body of Jesus to its burial place and was the first to learn of His resurrection (Matt. 28:1–8; Mark 16:9). Chapter 20 of John's gospel relates a touching story of Mary going to Jesus' tomb, finding it empty, then encountering the risen Jesus, whom she does not recognize at first. Mary goes to Jesus' disciples with the news "I have seen the Lord!"

"Magdalene" probably refers to her coming from the village of Magdala.

Mary Magdalene was a favorite subject for artists, who often portrayed her weeping over her past sins.

See 15 (maudlin).

520. Michal

Among David's many wives, Michal, daughter of Israel's first king, Saul, was probably the "stiffest." When the ark of the covenant, symbolizing God's presence, was brought into Jerusalem, King David danced joyously in the streets. "David danced before the LORD with all his might" (2 Sam. 6:14). Michal was watching this public display, "and she despised him in her heart." A grand celebration accompanied the affair, but when David came home, Michal gave him a chilly reception for his "indecent" dancing. (He had been wearing only a loincloth.) For her unkindness on this grand occasion, Michal was punished by never having children.

521. Miriam

Sister of Moses and Aaron, who played a part in hiding the infant Moses when the Egyptians were murdering Hebrew children (Ex. 2). As an adult she was referred to as a prophetess. After the dramatic parting of the Red Sea and the drowning of the Egyptians, she led the Israelite women in a song of victory (Ex. 15:20–21). Later she and Aaron criticized Moses, and the Lord temporarily punished her with leprosy.

522. the perfect wife

Proverbs 31:10–31, written in a pre-feminist age, gives a description of the perfect wife and household manager. The passage begins, "Who can find a virtuous wife? For her worth is far above rubies." The woman described is certainly no doormat or bubblehead, but a sort of queen of her domain. The passage ends, "Give her of the fruit of her hands, and let her own works praise her in the gates."

523. Peter's mother-in-law

The New Testament gives few details about the families of Jesus' disciples. We know that Peter had been married, because Jesus healed his mother-in-law of a fever. The healing had immediate (and practical) consequences: "She arose and served them" (Matt. 8:14–15).

524. the queen of Sheba

Solomon, Israel's king, was known for being wise and maintaining a splendid court. In 1 Kings 10 is the account of a visit from the queen of Sheba, who arrived in Jerusalem with a caravan of spices, gold, and gems. The queen tested his wisdom and was in awe. She sang the praises not only of Solomon but also of his God.

Sheba was probably an area in Arabia, noted for its spices and other luxury items.

Jesus referred to the queen's long journey to meet the wise king, noting that His own people were ignoring One who was greater than Solomon (that is, Jesus Himself).

For centuries the emperors of Ethiopia claimed to be descendants of Solomon and the queen of Sheba.

525. Rachel and Leah

Jacob, later named Israel by God, was a crafty man, but on one occasion he was outsmarted by his own uncle. Jacob fell deeply in love with his cousin Rachel, so much so that he promised to work for his uncle Laban for seven years. On his wedding night Jacob found that Laban had substituted Rachel's less attractive sister, Leah. (Laban's excuse: The elder daughter had to be married off first.) Jacob kept Leah as his wife and worked for another seven years so he could have Rachel. As a consolation for being the less loved wife, Leah produced children before Rachel did. The romantic (and somewhat comical) story is told in Genesis 29–31.

Jacob's twelve sons, ancestors of the twelve tribes of Israel, were born to Leah, Rachel, and the two wives' maids, who served Jacob as concubines (see 715).

526. Rahab the harlot

The Israelites captured the city of Jericho by a miracle of God (see 475 [Joshua]). Earlier, Israel had sent spies to scope out the city, and the spies encountered a kind prostitute, Rahab. When the ruler of Jericho sought out the spies, Rahab hid them on her roof under stacks of flax. For her kindness, the Israelites spared her when they captured Jericho.

In spite of her profession, she was regarded as a good woman, included in the "faith hall of fame" in Hebrews 11.

527. Ruth

This brief Old Testament book takes place "in the days when the judges ruled." Its chief character is the faithful Ruth, a woman of Moab whose Israelite husband died, leaving her to live with her mother-in-law, Naomi. When Naomi left Moab to return to Israel, Ruth promised to leave her homeland and go with her. Her words to Naomi are often quoted: "Wherever you go, I will go; and wherever you lodge, I will lodge; your people shall be my people, and your God, my God" (1:16). In Israel, Ruth married a man named Boaz and was the great-grandmother of King David. Considering the hostility between Israel and Moab, the book is remarkable for including a Moabite woman as an ancestor of David. Matthew's genealogy of Jesus mentions Ruth.

528. Tabitha / Dorcas

Both names mean "gazelle." She was a saintly woman of Joppa, widely loved for her making of clothes for the poor. When she died, her friends sent for the apostle Peter, who brought her back to life. "And it became known throughout all Joppa, and many believed on the Lord" (Acts 9:36–43).

529. the woman at the well

Jews and Samaritans detested one another in the New Testament period, and Jesus and His disciples, like most Jews, usually avoided Samaritan territory. Yet John 4 records His remarkable dialogue at a well with a Samaritan woman. The dialogue begins when Jesus asked her to draw Him some water, but soon they are discussing spiritual longings. Jesus explained that soon both Jews and Samaritans would abandon their ancient rituals and worship God "in spirit and in truth." Jesus revealed He knew of the woman's immoral past, and she saw that He was the Christ. The story shows the outreach of Christianity to a formerly despised people (see 301 [Samaritans]).

530. the woman caught in adultery

The scribes and Pharisees, the Jewish "establishment" that despised Jesus, often tried to test Him with moral questions. They brought to him a woman caught in adultery ("caught" meaning literally "in the act of it," not just a rumor of adultery). Technically, the Old Testament law indicated stoning her to death as the right punishment. Jesus, asked for His opinion, "wrote on the ground with His finger, as though He did not hear." Then followed His famous reply: "He who is without sin among you, let him throw a stone at her first." The angry mob dispersed, leaving only the woman. Jesus had condemned their self-righteousness, but He also said to the woman, "Go and sin no more" (John 8:3–12). It is one of the most touching stories in the Bible.

11

History, from Papyrus to the Present

THE BEGINNINGS

531. papyrus

We get our word *paper* from the *papyrus* plant, a tall marsh reed that ancient folk cut into thin strips, which they placed in a crisscross fashion to form a flat surface to write on. Its texture was something like heavy wrapping paper. In dry regions like Egypt papyrus can last for centuries, and in Egypt archaeologists have found the oldest manuscripts of the Bible—not complete books, but scraps and pieces of both Testaments. The oldest scraps date back to the second century.

Not all writing was done on papyrus. Skins of sheep and goats were made into a material called *parchment*—more durable than papyrus, but also more expensive.

Do we have the original manuscripts of the Bible authors themselves? No. But the pieces from the second century are a witness to how carefully people copied the Scriptures without (for the most part) making alterations.

532. scrolls

When you see the word *book* in the Bible, it means "scroll." These were made of either papyrus (see 531) or parchment, glued together to form long continuous rolls that were wound on a pair of rods. The beginning of a scroll was on the right and the end on the left (since the Hebrews wrote from right to left). Scrolls are still used in synagogues.

Our modern form of book, with pages attached at one side, was first called a *codex,* and did not come into use till around A.D. 100. They were an improvement, obviously, and for the first time it was possible to have the whole Bible together, which was never possible with scrolls. The Bible on one scroll would have been far too bulky.

533. "God's poor Greek," Koine

Rome was the chief political power in the New Testament age, but languagewise, Greek ruled. The common (*Koine*) Greek used throughout the Roman Empire was a convenient language allowing communication between merchants, officials—and preachers of the gospel. *Koine* was not the beautiful (but difficult) "classical" Greek of Homer and Plato, but a more flexible, easily mastered Greek. The entire New Testament was written in Greek, mostly by authors for whom it was a second language. It was sometimes referred to as "God's poor Greek," but it was a perfect language for spreading a new faith across an empire.

534. Hebrew to Greek—the Septuagint

The Old Testament was written in Hebrew, which in the course of time became a dead language. Jews were scattered over the Middle East and elsewhere, and Greek, not Hebrew, became a commonly used language. The Septuagint was the Old Testament translated into Greek, and it was enormously popular. A Jewish tradition says that seventy-two men translated it, which is why Bible scholars use LXX (Roman numerals for seventy) as an abbreviation for Septuagint.

The early Christians, who used Greek as their common language of communication, accepted the Old Testament as sacred, and they knew it in the Septuagint version. When the New Testament quotes the Old, it is usually quoting the Septuagint, not the Hebrew original.

One interesting note: Hebrew used the words *YHWH* (the name for God) and *Adonai* ("Lord"), sometimes together as *YHWH Adonai* ("Lord God"). The Septuagint translators used the same Greek word, *kyrios* (meaning "Lord"), for both *YHWH* and *Adonai*. Later translations of the Bible into other languages, including English, followed the same practice.

See 631 (Lord / LORD).

535. the pseudepigrapha

The period between the Old and New Testaments was busy, notably in the number of Jewish books being written. A few of these became known as the Apocrypha (see 552) and are found in some (but not all) Bibles. But many inter-Testament books were never accepted as sacred by Jews or Christians. They are known as the pseudepigrapha—Greek for "false writings." They include such writings as: Testaments of the Twelve Patriarchs, Psalms of Solomon, Testament of Job, Assumption of Moses, Martyrdom of Isaiah, Life of Adam and Eve, and many others. Most (as the titles indicated) claim to be written by, or tell the story of, some important Old Testament character.

Though these books weren't accepted as sacred, they do contain traditions that many people believed. One example: In the New Testament, Hebrews 11 (the "faith hall of fame") mentions martyrs for their faith and states that some were stoned, flogged, and even "sawed in two." This undoubtedly refers to an old tradition that the great prophet Isaiah was executed by being sawed apart. That old tradition is found in Martyrdom of Isaiah, part of the pseudepigrapha.

536. vowel men—the Masoretes

A language with only consonants and no vowels? That's what Hebrew is. The Masoretes were Jewish scholars who wanted to preserve an accurate form of the Scriptures for all ages. Over a period of centuries they faithfully copied the books of the Old Testament and (we can be very thankful for this) added "vowel points" to aid in pronouncing the words. For the past ten centuries there has been almost no variation in the text of the Hebrew Scriptures, thanks to the preciseness of the Masoretes. The "official" Hebrew text still used today by both Christian and Jewish translators is the "Masoretic text."

537. Codex Sinaiticus

Scrolls were the typical form of "book" in Bible times. The "upgrade" came with *codices* (plural of *codex*), pages bound at one side the way modern books are (but copied by hand, since this was long before the printing press). The British Museum in London holds the world's oldest copy of the complete Bible, the Codex Sinaiticus. Written in Greek, it dates from around A.D. 350.

538. the name "Bible"

The name comes from the Greek word *biblia,* plural of *biblion,* meaning "book." Going back even earlier, *byblos* meant "papyrus," the plant used in making the early form of paper. And, one step farther back in time, *Byblos* was the name of an ancient city noted for exporting papyrus.

When did the Bible come to be called the Bible? Probably by A.D. 400, when Christians throughout the Roman Empire were referring to their Scriptures (both Old and New Testaments) as "the Book."

The old Greek name, *biblia,* is plural, which is appropriate since "the Book" is a collection of sixty-six books.

539. the first translations

Koine Greek (as explained in 533) was an ideal language for carrying the Bible far and wide, since it was spoken over the whole Roman Empire. But as the faith spread, translations were needed. Probably the earliest translation of the New Testament was from the original Greek into Latin, done around A.D. 150. Around that same date it was also translated into Coptic, the ancient language of Egypt.

540. Marcion the heretic

He was a wealthy ship owner, converted to Christianity sometime around 140. But by 144 the Christians had excommunicated him for his beliefs. He started a religion that was a serious rival to Christianity. Marcion claimed that Christianity was a clean break from Judaism, and that the Creator God of the Old Testament was a different Being from Jesus' loving Father. Marcion rejected the Old Testament as sacred Scripture. He put together his own "sacred book," consisting of Luke's gospel and the letters of Paul—but from these he omitted all references to God as Creator.

In Marcion's time the New Testament as we know it had not been fully formed. The activity of people like Marcion gave Christians an incentive to decide definitively which writings they were to label as "sacred."

541. Justin Martyr (d. 165)

As his name indicates, Justin died as a martyr for his faith. Raised as a pagan, he spent his youth looking for a philosophy that would bring him inner peace. Talking with an old man at the beach, he discovered that Christianity was the "one true worthy philosophy." Justin wrote several books defending the truth of his newfound religion. *Dialogue with Trypho* narrates his conversation with an educated Jew. It is interesting for the light it sheds on how the early Christians interpreted the Old Testament. Justin also described how Christian worship services included readings from the "memoirs of the apostles" (the Gospels and the Epistles) followed by a sermon on the reading.

542. Irenaeus

He lived around A.D. 180 and was bishop of Lyons in what is now France. During his lifetime Christianity was in competition with a rival belief system known as Gnosticism. Gnostics borrowed Christian ideas but claimed that God is distant from the world and that salvation comes not from faith in Christ but in learning special secret teachings. Gnostics believed that matter is evil, not the good creation of God. Irenaeus wrote *Against Heresies,* an enormous book that compared the foolishness of the Gnostics with the truth revealed in the Bible.

543. Origen

He was born sometime around A.D. 185 and died as a result of injuries received from Roman persecution. He also inflicted one injury on himself: Taking literally Jesus' words about some people "making themselves eunuchs," he had himself castrated.

Origen was one of the great Bible scholars of his day, well read in the Hebrew and Greek originals. He wrote massive Bible commentaries, putting forward his idea of Scripture being interpreted on three levels: literal (what actually happened), moral (how it applies to life), and spiritual (how it delves into mysteries of faith). Regrettably, the spiritual interpretation came to dominate Christian scholars for centuries, and Bible commentators often lost interest in the literal and moral meaning of the Bible.

544. "New Testament"

Writing around the year 200, Tertullian was the first theologian to write in Latin (showing a shift from Greek to Latin as the "church language"). He coined the Latin term *Novum Testamentum,* meaning "New Testament," which we still use. He also coined the term *Trinity* to refer to God as Father, Son, and Spirit. He wrote the first commentary on the Lord's Prayer.

545. *traditors*

Their name is the Latin word for "traitors." During the brutal persecution of Christians under Emperor Diocletian, not all Christians were willing to be martyrs for their faith. Some obeyed the imperial edicts and turned over their copies of the Scriptures to the Romans. This provoked scorn from many Christians, particularly when some of the *traditors* later wished to become pastors. Opponents said that people who had been unwilling to suffer for their faith were not worthy to be ministers of the church. For several years the Donatists, a splinter group, existed in northern Africa because of the *traditor* controversy.

546. Emperor Julian the Apostate (331–363)

This Roman emperor got his famous nickname because he tried to turn the empire from Christianity back to paganism. His uncle was the famous Constantine, Rome's first Christian emperor. Julian looked down on the "Galileans" (the name he called Christians) and took steps to undermine their influence. He was not an active persecutor, but he did prohibit Christians from teaching their holy books in the schools. Some Christian teachers found a way around Julian's rule: They translated the Old Testament into an epic poem and the New Testament into a Platonic dialogue.

547. Ulfilas

He lived around A.D. 350 and was missionary to the Goths of northern Europe (who gave us our word *Gothic*). These warlike people had no written language, so Ulfilas developed an alphabet so as to give the Goths the Bible in their own language. In translating the Bible for them, he omitted 1 and 2 Kings. He believed the war-loving Goths would be better off not reading about the many wars of the kings of Israel.

548. Anthony the hermit (c. 300)

Anthony was born to well-to-do Egyptians, who died when he was twenty, leaving him all the wealth. He experienced a spiritual crisis when he heard a sermon on Jesus' command to the rich young ruler, "If you want to be perfect, go, sell what you have and give to the poor" (Matt. 19:20–23). Anthony gave away his land and donated his money to the poor. He lived a simple life, sleeping on the ground and existing on one meal a day (bread and water). He lived for years in an abandoned fort, seeing no one. Yet he attracted followers, who believed Christianity had become worldly and materialistic. Many people saw hermits like Anthony as practitioners of a purer Christianity, the faith of the New Testament. After he died, a popular *Life of Anthony* was widely circulated, attracting more people to become desert hermits.

The life must have been healthy. Anthony lived to be 105.

549. Athanasius and the canon

Canon means "standard." When applied to the Bible, it means "the books we accept as holy and inspired by God." In the New Testament period, the "canon" was what we now call the Old Testament, the thirty-nine books from Genesis to Malachi. The early Christians, both Jews and Gentiles, accepted these as holy and inspired. But Paul,

Peter, and other apostles were writing letters that Christians also believed were inspired, and other authors were producing "gospels," stories of Jesus' life and teachings. For years there was no "canon" of these Christian writings. Some people accepted certain Christian writings as holy, while others did not.

In the year 367 a prominent bishop named Athanasius circulated his "Easter letter" to his churches. In his letter he listed the twenty-seven writings that we now call the New Testament. Hoping to keep his people from error, Athanasius said that these books—and no others—were Christian holy writings. Later, a major church council confirmed Athanasius's list.

What did he base his "canon" on? Simply put, it excluded writings that didn't fit with Christians' core beliefs. Over time, Christians had learned that certain writings were clearly "inspired"—because the writings inspired those who read them, and also because the writings reflected the beliefs of Jesus' original apostles, passed down by word of mouth. Christians believe this gradual process of accepting some writings and rejecting others was guided by God.

550. New Testament Apocrypha

The New Testament has twenty-seven books, but in the period these were written there were dozens of other gospels and epistles being written. These were not accepted by Christians at large as being sacred and inspired. Most of the books that never made it into the New Testament are of very doubtful value—for instance, the many so-called "infancy Gospels" that show Jesus working pointless miracles as a child, or gospels that put into Jesus' mouth the words of some bizarre philosophy. The Gnostics, rivals to Christianity, produced their own gospels.

There were several "Acts" books, reporting the activities of a particular apostle or other person (such as Pilate) connected with Jesus' life. Stories about Jesus' mother, Mary, were widely circulated, and some of these became part of Catholic belief (for example, the beliefs that she remained a virgin and that she was taken bodily into heaven).

551. Jerome and the Vulgate

The Vulgate, the Latin translation that was *the* Bible for hundreds of years, was the one-man accomplishment of Eusebius Hieronymus Sophronius—better known as Jerome. Living in a cave in Bethlehem, Jerome translated the Hebrew Old Testament and the Greek New Testament into Latin, completed in 405. He knew all three languages well and made a fine translation.

Jerome did not want to include the books of the Apocrypha, since the Jews he knew did not accept them as holy books. But the church authorities insisted he include them in his Bible, and to this day the Catholic church follows the tradition of including the Apocrypha, while most Protestants follow Jerome's lead and omit them.

As time passed, Latin, a commonly spoken language in Jerome's day, became a dead language, used only by scholars and priests. It was the "church language" in Europe long after the common people had ceased to speak it. But the Catholic church decreed that the Vulgate was inspired just like the Greek and Hebrew originals, so it was forbidden to translate the Bible into people's spoken languages. The result: For hundreds of years—until the Reformation in the 1500s—the Bible was a book to be read by scholars, not by ordinary Christians.

552. Apocrypha

Apocrypha means "hidden things." The books were mainly written in the period between the Old and New Testaments. The books are: 1 and 2 Maccabees, Tobit, Judith, Wisdom of Solomon, Ecclesiasticus (not the same as Ecclesiastes), Baruch, and additions to Esther and Daniel. Of these books, most readers find the most profit in Wisdom and Ecclesiasticus, which are similar to Proverbs in their wise advice. Valuable information about the period between the Testaments is found in 1 Maccabees. Esther in the Apocrypha is a longer version of the one found in the Old Testament; the "extended" version does mention God and prayer.

Centuries ago, Bible translators struggled with a question: Do we include the Apocrypha? Around A.D. 400, the scholar Jerome was working on his great translation into Latin. Living in the Holy Land (a good place to be doing Bible translation), Jerome learned that the Jewish rabbis had chosen not to include certain books in their Bibles (what Christians call the Old Testament). He and other Christian scholars agreed that if the Jews did not consider these books sacred, neither should Christians. But these "questionable" books had been around a long time, and Jerome was pressured to include them in his Latin Bible, the Vulgate (see 551 [Jerome and the Vulgate]).

With the Reformation in the 1500s came a renewed interest in translating the Bible from the original Hebrew and Greek. The Reformers went back to Jerome's question: Should we include these books that the Jews do not consider sacred? Some said yes, some said no. Martin Luther included them in his German translation. He said they were not equal to the other books but were "profitable and good to read."

The Catholic position was fixed at the Council of Trent (1546), which said that, yes, the Apocrypha was definitely sacred Scripture, inspired by God. The council also pronounced damnation on anyone who took a different view. But, in time, that's exactly what Protestants did. Today, Catholic Bibles include the Apocrypha; most Protestant Bibles do not.

553. Augustine (354–430)

He is still one of the most widely read Christian authors, and his *Confessions* can be found in any bookstore. Augustine was a restless intellectual in his younger days, trying to find a philosophy that would bring him happiness. He struggled with sexual morality and had a son by his mistress. But in 386 he experienced a conversion to Christianity, which began with a solitary reading of Romans 13:13–14: "Let us walk properly, as in the day, not in revelry and drunkenness, not in lewdness and lust . . . But put on the Lord Jesus Christ, and make no provision for the flesh, to fulfill its lusts." As Augustine tells the story in his *Confessions,* he was sitting in a garden and heard a child's voice saying, "Take it and read it, take it and read it," and he saw the scroll of

Romans lying nearby. The incident was the turning point in his life, and he became one of Christianity's most notable theologians.

A.D. 500 to 1500

554. the Middle Ages

The Middle Ages is considered a low point in Bible reading. Although every person in Europe was (in theory) a baptized Christian, people could not read the Bible on their own. The clergy read from a Latin Bible—but only a tiny minority of people knew Latin. Church authorities feared letting laypeople have access to the Bible—they might get "revolutionary ideas." Worse, they might see the corrupt, immoral clergy in its true light. So for hundreds of years, reading the Bible in one's own language was a rarity—and a danger to boot.

555. the Jesus Prayer

This ancient prayer goes "Lord Jesus Christ, Son of God, have mercy on me, a sinner." It is based on the prayer of the tax collector in Luke 18:13. In the Middle Ages the prayer was popular in monasteries as a guide to devotions. Some people would repeat the prayer endlessly and go into a trancelike state.

556. *Biblia Pauperum*

Latin for "poor man's Bibles," *Biblia Pauperum* were picture books used during the Middle Ages by the illiterate. They illustrated the key events and themes of the Bible and were some of the earliest books produced in Europe.

557. relics

Not long ago a string of fake pearls once owned by Jackie Kennedy was auctioned off for an amazing sum. People have always been dazzled by celebrity, and people have wanted to own—or at least to see and touch—objects associated with famous people. In the past, people attributed supernatural power to such objects. In the Middle Ages, the wealthy and powerful would buy (or steal) objects associated with Jesus, Mary, the apostles, and other saints. These were known as relics. Since Jesus had been resurrected, there were no actual relics of Him but there were plenty associated with His mother, Mary, (bottles containing drops of her milk, for example), or His apostles (the skull of the apostle Andrew, a tooth from Paul, etc.). Many of the great cathedrals were built over the (alleged) tomb of some famous saint. (Peter's body is supposed to be buried in the enormous St. Peter's Basilica in Rome, for example.) People became extremely superstitious about relics and their supposed powers. Most of the relics were fakes—the bones and clothing of beggars, or even the teeth of animals.

With the Protestant Reformation in the 1500s came a skepticism about relics. The Protestant leaders emphasized living the Christian life, not being superstitious about the bones and teeth of people long dead. The cult of relics died out in Christianity—but as the Jackie Kennedy pearls prove, people will always be relic hounds.

The Bible emphasizes that only God is to be worshiped—not things, and not places.

558. the Book of Kells

This is considered one of the most beautiful books in the world, a grand example of an *illuminated manuscript,* a handwritten and lavishly decorated book from the Middle Ages. The book contains the Latin text of the four Gospels and was probably written somewhere in Ireland around the ninth century. It can be seen today at Trinity College in Dublin, Ireland.

559. florilegia

These are collections of Bible quotations, sometimes on a particular topic. In the days before printing presses, possessing an entire Bible was a rarity, but florilegia might serve to teach basic Christian doctrines. The word comes from Latin *flores legere,* "to gather flowers."

560. the Crusades

The notorious Crusades of the Middle Ages were not a matter of Christian warriors trying to convert Muslims to the faith. They were a matter of clearing a path for Christians wanting to visit the Holy Land sites. After the Muslims had conquered the land, they made life difficult for

Christian inhabitants and tourists. So the Crusaders had the goal of reconquering the land on behalf of Christians having access to the holy places they'd read of in the Bible. See 873 (the Holy Land).

561. Bernard of Clairvaux (1090–1153)

In the Middle Ages the monasteries were often places of idleness and immorality—but not always. Some of the monks were saintly people, and one of the best was Bernard of Clairvaux, whose life was truly a "love affair with God." He wrote dozens of books of hymns, devotions, and commentaries on the Bible. Like most medieval authors, he did not take the Bible at face value but looked for symbolic and allegorical meanings. Thus he read the Song of Solomon and preached eighty-six sermons on it, interpreting it allegorically and finding deep Christian meanings—even though the Song mentions neither Christ nor God.

562. glosses

In the Middle Ages the Catholic church prohibited Bibles in any language but Latin (which only scholars could read). Some Latin Bibles have been found in which someone wrote, in between the Latin lines, literal translations of the words. These were known as "glosses," and they give a new meaning to the old expression "reading between the lines."

563. Francis of Assisi (1182–1226)

Francis is one of the most appealing personalities of the Middle Ages, and many backyard gardens have statues of him. He was the son of a wealthy Italian merchant but after hearing a sermon on Matthew 10:7–10, Jesus' instructions to His disciples to preach the kingdom of God and give no thought to their material possessions, he decided to give up his worldly belongings and to live poor as the apostles had. He attracted a following, and in 1212 the Catholic church gave its official approval to his followers, the Franciscans. The "brothers," as they called themselves, met every year at Pentecost, but the rest of the time they wandered about Europe, preaching and aiding the poor, begging for what little food they had.

In the Middle Ages, Christians practically forgot the New Testament commands to preach the gospel to the world. Francis was one of the few medieval Christians to be a missionary, carrying the gospel to Syria and Morocco.

Some of Francis's followers claimed that his body showed the same wounds as Jesus received on the cross, the stigmata (see 178).

564. dividing into chapters

Hard as it is to believe, the Bible wasn't always neatly divided into chapters. The man who did this was archbishop of Canterbury, England's chief clergyman, Stephen Langton (d. 1228). Langton locked horns on more than one occasion with the unscrupulous King John. Langton also wrote Bible commentaries and theological works.

Anyone who studies the Bible owes Langton a debt of gratitude. It is much more helpful to say, "Oh, you'll find that in Matthew 5" than to say, "Oh, you know, it's somewhere in Matthew."
See 579 [dividing into verses].

565. Scholasticism

The Latin Bible was *the* Bible in the Middle Ages, so only priests and monks could read it. Priests and monks wrote Bible commentaries and other Christian books (all in Latin) for one another, not for ordinary people. The developments in theology and Bible studies in this period are known as Scholasticism, and it has come to symbolize a religion that is out of touch with ordinary Christians. Authors seemed to compete with one another in finding clever interpretations of the Bible. They believed that *all* of the Bible had some deep meaning, so when they encountered parts of the Bible like the bloody wars in Judges or the erotic poems in the Song of Solomon, they decided there *must* be a deeper spiritual meaning. In other words, they threw aside reading the Bible *at face value*. The Bible was not, they believed, a history of Israel and Christianity, but a kind of symbol-book, an allegory waiting to be interpreted. The great leader Bonaventure, writing in the 1200s, said that each verse of the Bible can be interpreted in seven ways: historical, anagogical, symbolical, allegorical, tropological, synecdochical, and hyperbolical. Another scholar said that "the sense of God's Word is infinitely varied, and like a peacock feather glows with many colors." No wonder that in the 1500s Martin Luther and many other faithful people were eager to translate the Bible into people's own languages so that it could be studied by someone besides the "experts."

566. Thomas Aquinas (1224–1274)

For centuries he was the most widely read Catholic theologian, and his multivolume *Summa Theologica* was considered the masterpiece of theology. Like most theologians of the Middle Ages, he was also a Bible scholar; also like the others, he was not satisfied to read the Bible at face value. For example, he interpreted Genesis 1:3, "Let there be light," in four ways: historical ("God created the light"); allegorical ("Let Christ be love"); morally ("May we be illuminated by Christ"); and anagogically ("May we be led to glory by Christ").

Thomas was a gentle, humble soul, and shortly before his death he had some sort of mystical experience that made him doubt the value of his many writings. He wanted to burn them all, but friends stopped him.

567. Nicholas of Lyra (1265–1349)

He died before the printing press was invented, but his commentary on the Bible was one of the first books printed. Nicholas was one of the few scholars of the Middle Ages who studied Hebrew, and from Jewish scholars he picked up an interesting idea: Read the Bible in the literal sense, at face value. This was not common practice in that era, when authors found all kinds of symbolic and allegorical meanings in the Bible (see 565 [Scholasticism]). Years later,

Martin Luther said he had learned much about Bible interpretation from Nicholas.

568. John Hus (1374–1415)

Before the Protestant Reformation of the 1500s, Hus was preaching reform, and it cost him his life. Hus (his name means "goose") was a Czech priest and professor who found much to criticize in the corrupt Catholic church of his day. Hus taught that only the Bible, not bishops nor even the pope, could establish Christian beliefs. More radically, he taught that any church teachings contrary to the Bible could be disobeyed. Hus was called before a church council to defend his beliefs. He was condemned and burned at the stake, but his teachings stirred the Czech people to establish their own church.

PRINTING, PROTESTANTS, AND OTHER DEVELOPMENTS

569. the first printed Bible

Johannes Gutenberg was the German printer who is considered the inventor of the printing press. The first book printed, in 1456, was, naturally, the Bible—Jerome's Latin Vulgate Bible, to be specific. A few Gutenberg Bibles are found in world museums, and some people say that the first printed book was also the most beautiful book ever.

Printing was at first a closely guarded secret craft, but by the time Martin Luther launched the Reformation in 1517, books were being printed all over Europe. The ability to mass-produce books—the Bible in particular—was one of the most dramatic changes in human history. More people learned to read, more people wanted the Bible in their own language, and the Bible became the possession of all Christians, not just the priests and scholars.

570. the Complutensian Polyglot

Gutenberg's Bible, the first printed Bible, was in Latin, the official "church" language of that day. The first Bible printed in the original languages of Greek and Hebrew was the Complutensian Polyglot, published in Spain in 1522. Only six hundred copies of the huge six-volume work were printed.

571. Nicolaus Copernicus (1473–1543)

The Polish astronomer's great contribution to science was his theory that earth and the other planets revolve around the sun. His theory appeared in his book *De Revolutionibus,* not published till after his death. The Catholic church officially condemned the theory.

The men who wrote the Bible were not astronomers, and the Bible's references to the sun and the planets revolving around the earth reflect what men of that age knew. We still speak of the sun "rising" and "setting," even though we know technically that it is the earth that is moving.

See 580 (Galileo).

572. Erasmus (1467–1536)

Desiderius Erasmus never joined with the movement known as the Reformation, even though its aims and his were almost the same. A noted scholar, Erasmus wanted to get "back to the Bible"—in the original languages, that is. Believing that the church's Latin Bible, the Vulgate, had errors, he published a Greek New Testament in 1516. It went through several editions and helped to break the centuries-old tradition of reading no Bible but the Vulgate. Erasmus's main motive was to make the Greek New Testament available so that other scholars could translate it into the spoken languages of Europe.

Like the Reformation leaders, Erasmus emphasized not only reading the Bible in its original language but also stressed a genuine Christian lifestyle instead of the external rituals of the church. He also wrote books ridiculing the corruption and immorality of the Catholic clergy. Even so, he lived and died a Catholic and was buried in a cathedral in Switzerland.

573. the Reformation

The great religious movement launched by Martin Luther and others in the 1500s was essentially a "back to the Bible" movement. A key belief of the Reformation was that the Bible alone was man's guide to Christian belief and morals. Luther and other reformers believed the Catholic church had traditions and practices at variance with the New Testament, and this was why the church had become corrupt and ineffective. Catholics said that the Bible *and* the many centuries of church tradition were authoritative, but the Reformers said, no, the Bible alone was the guide. One key result of the Reformation was many new translations of the Bible into the people's spoken languages, ending the many years of the Bible being only in Latin, a language the people no longer understood.

574. Martin Luther (1483–1546)

Luther's claim to fame is that he launched the Protestant Reformation. That whole movement was a "back to the Bible" movement, because Luther and other Protestants believed the Catholic church had strayed a long way from the Christianity taught in the Bible. In 1517 Luther, a monk and teacher, posted his famous Ninety-five Theses, concerned with church corruption. From that point on his life was one of controversy and drama. He was asked to retract his views, but before a council he made his famous statement: "Here I stand. I can do no other. God help me. Amen." He was excommunicated, and there were threats on his life, but he pursued his vision of Christian beliefs and morals based on the Bible. In his busy life he managed to write dozens of theological works and commentaries on large parts of the Bible.

Luther's great contribution was his one-man Bible translation, completed in 1534. Somehow he completed the entire New Testament in a little over two months. It was *the* German Bible for centuries and one literary critic called it "the first work of art in German prose."

575. "an epistle of straw"

The epistle of James in the New Testament is famous for its statement that "faith without works is dead" (James 2:26). The epistle talks little about the theology of salvation and instead focuses on living a moral Christian life, since faith must be put into action. The great Reformation leader Martin Luther was bothered by this. He believed the Catholic church had neglected the belief in salvation by faith and had focused on being saved by deeds. (These "works" included contributing vast sums of money to the church.) Luther was so convinced that salvation by faith was *the* key doctrine of Christianity that he called James "an epistle of straw" (meaning worthless) since it suggested (or so Luther thought) a religion of deeds, not faith. Even so, when Luther made his translation of the Bible into German, he did not omit James.

576. Ulrich Zwingli (1484–1531)

At the same time Martin Luther was launching the Reformation in Germany, a Swiss pastor named Zwingli started his own reforms in Switzerland. Zwingli's first innovation was that instead of preaching on the Catholic church's required Bible texts for each particular Sunday, he chose to preach through the entire gospel of Matthew. Zwingli also announced that the Catholic teaching that the Communion bread and wine actually become the body and blood of Christ is not true, that the service is only a memorial.

577. small group Bible study

In the 1500s, the religious movement called the Reformation caused a major change in people's Bible-reading habits. The Bible began to be translated from Latin into the living languages people spoke. It is hard to overstate how new and shocking this was: being able to possess and read a Bible in one's own language. Bibles (and all books) were fairly expensive in those days, so chances were good that there might be only one Bible per household (assuming the home could afford any book at all). So the first Bible study groups were family groups, gathered around the hearth, listening to someone read aloud from this book that had always been in Latin, a language they knew nothing of. And "family groups" meant more than Dad, Mom, and two kids. Chances are each household contained grandparents, in-laws, uncles and aunts, etc.

578. John Calvin (1509–1564)

Raised as a Catholic, Calvin got caught up in the Protestant Reformation and became one of its leaders, and probably its most noted theologian. Like all Reformation leaders, he emphasized the necessity that each Christian (not just ministers) know and follow the Bible in daily life. He believed that Christian doctrine should be based strictly on the Bible. The Catholic church had, he thought, neglected the Bible and placed too much reliance on ritual and meaningless theological debates. He produced a theological classic, *The Institutes of the Christian Religion,* which he claimed was based solely on the Bible. He also wrote lengthy commentaries on most books of the Bible and was a powerful influence in the city of Geneva, Switzerland, where he tried to bring the citizens' lives into line with biblical standards.

579. dividing into verses

Sometime in the 1200s Stephen Langton, archbishop of Canterbury, divided each book of the Bible into chapters. More than three hundred years later a French printer took the process a step further and divided each chapter into verses. Robert Estienne was a Protestant convert and an associate of Reformation leader John Calvin in Switzerland. Estienne believed strongly in the Protestants' emphasis on understanding the original Hebrew and Greek texts of the Bible, and his printing house produced a Hebrew Old Testament and Greek New Testament for scholars to study. Believing that study would be easier if each chapter was divided into numbered verses, Estienne took on the job. According to his son, he did most of the work while riding horseback from Paris to southern France. Perhaps the movement of the horse explains why some of the verse divisions seem to appear in strange places.

See 564 (deviding into chapters).

580. Galileo (1564–1642)

Italian scientist Galileo discovered, using his telescope, that the earth and the other planets revolve around the sun—not (as the Catholic church officially taught) that the sun and planets revolve around the earth. Galileo's findings supported what the Polish scientist Copernicus had believed. But the Catholic Inquisition prohibited Galileo from teaching what he'd found. His book *Dialogue on the Two Chief Systems of the World* led to his trial by the Inquisition. He recanted his views, but lived under house arrest until his death.

The church at that period claimed its scientific views were based on the Bible, and they condemned anyone who differed. They overlooked an obvious fact: The Bible was not written as a science textbook, and its references to the motion of the earth, sun, and planets were written by nonscientists describing things as best they could. Galileo wrote, "The intention of the Scripture was to persuade men of the truths necessary to salvation. Science could not do this, but only the Holy Spirit."

See 571 (Copernicus).

Moving Toward the Modern

581. Isaac Newton (1642–1727)

The familiar image of Isaac Newton is of the man discovering the law of gravity when an apple drops on his head. Newton was one of the greatest scientists of all time, and his theories on the law of gravitation were only a part of his many amazing discoveries. Newton so impressed his contemporaries that he was knighted—that is, he became "Sir Isaac."

In modern times, many scientists are nonbelievers, not men of faith. This wasn't true of Newton. Newton claimed that each of his discoveries was communicated to him by the Holy Spirit. He was fascinated by the Bible and wanted to reconcile science with religion. Throughout his life Newton believed that man's paramount aim was to understand the Bible and God's purposes. His scientific discoveries only made him more certain that a divine Creator still watched over the world.

Newton wrote that "no sciences are better attested than the religion of the Bible."

582. Pietism

Bible study has a way of renewing faith. This certainly was true in Germany in the 1600s, when Lutheranism had settled in as the unexciting "established" church in the land. The Lutherans had a well-thought-out theology but little appeal to people's sentiments. A pastor named Philipp Jakob Spener published *Pia Desideria,* calling for a reform that would make faith a matter of the heart as well as the head. Spener's book called for the laypeople, not just the ministers, to be more familiar with the Bible. The movement came to be called Pietism. It led to some notable charitable institutions, mission work, and more lively preaching.

583. the Enlightenment

Europe had been (in theory, anyway) Christian for many centuries. But in the 1700s many people, particularly intellectuals, began to put more faith in human ability than in Christianity and the Bible. Enlightenment philosophers stressed mankind's rationality, which could serve as a better guide to life than the Bible and the church, which were "superstitious." Many Enlightenment leaders called themselves "deists," believers in one God, but a God that pretty much left mankind to itself. Christ was seen as a good moral teacher, but not the Savior of mankind. Sin, said the intellectuals, was not man's problem—ignorance was. Authors like Voltaire (see 584) helped popularize Enlightenment thought. It was a powerful influence on America's Founding Fathers, particularly Benjamin Franklin (see 61) and Thomas Jefferson (see 63).

584. Voltaire (1694–1778)

He was one of the world's most admired authors and public commentators of his day, still much loved in his native France. Like many leaders of the movement we call the Enlightenment (see 583), Voltaire was extremely critical of Christianity and the Bible. He called himself a theist, saying he believed in one God but not in Christianity. He said he admired Jesus as a great man, and that the morality taught in the New Testament was good—if it agreed with morals taught in other world religions.

585. John Wesley (1703–1791)

The founder of Methodism, along with his brother, Charles, concluded that the English church of his day was spiritually dead. Methodism emphasized small group fellowship, more emotional preaching, Bible study, and hymn singing. Wesley wrote, "I am a Bible bigot. I follow it in all things, both great and small."

586. Joseph Priestley (1733–1804)

Priestley's greatest contribution to history was as a scientist, noted for his work in the chemistry of gases. He was also a minister, one who became convinced that Jesus was not divine, so he became a Unitarian. He published *History of Early Opinions Concerning Jesus Christ* to prove that, contrary to the New Testament, the early Christians did not believe Jesus was divine.

587. William Carey (1761–1834)

A shoemaker by trade, he became one of the greatest missionaries in history. Carey became a pastor and in 1792 preached a famous sermon—"Expect Great Things from God, Attempt Great Things for God"—in which he urged a ministers conference to evangelize India. Carey lived in poverty in Calcutta while he mastered Bengali, Sanskrit, and other Indian languages. He translated the Bible into Bengali, the first Bible in an East Asian language. Carey is often called "the Father of Modern Missions."

588. Adoniram Judson (1788–1850)

Judson was a leading American missionary. He and his wife settled in Burma, where he learned the language and translated the entire Bible into Burmese. Judson was one of many dedicated missionaries in the 1800s who proved to be not only tireless ministers but also skilled translators.

589. David Friedrich Strauss (1808–1874)

Strauss, a German Bible scholar, achieved instant notoriety in 1835 with his two-volume *Life of Jesus, Critically Examined*. Like several other "biographies" of Jesus written in the 1800s, it threw out all the supernatural elements from the Gospels and claimed that the early Christians based their religion on myth, not real events.

590. Charles Darwin (1809–1882)

He was a mild man, but his scientific books changed the world's view of humanity and traditional religions. *The Origin of Species* (1859) and *The Descent of Man* (1871) cast doubt on the creation story in Genesis and led people to believe that evolution, not God, was the ultimate truth. Darwin was an agnostic, and his teachings helped spawn many more agnostics or atheists. Darwin's wife despaired for her husband's soul, and she found consolation in prayer and Bible reading. Darwin was buried with honor in England's most famous church, Westminster Abbey.

591. T. H. Huxley (1825–1895)

Huxley, a British scientist and author, was called "Darwin's Bulldog" because he defended and popularized the theory of evolution. Huxley despised Christianity and the Bible, yet he grudgingly admitted the Bible had played a social role in history: "Throughout the history of the Western world, the Scriptures have been the greatest instigators of revolt against the worst forms of tyranny."

592. Bruno Bauer (1809–1882)

In the 1800s Germany was home to many Bible scholars who published their doubts about the miraculous elements in the Bible. Bauer went a step further and claimed that Jesus never existed at all, and the New Testament was pure fiction. Bauer was an extremely bitter man, rebelling against the faith of his youth, but his skepticism became popular among intellectuals. In the late 1800s it was common for sophisticated people to share his view that Jesus never existed.

593. Joseph Ernest Renan (1823–1892)

Renan published his *Life of Jesus* in 1863 and it was amazingly popular—and controversial as well. Renan admired Jesus as a wise teacher and charismatic personality—but not as the Son of God. He later wrote a seven-volume *Origins of Christianity,* which also ruled out any belief in the supernatural. His *History of Israel* applied the same skepticism to the Old Testament. Renan had been a professor of Hebrew but was fired because of the controversy his books generated.

594. Søren Kierkegaard (1813–1855)

Denmark's great Christian philosopher believed that the faith had become dull and matter-of-fact, and that most people were Christians only on the surface. In his many books he emphasized the duty of making a "leap of faith" in life, genuinely accepting the deep truths of the Bible, and pursuing a personal relationship with God. One of his books, *Fear and Trembling*, takes its title from Philippians 2:12: "Work out your own salvation with fear and trembling."

595. Julius Wellhausen (1844–1918)

A respected professor of the Old Testament, Wellhausen, a German, changed the whole course of Bible studies with his theory that the Torah, the first five books of the Old Testament, were not written by Moses nor by any one author, but compiled over several centuries. He came up with the JEDP theory of the Torah, "J," "E," "D," and "P" being the four "strands" that editors eventually wove into the "books of Moses." His clever theory had the unfortunate effect of making many people doubt that the Old Testament was truly inspired.

596. Adolf Von Harnack (1851–1930)

Harnack, like most famous German scholars, was skeptical about the supernatural elements in the Bible. His classic book, a best-seller, was *What Is Christianity?* in which he explained his idea that Jesus' gospel was not about Himself but about the Father. Jesus, Harnack thought, was not truly divine, and most of His miracles were legends. He wrote scholarly books such as *Luke the Physician* and *The Sayings of Jesus*, but is best remembered for *What Is Christianity?* and the skepticism it helped popularize.

597. Sir William Ramsay (1851–1939)

The 1800s were years of skepticism about the Bible, as scholars cast doubts on the historical value of the Bible (not to mention throwing out anything miraculous). Ramsay, an archaeologist, began as a skeptic, but the more he studied the artifacts from the New Testament period, the more convinced he was that the New Testament was grounded in fact. Ramsay concentrated on Luke and Acts and concluded that Luke was a careful historian. Ramsay's most famous book was *St. Paul the Traveler and Roman Citizen.*

598. Sigmund Freud (1856–1939)

Freud, the founder of psychoanalysis, was a Jew and an atheist. He considered religion a neurosis based on human illusions. One notable antireligion (and anti-Bible) book he wrote was *Moses and Monotheism,* published the year he died.

599. J. Gresham Machen (1881–1937)

Machen was a key player in the "great divide" between liberals and conservatives in the 1920s. As a Presbyterian seminary professor, Machen opposed the liberal drift of his denomination, and the Presbyterians suspended him from the ministry. He started another denomination, the Orthodox Presbyterians. Machen wrote several books, including the classic *Christianity and Liberalism,* which is still the best definition of what separates traditional Christians from liberals. He defended the traditional view of the Bible in *The Virgin Birth of Christ* and also wrote *The New Testament for Beginners.*

600. Karl Barth (1886–1968)

The Christian liberal of the 1800s was skeptical about the Bible (its supernatural elements, anyway) but optimistic about human nature. World War I dampened that optimism, and World War II was like an ice-cold shower. A Swiss pastor and theologian, Karl Barth published his *Commentary on Romans* in 1919, and one reviewer called it "a bombshell on the liberal theologians' playground." Barth affirmed everything Paul's epistle to the Romans said about human sin. Barth went "back to the basics" in terms of Christian doctrine—exactly what the fundamentalists were doing at that time.

But Barth was not a fundamentalist. He emphasized the holiness of God, the depth of man's sin, and Jesus as Savior—but also doubted that the Bible was historically true in every detail. His position—which came to be called *neoorthodoxy*—was a way of having one's cake and eating it too. The neoorthodox believed in traditional Christian teachings, but were skeptical about the historical details. Fundamentalists said that the Bible is the Word of God; the neoorthodox said the Bible *becomes* the word of God when it inspires the reader. The neoorthodox flirted with universalism, the belief that all men will eventually be saved.

Barth set forth the neoorthodox position in thirteen massive volumes titled *Church Dogmatics.* His writings influenced a whole generation of Bible readers and theologians.

601. Albert Schweitzer (1875-1965)

Schweitzer wore many hats: medical missionary, world-renowned organist, theologian. He gave organ recitals to finance his hospital in Africa, and he was honored with the Nobel Peace Prize in 1952. Schweitzer's controversial contribution to Christian thought was his *Quest of the Historical Jesus.* He had serious doubts about the accuracy of the New Testament. Like many German scholars of his generation, he did a lot to undermine faith in the Bible. Admittedly, Schweitzer was a compassionate and saintly man.

602. Rudolf Bultmann (1884-1976)

This German professor of the New Testament did (so his critics say) tremendous harm to belief in the New Testament. A key word that Bultmann made popular was *demythologize.* He believed that modern man could no longer believe the supernatural elements in the Bible, so readers must "demythologize" the miracles and reinterpret the Bible in ways meaningful to contemporary life. Bultmann was noted for saying, "One cannot believe in the electric light bulb and in the resurrection of Jesus."

603. Watchman Nee (1903-1972)

The noted Chinese author and evangelist founded the Little Flock movement, which takes its name from Luke 12:32: "Do not fear, little flock, for it is your Father's good pleasure to give you the kingdom." The group began as a student fellowship for prayer and Bible study. Nee was arrested and imprisoned by the Communist Chinese for many years.

604. the Dead Sea Scrolls

In 1947 a goat herder stumbled upon a stash of ancient scrolls in caves near the Dead Sea. They turned out to be the oldest manuscripts ever found of the Old Testament, with fragments of every book except Esther. The site came to be known as Qumran, and scholars believe the residents of the desolate site were Jews who lived like monks and devoted themselves to studying the Old Testament.

605. the Vatican II Council

The Second Vatican Council, meeting 1962–65, produced dramatic changes in the Roman Catholic Church, many of them affecting the church's use of the Bible. The council (usually referred to as "Vatican II") decreed that preaching must be nourished and ruled by the Bible. The Bible should be translated from the Greek and Hebrew—not, as the old rules stated, from the Latin Vulgate. Translators and Bible scholars can work with non-Catholics. The study of the Bible is declared to be the soul of theology. Clergy must be well trained in the Bible for preaching and teaching. Bishops should encourage people to read the Bible and appropriate commentaries.

In brief, Vatican II sent a message to Catholic clergy and laity: more Bible.

606. Billy Graham (b. 1918)

William Franklin Graham is probably one of the most respected—and certainly one of the best-known—religious figures of the century. Though ordained a Southern Baptist, Graham has successfully downplayed denominations and emphasized a basic, Bible-centered Christianity in his evangelistic preaching around the world. His many sermons and books are strictly rooted in the Bible.

607. the Shroud of Turin

No piece of fabric has ever been put through as many scientific tests as this piece of linen that many believe was Jesus' burial cloth. The shroud has been held, at least since 1578, in Turin, Italy. It shows front and back images of a man laid out in death and covered with wounds. The wounds correspond to all of Jesus' humiliations: nail wounds through the wrists and feet (John 20:27); beating about the face (Matt. 27:30); a piercing of the right side (John 19:34); "crown" wounds from some spiked round object (Mark 15:17); and scourge wounds with pellets of bone and metal (Mark 15:15). Scientists believe the man was between thirty and forty-five years old (Luke 3:23).

While "the jury is still out" on the Shroud of Turin, many firmly believe that it is indeed the burial cloth of Christ.

12

Holy Days and Holidays

ISRAEL'S HOLY DAYS

608. Sabbath

According to the Bible, the Sabbath dates back to the world's creation: "God blessed the seventh day and sanctified it, because in it He rested from all His work" (Gen. 2:3). In the Ten Commandments man is told that the seventh day is to be a day of rest, for in six days God made the heavens and the earth but rested on the seventh day. So the Lord blessed the Sabbath day and made it holy (Ex. 20:11).

The pagan world saw every day as a workday, so requiring one day of rest out of seven was an enlightened view. No other religion had this concept, and we can thank God and the Israelites for the fact that we have a concept of a "weekend."

609. Passover

Still celebrated by Jews, Passover commemorates God's "passing over" the Hebrews' homes as He caused the death of the firstborn of the Egyptians. Moses had told the people to mark their homes with blood, and the angel of death "passed over" them (Ex. 12:29). This last of the ten plagues on the Egyptians had the desired effect: Pharaoh released the Hebrew slaves, whom God had told to prepare unleavened bread (bread without yeast), since they would be leaving hastily.

Passover is followed by the Feast of Unleavened Bread (Ex. 23:15), in which the bread without yeast is eaten for seven days. The festival begins with killing and eating the Passover lamb. Both Passover and unleavened bread were reminders to the Jews of the key event in their history, the divine deliverance from slavery in Egypt.

These holy days were forgotten once the people settled in Israel. Not until the time of the reformer kings Hezekiah and Josiah was Passover again celebrated (2 Chron. 30:1; 2 Kings 23:21). Afterward it was—and is—celebrated faithfully.

Jesus' crucifixion and resurrection occurred near the date of Passover (which allows Christians to determine the dates for Good Friday and Easter). Since the first Christians were Jews, they made the connection that Jesus' crucifixion was like the sacrifice of the Passover lamb occurring at the same time, and that God's deliverance of the Hebrew slaves was like mankind's delivery from sin because of Jesus' crucifixion: Both indicated a new life. Paul, in 1 Corinthians 5:7 (NIV), refers to Christ as the Passover lamb. Many times in the New Testament, Jesus was referred to as the "Lamb of God," the perfect and final sacrifice for human sin.

610. Day of Atonement / Yom Kippur

The purpose of this holy day was to remind people of the collective sins of the whole year. On this day Israel's high priest made confession for all the people's sins and entered on their behalf into the Holy of Holies (see 116), where he sprinkled blood on the ark of the covenant. He also sent the scapegoat, on which he symbolically placed the people's sins, into the desert (see 2 [scapegoat]). The solemn day involved godly sorrow over sin but also rejoicing over God's forgiveness. Leviticus 23:26–32 prescribes the rituals.

611. Feast of Tabernacles

This popular festival commemorated the forty years the Israelites spent in the wilderness after liberation from Egypt. It began five days after the Day of Atonement, and during the feast people lived in booths or tents ("tabernacles") to remind themselves of how their ancestors lived in the wilderness. The seven-day feast is described in Leviticus 23:33–43.

612. the year of Jubilee

Every fiftieth year was to be the Jubilee year, a sort of "freedom" year: Israelites enslaved to other Israelites were freed, ancestral lands were returned to the original owners, and the land rested from agriculture (Lev. 25:8–55).

There is no mention in the Bible that Israel ever actually observed the Jubilee year.

613. Hanukkah / Dedication

This Jewish holiday originated in the period between the Testaments. It is mentioned in the New Testament once, in John 10:22, which only mentions that Jesus was in Jerusalem at the time of the Feast of Dedication (another name for Hanukkah).

CHRISTIANITY'S HOLY DAYS

614. Sunday / the Lord's Day

The Christian Sunday—"the "Lord's Day" in the Bible—is not the same as Sabbath. Jesus the Jew observed the Sabbath, but He also claimed that "the Sabbath was made for man, and not man for the Sabbath" (Mark 2:27)—His response to the too-strict rules about Sabbath observance. The first Christians, being Jews, observed the Sabbath, but it eventually lost its importance, especially among Gentile Christians. For Christians, the first day of the week—the day of Jesus' resurrection—was more important than the seventh day. But in a sense the Christians continued the Jewish tradition: one day out of seven for rest and worship.

See 995 (seven).

615. Annunciation

The word simply means "announcing." It refers to the angel Gabriel visiting the Virgin Mary and telling her she is to bear the child Jesus. It was a popular subject with artists, and art museums are filled with *Annunciation* paintings. The Catholic and Orthodox churches celebrate the Feast of the Annunciation on March 25 (exactly nine months before Christmas, if you see the connection).

616. the Visitation

Two amazing pregnancies are recorded in Luke 1: the Virgin Mary and her previously barren relative, the elderly Elizabeth, wife of the priest Zechariah. Elizabeth gives birth to John the Baptist, and Mary gives birth to Jesus. Both the pregnancies and births are foretold by the angel Gabriel.

Luke 1:46–55 records Mary's song of praise, the Magnificat (see 140).

Catholics and some others celebrate the Visitation on May 31.

617. Christmas

The word does not occur in the Bible, and it wasn't celebrated until about A.D. 450, called the Feast of the Nativity (see 856 [the Nativity]).

Matthew and Luke give us a lot of information about Jesus' birth—but no hint of what time of year it was. Frankly, we have no idea. The Romans celebrated December 25 as the festival of *Sol Invictus,* the unconquered sun. This was a winter holiday celebrating the lengthening of days. Even as Christianity spread, the old holiday persisted, so the church adopted it, claiming it as the birthday of the Sun of Righteousness, Christ. The Romans had the practice of exchanging gifts during their Saturnalia (December 17–24), and the church chose to connect this with the gifts of the magi to Jesus (see 619 [Epiphany]).

618. the Holy Innocents

Beautiful as the Christmas story is, it has its gory side. Matthew 2 tells how the wise men came seeking the child Jesus, "the King of the Jews." This provokes the rage and paranoia of the Jewish king, Herod. Hearing that the child has been born in Bethlehem, Herod orders the killing of all boy babies there. The baby Jesus escapes death because a dream has warned Joseph and Mary to flee. The massacred infants are traditionally known as the Holy Innocents. Catholics and some others celebrate the Feast of the Holy Innocents on December 28.

619. Epiphany

This holy day, celebrated on January 6, commemorates two key biblical events: the visit of the wise men to the baby Jesus, and Jesus' baptism by John in the Jordan River. The Greek word *epiphaneia* means "appearance" or "manifestation." The wise men's visit means Christ has appeared to the Gentiles (non-Jews), and His baptism means His adult ministry has begun. The "twelve days of Christmas" refers to the span of time from Christmas to Epiphany.

620. the presentation of the Lord

Luke 2:22–38 speaks of Mary and Joseph taking the baby Jesus to the temple to "present Him to the Lord" according to Jewish custom. There they meet the devout Simeon, who has been waiting all his life for the Messiah and who sees that it is the baby Jesus (see 139 [Nunc Dimittis]). The family also encounters the elderly Anna, who recognizes the child as Israel's savior. The Presentation has been a popular subject for artists.

Catholics and some others celebrate this on February 2.

621. Lent

Some churches observe the forty days before Easter as Lent, a time of soul-searching and penitence. The practice dates from around A.D. 300 and was based on Jesus' forty days of fasting during the time He was tempted by Satan (Matt. 4:2; Luke 4:2). In earlier times, Christians did fast during Lent, but later the idea developed of some form of self-denial—"giving up something for Lent," as many people phrase it.

622. Palm Sunday

The Sunday before Easter commemorates Jesus' welcome by crowds carrying palm branches as He made his way to Jerusalem. They took palm branches and went out to meet Him, shouting, "Hosanna!" and "Blessed is He who comes in the name of the LORD!" (John 12:13). This is known as His "Triumphal Entry." By the following Friday He was crucified. Some churches still stage processions using palm branches.

See 623 (Holy Week).

623. Holy Week

This is the week from Palm Sunday to the following Sunday, Easter, and includes the days known as Maundy Thursday (see 624) and Good Friday (see 625). In some ways it was the most important week in Jesus' life, with such critical events as His cleansing the temple (see 419), the Last Supper (see 421), His arrest, trial, and crucifixion, and, on Easter, His resurrection from the dead. Because the New Testament connects these key events with mankind's salvation, Christians made their celebration a significant part of worship.

624. Maundy Thursday

The Thursday before Easter commemorates the night before Jesus' crucifixion. It was an eventful night: Jesus' Last Supper with His disciples, the agony in Gethsemane, the arrest. *Maundy* comes from the Latin word *mandatum*, meaning "commandment." In John's account of the evening, Jesus told His disciples, "A new commandment I give to you, that you love one another; as I have loved you, that you also love one another" (John 13:34).

625. Good Friday

In a way it is an odd name for a sad day—the day of Jesus' crucifixion. It came to be called "good" because Jesus' death on the cross was regarded as the perfect sacrifice that canceled out human sin and allowed man to be reconciled to God.

The following day, when Jesus was in the tomb, is sometimes called Holy Saturday.

626. Easter

The celebration of the resurrection of Jesus occurs every Sunday (which Christians came to call "the Lord's Day"), and it was about a century before anyone began observing the annual event that came to be called Easter. It was first called *Pascha,* the Greek word for Passover, which was natural since Jesus' death and resurrection occurred near the Jewish Feast of Passover. The apostle Paul referred to Jesus as "our Passover lamb" (1 Cor. 5:7 NIV). Jesus, called the "lamb of God" several times in the New Testament, was regarded as the perfect and final sacrifice for man's sins.

In the year 325 the Council of Nicaea decreed that Easter would be celebrated each year on the Sunday following the first full moon after the spring equinox (March 21).

Easter was, until the last century or so, considered a much more important holy day than Christmas.

The word *Easter* is not actually found in the Bible.

627. Ascension

All four Gospels report that Jesus rose from the dead and appeared to His disciples. Only Luke reports what became of Him afterward: "Now it came to pass, while He blessed them, that He was parted from them and carried up into heaven" (Luke 24:51). In Acts 1:10–11, he adds more detail to this account: "While they looked steadfastly toward heaven as He went up, behold, two men stood by them in white apparel, who also said, 'Men of Galilee, why do you stand gazing up into heaven? This same Jesus, who was taken up from you into heaven, will so come in like manner as you saw Him go into heaven.'" This is known as the Ascension, and it is mentioned several times in the New Testament. The early Christians believed that, just as Jesus had left the earth to ascend to heaven, He would soon return from heaven and take His followers home.

628. Pentecost

This is celebrated by both Jews and Christians, but in different ways. Israel's Feast of Pentecost (also called Feast of Weeks) was (and still is) celebrated fifty days after Passover (*Pentecost* means "fiftieth"). It marks the completion of the wheat harvest, and part of the ritual involved offering the Lord the firstfruits of their produce (Lev. 23:15–21).

Christians celebrate Pentecost as the day the Holy Spirit came upon the believers gathered in Jerusalem to celebrate the Old Testament Pentecost. Acts 2 dramatically describes the incident in which the apostles were filled with the Holy Spirit and began to speak in other tongues. Many Jews from various nations gathered for the Pentecost celebration. The apostle Peter preached to them a stirring sermon, resulting in three thousand new Christians. This fulfilled Jesus' words to them in Acts 1:8, predicting they would receive power when the Holy Spirit came on them, and they would be His witnesses across the earth. Christians often refer to Pentecost as "the birthday of the church."

629. Advent

In many churches Advent refers to the four weeks prior to Christmas, a "season of preparation" for Jesus' coming at Christmas. This was not celebrated in the New Testament period (nor was Christmas, for that matter). The early Christians paid little attention to Jesus' nativity and the time before it because they were more concerned with Jesus' *coming again.* Some churches today bring this into their Advent celebrations, reminding people that Advent is not just a remembering of the past (Jesus came to earth) but a look toward the future (Jesus' triumphant return).

13

Ideas

IDEAS ABOUT GOD

630. holy

In Isaiah 55:8–9, God says, "My thoughts are not your thoughts, nor are your ways My ways . . . For as the heavens are higher than the earth, so are My ways higher than your ways." This is a good definition of *holiness*—God is distinct from, and greater than, His creation. The Bible speaks again and again of God as holy. This meant He was greater than the many fertility gods of the pagan peoples, gods who were powerful, but not moral. Israel's God was all-powerful *and* righteous. Not only was God holy, but His chosen people, Israel, were to be like Him: "You shall be holy; for I am holy" (Lev. 11:44). The people were to practice a higher morality than the idol-worshiping peoples around them. They were to worship only one righteous God, not forces of nature.

The New Testament continues the idea of a holy God and His holy people—but the holy people are no longer those born Jews, but anyone who puts his faith in Christ, the "Holy One of God."

631. Lord / LORD

If you look closely at your Old Testament, you'll notice the word *Lord* appears in two ways: *Lord* and *the LORD*. What's the difference?

Lord translates the Hebrew word *Adonai,* meaning "lord" or "master." The word could refer to God, or to a human master.

The LORD (note the caps and small caps) translates the Hebrew *Yahweh,* the mysterious name of God. The actual name Yahweh means something like "I Am" or "I Cause Things to Be." (One loose translation might be "Supreme Being.") For hundreds of years, English Bibles have chosen to translate Yahweh as *the LORD* instead of fumbling for a way to translate Yahweh. This choice goes back to the Jews, who had formed the habit of never actually saying the name Yahweh. Since it was the true name of God, they felt it was too holy to pronounce. So they got into the habit of saying *Adonai* instead of *Yahweh.* The translators followed this practice, and they use the small caps so you'll always know that *Lord* and *LORD* are translating two different words. (In some isolated areas of the world, tribes still have a high god that is known by a name that the people believe is too holy to say aloud.)

Couldn't we use *Yahweh* in our English Bibles? One version, the New Jerusalem Bible, does. In this version, Psalm

23 begins "Yahweh is my shepherd." Does that sort of jar your ears? Most people think so. After all these centuries of calling God "Lord," we could probably never adjust to calling Him "Yahweh."

In the original Hebrew, *Adonai* and *Yahweh* sometimes appear together when referring to God. How do we translate that? Wouldn't it seem clumsy to say *Lord LORD?* Most translators think so; they came up with alternate phrases. The New International Version and Today's English Version use "Sovereign LORD," for example. Some other versions use *Lord GOD.*

In the New Testament, the term *Lord* applies not only to God but to Jesus. The early Christians saw Jesus as the Son of God. You will find "the Lord Jesus" many times in the New Testament. "Jesus is Lord" was probably the earliest statement of faith in Jesus Christ. Calling Jesus "Lord" meant that the person believed Jesus was the one he followed and worshiped.

See 656 (Christ); 937 (Jehovah).

632. covenant

It's hard to understand the Bible without grasping the idea of *covenant.* A covenant was an agreement—a *contract,* to use a popular word of today. There were covenants between human beings, but the Bible is interested in the covenants between man and God.

Another word for covenant is *testament.* Christians see the first part of the Bible as the older covenant with God— the Old Testament. Jesus and the faith centered on Him are something new—the New Testament.

633. the rainbow covenant

The first covenant mentioned is the one between God and Noah. After surviving the worldwide flood with his family, Noah is told by God that this disaster will never again happen. As a reminder of the covenant, God gives Noah the rainbow. This covenant carries no condition on man's part. It is simply God's promise—not just to man, but to all created things—that He will never again blot out all life with a flood (Gen. 9).

634. circumcision covenant

Abraham, considered the father of the Hebrews (or Israelites) had an agreement with God: All males in his household and all his male descendants would be circumcised (Gen. 17). Circumcision was a sign that Abraham and his descendants were God's special people, the "people of the covenant." Failure to circumcise was so serious that the person could be expelled from the faith community.

See 118 (circumcision).

635. the Sinai covenant

The book of Exodus (which contains the Ten Commandments) depicts the leader Moses guiding the Israelite slaves out of Egypt toward their new homeland in Canaan. At Mount Sinai in the desert, Moses passed on to the people the laws given to him by God. The agreement was this: If the people would obey God's laws, they would settle in the promised land and prosper in it. If they disobeyed, they would bring disaster on themselves. It was a conditional covenant: Obey and thrive, disobey and suffer.

Much of the Old Testament is the story of how Israel failed to keep the covenant—only to be forgiven again and again by God. Still, the condition applied: The people didn't keep the covenant, so they suffered—ultimately by being deported by invading empires.

The Sinai covenant never assumed that people could be sinless. The Law provides a system of sacrifices—gifts of animals or grain given to the Hebrew priests. Israel's religion, like many world religions, provided that sinners could make up for their failings (and prove they were sorry) by giving something valuable to God—a sheep or cow, for example. The sacrifice did not "undo" the sin. But it did prove the person was aware of the sin and willing to give up something as a sign of repentance. The Old Testament makes it clear that there is nothing "magical" about sacrifices. That is, it isn't the slaughtered animal that heals the sin, but the fact that the person is aware of his sin and repents. Israel's system of sacrifices was far more humane than the neighboring nations that sacrificed their own infants to idols.

636. Jeremiah's heart covenant

The prophet Jeremiah watched tearfully as his sinning countrymen were carried off to exile in Babylon—a result of breaking the Sinai covenant. Jeremiah predicted a new covenant: "This is the covenant that I will make with the house of Israel after those days, says the LORD: I will put My law in their minds, and write it on their hearts; and I will be their God, and they shall be My people" (Jer. 31:33). This new covenant involved an inward motivation to please God.

637. the new covenant

According to the letter to the Hebrews, Christ is "the Mediator of the new covenant, by means of death, for the redemption of the transgressions under the first covenant, that those who are called may receive the promise of the eternal inheritance" (9:15). In other words, the old covenant (the laws given to Israel at Sinai) was no longer binding. The new agreement involved Christ who, in effect, "pays a ransom" so we don't have to suffer for the sins we've committed. Jesus Himself made this new covenant clear at the Last Supper with His disciples: "This is My blood of the new covenant, which is shed for many" (Mark 14:24). The "blood" He was referring to was the wine they were drinking at the supper. The wine symbolized the blood He was about to shed by being crucified. It is a key belief in the New Testament that Jesus' death was the ultimate sacrifice. It did away with the old system of animal sacrifices. Jesus' death cancels out all the sins we committed or ever will commit.

When Christians celebrate the Lord's Supper they remind themselves that Jesus' body and blood (symbolized by bread and wine) are the final sacrifice that cancels out our sins and makes us "right with God."

In the modern world we probably never see an animal being slaughtered, so we're repelled at the whole idea of animal sacrifice. Likewise we don't like the idea of Jesus as a sacrifice—as if God took pleasure in seeing Jesus bleed and die. But if we're going to grasp the Bible, we need to project ourselves back into that world. Yes, it is unpleasant to think about Jesus dying. It should be. The whole point of the New Testament is that Jesus, who lived a sinless life, willingly presented Himself as a sacrifice on behalf of sinners. A completely innocent man was willing to die to benefit guilty people.

See 656 (Christ); 118 (circumcision); 274 (Israelites); 277 (patriarchs); 231 (sin).

638. the Holy Spirit

The Bible's first mention of the Spirit is in the story of the Creation, Genesis 1, where the "Spirit of God was hovering over the face of the waters" (v. 2). The Spirit is God Himself, active in creation and endowing certain individuals for special tasks. The Hebrew and Greek words that we translate "Spirit" both mean "wind" or "breath"—something active, moving, energy-producing.

The New Testament teaches that all believers, not just a few, "have" the Holy Spirit, who endows each believer with some spiritual gift (1 Cor. 12). The Spirit is "God within," guiding the believer in his walk with God. Jesus referred to the Spirit as the "Counselor" (or "Comforter") who would guide His disciples once He had left them (John 14–15).

Because the Gospels mention that the Spirit appeared "like a dove" over Jesus at His baptism, the Spirit is usually represented by a dove.

See 700 (baptism in the Holy Spirit); 239 (the unpardonable sin).

639. the Trinity

The idea of God as three-in-one and one-in-three is present in the New Testament, although the actual word *Trinity* is not. Jesus, in His Great Commission (see 428) to His disciples, told them to baptize people "in the name of the Father and of the Son and of the Holy Spirit" (Matt. 28:19), and baptisms still use that formula. Paul, in Galatians 4:6, refers to God the Father, Son, and Spirit in the same verse.

640. loving-kindness

The Hebrew word *hesedh* in the Old Testament is hard to translate—just like the *agape* of the Greek New Testament, which has a similar meaning. The Bible authors used *hesedh* to refer to God's love, commitment, and care. One contemporary translation translates it as "unfailing love," which is adequate, while another uses "kindness"—fair, but not quite deep enough.

Coverdale (see 186) coined his own word: "loving-kindness." It passed into the King James Version and so generations of Bible readers were exposed to the word *loving-kindness*.

641. monotheism

This means belief in one God, and only one. Christians are monotheists, and so are Jews and Muslims. It is not always clear in the Old Testament that the Israelites were monotheists. The prophets constantly railed against the

Israelites worshiping other gods. It seems that many ancient people accepted the idea that their own god might be the best god without being the only one. (This is known as *henotheism*.) Many Israelites were willing to worship God but also pay respects to Baal, Molech, and other deities. But, as the prophets preached, the false gods were only idols, dumb images of wood and stone.

642. fear of God

The word *awesome* used to pack more of a punch than it now does. Only really amazing things were awesome, and God definitely was. The Old Testament depicts God as loving, merciful, and kind—but also a Being who strikes awe and even fear in man. As the Holy One, God strikes fear in men, since they are sinners. Moses told the people that fear of God should keep them from sinning (Ex. 20:20). And Psalm 111:10 repeats a common phrase in the Bible: "The fear of the LORD is the beginning of wisdom."

The New Testament presents us with God-in-the-flesh, Jesus, who is loving and compassionate. But the fear of the Lord is still a reality. Paul told Christians to "work out your own salvation with fear and trembling" (Phil. 2:12), and Hebrews reminds believers always to be conscious of sin, because "it is a fearful thing to fall into the hands of the living God" (Heb. 10:31).

Loving God was a radical idea in the ancient world. No one loved the pagan gods Zeus or Baal or Molech—they were feared, but not loved. The God of the Bible was One to be feared *and* loved.

643. God as Rock

"Rock" suggests durability and steadfastness, and the Bible calls God a "Rock" many times. Several times He is called "the Rock of Israel." In a long prayer, David stated, "The LORD is my rock and my fortress and my deliverer" (2 Sam. 22:2). Psalm 18:31 asks, "Who is a rock, except our God?"

644. inspired / "God-breathed"

Christians believe the Bible is inspired by God. The Bible's own classic statement on this is in 2 Timothy 3:16–17: "All Scripture is God-breathed and is useful for teaching, rebuking, correcting and training in righteousness, so that the man of God may be thoroughly equipped for every good work" (NIV). The Greek word *theopneustos* used to be translated "inspired by God," but "God-breathed" has the same meaning. Interestingly, the Scripture that Paul is referring to in this passage is in the *Old* Testament, since the New Testament (which this passage became a part of) was still being written.

645. anthropomorphism

It means "shape of man," and it refers to the practice of speaking of God's "body parts"—that is, speaking of God, an invisible spirit, as having hands, eyes, ears, fingers, etc. The Ten Commandments strictly forbid making an image of God, but the Bible authors couldn't help but speak of God as, figuratively anyway, using His hands, His mouth, etc. Exodus 31:18 speaks of the stone tablets holding the

Commandments as being inscribed by "the finger of God." The "fiery finger" shown engraving the tablets in the movie *The Ten Commandments* was taking "finger" literally.

646. grace

The word occurs again and again in the New Testament. It translates the Greek word *charis,* meaning simply "gift." Specifically, it refers to God's free and unmerited love and forgiveness shown to sinful humanity. It is a key belief for Paul, who repeatedly emphasized that God saves us out of His free choice—not because we *deserve* saving, but because He chooses to do so. Salvation is not through humans' good deeds but by *grace alone.* The classic statement of the Bible on grace is Ephesians 2:8: "By grace you have been saved through faith, and that not of yourselves; it is the gift of God." Paul loved the word so much that he used it as a form of greeting. All his letters open with "Grace to you and peace."

647. atheism

If *atheism* means a firm belief in no God, the Bible never speaks of that kind of atheism. Almost everyone in the ancient world worshiped some god or gods, and Israel's recurring problem was not disbelief in God but belief in too many false gods. According to Psalm 14:1, "The fool has said in his heart, 'There is no God.'" But this is not atheism so much as it is denying that God will watch and punish the evil ones.

There is no word in biblical Hebrew meaning "to believe in." In the Bible, humans do not doubt God's (or gods') existence. This is what makes human rebellion against God so amazing in the Bible: They *know* God exists, but rebel anyway.

648. glory

We think of glory as something invisible—fame, renown, respect. But in the Bible the glory of God is sometimes visible. His pillar of cloud and fire that led the Israelites through the wilderness was highly visible. Later the glory of the Lord settled on Mount Sinai. To the Israelites the glory of the Lord looked like a consuming fire on top of the mountain (Ex. 24:16). In the tabernacle, God's glory was also visible (Ex. 40:34).

The divine glory blazed around Jesus at the Transfiguration: As He was praying, the appearance of His face changed, and His clothes became as bright as a flash of lightning. Two long-dead men, Moses and Elijah, appeared in glorious splendor, talking with Jesus (Luke 9:29–31).

649. "long-suffering"

Older versions of the Bible, including the King James, use this word to refer to God's patience in dealing with humanity. The word was coined by Tyndale in the 1500s, and even though most modern versions don't use it, it is an excellent word. The Bible continually stresses that God is slow to anger, patient—holding off punishment when, by rights, it is long overdue. Paul lists it as one of the "fruits of the Spirit" that Christians should exhibit (Gal. 5:22).

650. names

You can't help but notice that many biblical names—especially in the Old Testament—are peculiar. They seem less so when you realize that a name was picked because it had a meaning, not just because it "sounded nice."

Notice how many Old Testament names contain an -*iah* or an -*el* at the end (or sometimes *El-* at the beginning of a name). The -*iah* (sometimes -*jah*) was the Hebrew word *Yah*, referring to God. *El* was another name for God. So every name with -*iah* or -*el* has some meaning relating to God. *Isaiah*, for example, means "Yah [God] saves." *Zechariah* means "Yah [God] remembers." *Daniel* means "El [God] is judge." *Elijah* combines the two names and means "Yah is God."

When the Old Testament original uses *Yah* (or its longer form, *Yahweh*), English Bibles translate it as LORD.

See 937 (Jehovah); 631 (Lord/LORD).

651. adoption

God has no children, genetically speaking. People *become* sons and daughters of God, so every child of God is an adopted child. Other religions had crude stories of gods literally producing children, but for Israel, God only has spiritual children—that is, those who obey Him as a Father. Paul several times refers to Christians as being "adopted" by God: "You received the Spirit of adoption by whom we cry out, 'Abba, Father'" (Rom. 8:15). While Christians are presently children of God, the "full" adoption occurs after death: Believers "groan within ourselves, eagerly waiting for the adoption, the redemption of our body" (Rom. 8:23).

652. election

Not political elections, but the act of choosing. The Old Testament makes it clear that God *chose* Israel, not vice versa. God called Abraham and his descendants to be His people. The prophet Amos summarized well: "You only have I known of all the families of the earth" (Amos 3:2). Amos and other prophets were aware that the choice was not made because Israel was moral (since it often wasn't). Running through the whole Old Testament is the idea that God's love was undeserved—which made it all the more remarkable.

In the New Testament the emphasis shifts from Israel to individuals. Jesus told His disciples, "You did not choose Me, but I chose you" (John 15:16). Jesus also said, "Many are called, but few are chosen" (Matt. 22:14).

If God is the chooser, where does human free will come in? The theologians and Bible scholars have been debating this for centuries. Does the Bible want it both ways—God as the One who chooses, but man with free will? Puzzling as it is, yes.

653. kingdom of God

"Kingdom of God" and "kingdom of heaven" are mentioned many times in the New Testament, usually by Jesus.

Mark 1:15 begins the story of Jesus in this way: "The time is fulfilled, and the kingdom of God is at hand. Repent, and believe in the gospel." But He made it clear that the kingdom is not a place or political entity. Jesus told Pilate, "My kingdom is not of this world" (John 18:36). "Kingdom of God," as Jesus used it, meant "rule of God"—the condition of God's will prevailing in men's lives. In a sense, the kingdom of God exists when men show that they love and obey God. As Jesus put it, "The kingdom of God is within you" (Luke 17:21). Jesus saw Himself as the establisher of this kingdom, for He spoke of it often as "My kingdom."

Jesus' enemies managed to have Him executed because they claimed He was a political threat to Rome—which the Roman governor Pilate knew was not so. The Jews had produced many political agitators wanting to be "king of the Jews," but Jesus was not one of these.

654. oaths

An oath is an appeal to God to witness the truth of some statement or agreement. The familiar oath phrase "as surely as the Lord lives" occurs many times in the Old Testament and was taken seriously. (This is why one of the Ten Commandments forbids taking God's name in vain—which occurs when an oath is made lightly or rashly.)

Jesus told His followers, "Do not swear at all . . . Let your 'Yes' be 'Yes,' and your 'No,' 'No'" (Matt. 5:34–37). Jesus was teaching a higher morality, in which a person's honesty would be so obvious that there would be no need to swear any kind of oath. James 5:12 repeats this important teaching.

Some Christian groups such as Quakers and Mennonites take Jesus' words on oaths literally and will not swear in a courtroom.

IDEAS ABOUT JESUS CHRIST

655. Savior

The word means "one who saves" or "deliverer." In the Old Testament the word applies to God, who saves people from their troubles—sickness, enemies, etc. The New Testament gives the word a different twist: Jesus is the One who saves people *from their sins.* He does not forget people's worldly sorrows, but mostly He is the Savior who blots out their sins so they can fellowship with a righteous God. This fits with the New Testament belief that our biggest problem in life is our own failings, our sins. Jesus is not a political or military deliverer, but a spiritual liberator.

656. Christ / Messiah

Was *Christ* the last name of Jesus? Hardly. In Jesus' day most people did not have last names (though they might be referred to as, for example, "John the son of Zechariah"). The New Testament many times uses the phrases *Jesus Christ, Christ Jesus,* and *the Christ.* Christ is not a name, but a title. It means "anointed one." Anointing—dabbing the head with a small amount of oil—was a ritual that marked a person for some special purpose in life—kings and priests, for example. Calling Jesus *the Christ* meant that He was

"God's anointed One," the One whom God had chosen for an extraordinary mission on earth.

Christ, a Greek word, has the same meaning as the Old Testament's Hebrew word *Messiah*. (You're familiar with this word from Handel's popular choral work, often performed at Christmas. Handel could have called his work *Christ*, except that *Messiah* does have a pretty ring to it.) In the Old Testament the word *Messiah* can refer to almost any person or even an inanimate object that is anointed. But as time passed, the Jews began to believe that God would send one special person, *the* Messiah, who would restore the nation of Israel to its political and spiritual glory. Many people saw this figure as a warrior king who would chase the foreign oppressors from the land. Groups of guerrilla fighters and terrorists banded together occasionally, trying to put the dream into action. One group of these was called the Zealots, and one of Jesus' disciples was a Zealot named Simon. No doubt Simon and some other followers of Jesus wondered if He was the long-awaited Messiah who would chase the Romans from the land.

Jesus failed to meet these expectations. He told the Roman governor, Pilate, "My kingdom is not of this world" (John 18:36). Yet many people had become convinced that Jesus *was* the Messiah, the Christ. They perceived that their expectation of a military-political strongman had been wrong. Jesus the Messiah was a *spiritual* Savior, One who would save people not from foreign armies but from their own sins (which, in the Bible, is more of a problem than war is).

Ironically, this spiritual Christ ended up being executed by those who believed He was trying to be the political

Messiah: "They began to accuse Him, saying, 'We found this fellow perverting the nation, and forbidding to pay taxes to Caesar, saying that He Himself is Christ, a King'" (Luke 23:2).

See 632 (covenant); 631 (Lord/LORD); 655 (Savior).

657. Son of man

The name occurs many times in the Old Testament, with the simple meaning "human being" or "mortal" (which is how some translations phrase it). It is used dozens of times in the book of Ezekiel, who always has God addressing him as "son of man."

More important, it was the name Jesus used for Himself. People impressed with Him might refer to Him as "Son of God," but He used "Son of Man" as His own designation, probably because it emphasized His humanness and His unity with mankind. He often used it in a "third person" form, saying "the Son of Man" instead of "I."

The New Testament continually stresses that Jesus was truly human but also God in the flesh. It was appropriate that the divine Savior was One who identified with the people He had come to save.

The only Christian who ever referred to Jesus as "Son of Man" was Stephen, just before his death by stoning: "I see the heavens opened and the Son of Man standing at the right hand of God" (Acts 7:56).

658. shepherd

In Bible times it referred to literal keepers of sheep, but it is often used figuratively to refer to God (see Ps. 23) or to authority figures (kings, priests, etc.) who look after the people. The prophets, Ezekiel in particular, railed against Israel's leaders who neglected the people: "Woe to the shepherds of Israel who only feed themselves! Should not the shepherds feed the flocks?" (Ezek. 34:2).

Jesus saw Himself as a shepherd: "When He saw the multitudes, He was moved with compassion for them, because they were weary and scattered, like sheep having no shepherd" (Matt. 9:36). To His disciples He said, "I am the good shepherd. The good shepherd gives His life for the sheep" (John 10:11). Paul told the Christian leaders at Ephesus to "shepherd the church of God" (Acts 20:28).

The word *pastor* originally meant shepherd. (See any connection between *pastor* and *pasture?*)

659. Word / Logos

John's gospel opens with "In the beginning was the Word, and the Word was with God, and the Word was God." The "Word," as the Gospel shows, was Jesus Christ. "Word" translates the Greek word *Logos,* which means more than "word"—*Logos* suggests communication, thought, ideas, wisdom. As John uses it, it means God revealing Himself to man—the divine mind in a way that man can grasp it. *Logos* was a commonly used word among Greek philosophers, and probably John used *Logos* as a point of contact with people influenced by Greek thought. The word is used only at the beginning of the Gospel, so John probably used it as a "hook" to lead readers into his story of Christ.

660. Son of God

Mark's gospel opens by saying it is "the gospel of Jesus Christ, the Son of God." Jesus never called Himself this, but many others did (including Satan when he tempted Jesus). In His teaching, healing, and casting out of demons, Jesus gave the impression that only the power of God could do such wonders. And of course, Jesus almost always referred to God as "My Father." At Jesus' baptism and transfiguration, God audibly spoke of Jesus as "My Son."

The one occasion when Jesus acknowledged Himself as Son of God was His trial before the Jewish council: "They all said, 'Are You then the Son of God?' So He said to them, 'You rightly say that I am'"(Luke 22:70). The council used this admission to condemn Him.

Belief in Jesus as the Son of God was a key part of accepting the faith. The point is well stated in 1 John 4:15: "Whoever confesses that Jesus is the Son of God, God abides in him, and he in God." The New Testament authors used the title many times.

661. the Lamb of God

Like many other animals, lambs were used in Israel's sacrifices for sin. The most notable slaughtering of lambs was in connection with Passover, in which each family was to kill and eat a lamb for the Passover meal. Like all sacrificial animals, the Passover lamb was to be "without defect."

In people's minds, a lamb combined images of innocence and sacrifice. Thus Jesus was referred to as the "Lamb of God"—most memorably by John the Baptist, who pointed Jesus out and said, "Behold! The Lamb of God who takes away the sin of the world!" (John 1:29). Since Jesus' crucifixion occurred near the time of Passover, the early Christians made a connection between His death and the killing of the Passover lamb. Paul stated that Christ, our Passover Lamb, had been sacrificed (1 Cor. 5:7). And 1 Peter 1:19 refers to Christ as "a lamb without blemish and without spot."

Revelation could be called "the book of the Lamb." In its many symbolic visions the Lamb represents Christ, who, at the end of the world, triumphs over the powers of evil. Revelation 5:12 speaks of a hymn of praise to the Lamb: "Worthy is the Lamb who was slain to receive power and riches and wisdom, and strength and honor and glory and blessing!" Handel set this to music in the last segment of his *Messiah*.

662. Redeemer

To "redeem" is to buy back, to repurchase. In Bible times slavery was common and many people became slaves because of debt or other problems. If a friend or relative could buy them out of slavery, they were said to be "redeemed." In the New Testament, "redeem" and "redemption" refer to being redeemed from slavery to sin. The words are frequently used in reference to Jesus, the great "Redeemer." Paul states that through Christ "we have redemption through His blood, the forgiveness of sins"

(Eph. 1:7), and we are "justified freely by His grace through the redemption that is in Christ Jesus" (Rom. 3:24).

Paul also uses "redemption" in a future sense: Just as believers are now redeemed from sin, so in the future they will be redeemed from the present body and given an incorruptible body (Rom. 8:23).

663. ransom

A ransom was the price paid to free someone from slavery or captivity. It could also be the fine paid as a substitute for the person's own life. The New Testament states that Christ paid a spiritual ransom on behalf of man's sins. Jesus made this clear Himself: "The Son of Man did not come to be served, but to serve, and to give His life a ransom for many" (Matt. 20:28). Paul echoed this idea, saying that Christ "gave Himself a ransom for all" (1 Tim. 2:6).

See 662 (redeemer).

664. Mediator

The New Testament uses many names to refer to Jesus' work as Savior. Because man's sin separates him from God, there is need of a mediator (the Greek word is *mesites*, meaning "middle man") to bring God and man together. Paul summarized this nicely: "There is one God and one Mediator between God and men, the Man Christ Jesus" (1 Tim. 2:5). The epistle to the Hebrews refers several times to Jesus as the divine Mediator (Heb. 8:6; 9:15; 12:24).

665. reconciliation

Jesus said, "Blessed are the peacemakers." The greatest peacemaker would be one who reconciles man and God. The Bible takes a serious view of sin and of the holiness of God. Result: Man's sin alienates him from God. The New Testament speaks of Jesus as the One who heals the breach. According to Paul, "God was in Christ reconciling the world to Himself, not imputing their trespasses to them . . . We are ambassadors for Christ, as though God were pleading through us: we implore you on Christ's behalf, be reconciled to God" (2 Cor. 5:19–20).

666. atonement

Look at the word closely and you see its meaning: at-one-ment. It means bringing two separated parties together, making them *at one*—in other words, reconciliation. The word isn't used much anymore, except that Jews still celebrate the annual Day of Atonement (Yom Kippur). Leviticus 16 spells out how ancient Israel observed the day, which included the ritual of the high priest symbolically placing his hands on the head of the scapegoat, transferring Israel's sins to it, and sending it away to the wilderness.

The key idea is that human sin offends a holy God, so something must occur to bring about a reconciliation between man and God. Israel, like most nations, practiced animal sacrifices. The dramatic change came with the New Testament, where the Christians perceived that Christ, the perfect and innocent man, suffered a horrible death and became the final, once-and-for-all sacrifice for human sin.

Paul affirmed that God presented Jesus as an atonement sacrifice, through faith in His blood (Rom. 3:25).

When theologians speak of "the Atonement" (often with a capital *A*), they are referring to Jesus' death as the great sacrifice that reconciles man to God.

See 2 (scapegoat); 126 (altars).

667. justification

It means "setting things right" or "making valid." The New Testament teaches that because Jesus was a perfect, sinless man, those who have faith in Him are also made righteous, with the penalty for their sin removed. The idea is that God is a righteous judge who has to punish human sin. Jesus, the innocent victim, takes the punishment Himself—the innocent suffering so the guilty won't have to. The Christian's awareness of this free gift of God—being "let off the hook"—should lead to gratitude and love for God. Paul talks about justification a great deal in his letters, notably Romans 4:6–8; 5:18–19; 2 Corinthians 5:19–21; Galatians 2:16–17.

668. the body of Christ

The church (in the sense of a building) is not mentioned in the Bible, but the church as a fellowship of Christians is (see 688 [church]). More than once the Christian fellowship is referred to as a *body*, that is, something alive, a unit with different parts that work together in a common life. And the head of the body is Christ. Paul stated the idea perfectly in Romans 12:5: "We, being many, are one body in Christ, and individually members of one another." In 1 Corinthians 12 he explained the importance of accepting one another as having different abilities, all working toward a common goal. Each Christian has something to contribute, and there is no place for snobbery or selfishness.

IDEAS ABOUT THE GOOD LIFE

669. born again

The concept of conversion, doing a moral and spiritual "about-face," is a prominent one in the Bible. The prophets of Israel constantly urged people to turn from their wicked ways, and in the New Testament Jesus and the apostles urged people to repent and turn to God. Only in John 3 is the actual phrase "born again" used. Jesus told the wise Jew Nicodemus that he had to be "born again"—although the Greek words could also be translated "born from above." With either translation, the idea is that one must experience a spiritual renewal.

670. conversion

Most people who became Christians in the New Testament period were adult Jews or Gentiles who made a dramatic break with their past when they accepted Christ as Lord. The most dramatic conversion is probably Paul's, related in Acts 9. Acts 2 relates the first "altar call," Peter's sermon followed by a call to come forward, repent, and be baptized.

Are there "gradual conversions," or is that a contradiction in terms? In 2 Timothy 1:5, Paul refers to Timothy's "genuine faith that is in you, which dwelt first in your grandmother Lois and your mother Eunice, and I am persuaded is in you also." Did Timothy "grow up in the faith" and never need to have a dramatic conversion experience? The Bible does not answer all our questions.

671. fruits of the Spirit

"The fruit of the Spirit is love, joy, peace, longsuffering, kindness, goodness, faithfulness, gentleness, self-control" (Gal. 5:22–23). These admirable qualities are listed by Paul—following a quite different list of qualities of people who follow their sinful natures.

"Fruits of the Spirit" are different from the list of "spiritual gifts" found in 1 Corinthians 12 (see 148 [gifts of the Spirit]).

672. faith, hope, and charity

This trio is found in 1 Corinthians 13:13, the end of Paul's famous statement on the nature of genuine love. In this chapter Paul defined the nature of unselfish love (the Greek word *agape*), stating that it was more desirable than any other "spiritual gifts." At the end of the chapter, Paul says, "Now abide faith, hope, love, these three; but the greatest of these is love."

Older translations of the Bible (the King James, for example) use "charity" instead of "love." This has an advantage, since people today assume that any discussion of "love" involves romance. "Charity," when the King James was written, did not mean "giving to the poor," but caring, nurturing, looking after someone's best interests.

Christians have sometimes referred to faith, hope, and charity as "the three holy virtues."

673. love / agape

The Old Testament depicts many kinds of love: friends, family, sexual, romantic, spiritual. It shows God's love for man as the greatest love—selfless, forgiving, merciful, at times "tough," but strong and durable. That sort of love appears in the New Testament, and the Greek word is *agape*. In fact, Greek had several words for love—*eros* ("attraction love," mostly sexual), *philia* (friendship), and *storge* (family love). But the word used by Jesus and His followers was *agape*, a love well defined in Paul's famous "love chapter," 1 Corinthians 13 (see 437 [the Love Chapter]). Jesus and the apostles had an important message: Love the way God does, unselfishly, seeking the other's welfare.

Agape has proved difficult to translate, since "love" for many people means the love found in romance novels, rock songs . . . or pornography. John Wycliffe and, later, the King James translators, understood this and translated the word as "charity." Tyndale and the popular Geneva Bible used "love," and so do all modern translations. It is an inadequate translation, but no one has thought of an alternative—except for reading 1 Corinthians 13 frequently to recall just what *agape* means.

674. faith

The word occurs hundreds of times in the Bible. It refers to man's spiritual trust in God, in Christ, in the divine commandments. Paul wrote often about faith in his epistles. For him it was the submissive trust in Christ (1 Cor. 15:1–3). To be a Christian meant not just saying "yes" to a set of beliefs but basing one's life on those beliefs, trusting that Christ the Savior restored man's broken relationship with God.

675. hope

The word is used in the usual sense in the Bible, but it also had some deeper meanings. In the Old Testament, Israel's supreme hope was that God would finally deliver the nation from all political oppression and the people would live the holy lives God expected of them. In the New Testament, the key hope is for eternal life. This is not just a wish or dream, but an expectation, based on the promises of Christ. Paul emphasized that even though faith in Christ brought satisfaction in this earthly life, even more important was what lies ahead: "If in this life only we have hope in Christ, we are of all men the most pitiable" (1 Cor. 15:19).

676. forgiveness

It is one of the loveliest words in the English language, and a concept the Bible constantly harps on. God, the Holy One, is constantly willing to forgive people if they repent. Out of gratitude for such mercy, people should be willing

Ideas

to forgive others. How many times must we forgive someone who wrongs us? "Peter came to Him [Jesus] and said, 'Lord, how often shall my brother sin against me, and I forgive him? Up to seven times?' Jesus said to him, 'I do not say to you, up to seven times, but up to seventy times seven'" (Matt. 18:21–22). Jesus' point was that there is no "right" number of times to forgive; rather, the emphasis is on the attitude, not the number of times.

677. a new heart

The book of the prophet Ezekiel is most remembered for the prophet's strange visions (such as the valley of the dry bones, and the four cherubim). But Ezekiel also prophesied something more centered on individuals, predicting a time when God would transform a sinful people: "I will give you a new heart and put a new spirit within you; I will take the heart of stone out of your flesh and give you a heart of flesh" (36:26).

678. Christian freedom

Paul, the former Pharisee who had been obsessed with following the many regulations of the Jewish law, rejoiced that Christianity gave more freedom—not freedom to be immoral, but freedom from fastidious details. Chapter 5 of his epistle to the Galatians is the Bible's great "freedom chapter." Paul affirmed that Christians please God by being led by the Spirit, not by obeying rules. He told the Galatians: "Through love serve one another. For all the law

351

is fulfilled in one word, even in this: 'You shall love your neighbor as yourself'" (5:13–14).

679. the priesthood of all believers

Israel had priests, but the New Testament (particularly the epistle to the Hebrews) teaches that Christ is the Great High Priest, the only mediator needed between God and man. So the old system of priests and rituals is no longer needed. But 1 Peter goes a step further: All Christians are, in a sense, priests—that is, people with direct access to God. Peter told his readers, "You are a chosen generation, a royal priesthood, a holy nation, His own special people" (2:9).

When the Reformation began in the 1500s, its leaders reacted against the Catholic priesthood (which was often corrupt) and emphasized the priesthood of all believers. This is the reason that most (though not all) Protestant churches today do not refer to their pastors as "priests."

680. peace

To us it means "no war." In the Bible it meant much more: the state of well-being, security, the condition of being in a right relation with both God and man. The Hebrew word *shalom* and the Greek *eirene* both convey this rich meaning. For one with faith in God, this type of peace could be had even if war was raging. Christ the Savior is referred to as "our peace" (Eph. 2:14). The Bible's view of peace is summarized nicely in Isaiah 26:3: "You will keep him in perfect peace, whose mind is stayed on You, because he trusts in You."

681. sanctification

It means "to make holy" or "to make pure." The Bible continually contrasts God's holiness with human sin. The New Testament speaks of this process as something God does in us, and also something we do ourselves. Paul, in Romans 12:1, tells believers, "I beseech you therefore, brethren, by the mercies of God, that you present your bodies a living sacrifice, holy, acceptable to God." Paul also points to the role Christ and the Spirit play in sanctifying the believer: "You were washed . . . you were sanctified . . . you were justified in the name of the Lord Jesus and by the Spirit of our God" (1 Cor. 6:11). The Bible presents two sides of the coin: Christ sanctifies us, cleansing us from our sins. But believers must continually strive to keep themselves morally pure.

682. meekness, humility

The whole Bible is "anti-pride"—if pride means arrogance, thinking too highly of oneself, making oneself a god. Meekness and humility are praised—not the meekness of milksops or people harping on their own faults, but simply a realistic view of one's pluses and minuses, and an awareness that only God is worthy of worship. Moses, the great deliverer of Israel, was called "very humble, more than all men who were on the face of the earth" (Num. 12:3). Jesus, in His Beatitudes, pronounced, "Blessed are the meek, for they shall inherit the earth" (Matt. 5:5). Paul echoed this view when he said, "Let nothing be done through selfish ambition or conceit, but in lowliness of mind let each esteem others better than himself" (Phil. 2:3). Paul also described Christ Himself as "meek and gentle," the Son of God who lived humbly.

683. servant of Christ

Jesus described Himself as a "servant" and encouraged His disciples to be servants, not dominators. He followed the Old Testament idea that a righteous man is the "servant of God," but also showed that one is to be servant to one's fellow man.

Paul liked to refer to himself as "a servant of Jesus Christ," as did James, Jude, and Peter in their epistles. This was a way of saying, "Yes, you regard us as authority figures in the Christian fellowship, but we are all *servants* of the true Master, Christ."

One of the titles of the Catholic pope is "servant of the servants of God."

684. the Way

"Beliefs" are not important in the Bible—unless they result in a way of life, that is. For this reason the New Testament refers several times to the life of faith in Christ as "the Way." Christianity is not so much a system of ideas as a way of life. Jesus referred to Himself as "the way, the truth, and the life" (John 14:6). Acts refers several times to Christians as followers of "the Way" (9:2; 18:25; 19:9).

IDEAS ABOUT MAN

685. original sin

Original here means "from the origin." The term *original sin* does not appear in the Bible, but the idea is prevalent, particularly in the New Testament. Paul gave a classic statement on it in Romans 5:12–19. The key idea is that Adam, the original man, disobeyed God. This not only alienated him from God, but the condition of being separated from God was "inherited" (spiritually, not biologically) by all human beings. As Paul explains it, sin (disobeying and thus offending God) and death (the punishment for sin) are part of the human condition, a condition that can only be remedied by the divine Savior, Jesus.

See 232 (the fall of man).

686. image of God

Human sin is referred to again and again in the Bible, but the Bible authors never completely forgot that man was made, as Genesis 1:26–27 says, "in the image of God." God gave life to all other living things, but man was special, made to be "like" God. This "image" was not physical (since God is a spirit) but a matter of mind, will, emotion— what we normally call a "soul" as opposed to existing only to eat, sleep, and reproduce. Man, unlike animals, has a spiritual and moral nature. He can sin—which is exactly what happens in Genesis 3 (see 232 [the fall of man]). Sin touches all of human life, but never is the image of God completely erased.

Part of the New Testament message is that relationship with God can be restored and we can be more like God—the whole meaning of "image." Paul urged Christians to "put on the new man which was created according to God, in true righteousness and holiness" (Eph. 4:24). In Colossians 3:10 he refers to "the new man who is renewed in knowledge according to the image of Him who created him."

687. righteous remnant

Throughout the Bible is the idea that the human race as a whole is sinful, but there is always a "righteous remnant" that God wishes to preserve. This lies behind the saving of Noah and his family from the global flood. Later, Israel was supposed to be God's holy, righteous nation, but the nation as a whole was never very righteous. Israel's prophets saw this clearly and spoke of a remnant that would be preserved by God. Isaiah mentions the righteous remnant dozens of times, as do most of the other prophets. Zephaniah predicted a time when "the remnant of Israel shall do no unrighteousness and speak no lies, nor shall a deceitful tongue be found in their mouth; for they shall feed their flocks and lie down, and no one shall make them afraid" (Zeph. 3:13).

IDEAS ABOUT THE CHURCH

688. church

In the Bible, "church" never refers to a building, but only to a fellowship of Christian believers. The Greek word is *ekklesia* (from which we get our word *ecclesiastical*) and it means "assembly" or "gathering." Jesus Himself used the word twice (Matt. 16:18 and 18:17), but it is used often in Acts and the Epistles. It could refer to a local fellowship of Christians but could also refer to Christians everywhere, as in Colossians 1:18: "He [Christ] is the head of the body, the church." This obviously refers to something larger than the local group.

It is unfortunate that we translate *ekklesia* as "church," because "church" suggests not only a building but also an institution, while the *ekklesia* in the Bible is clearly a voluntary fellowship of believers in Christ.

689. tithing

A "tithe" is a "tenth," and in the Old Testament it refers to giving 10 percent of everything to the Lord. Tithing laws are spelled out in Deuteronomy 12:6–17 and 14:22–28. In practice, of course, no one can actually give money or produce to God Himself. Israel's practice was to give the tithe to the Levites, those who served in the temple. The tithes also helped support the poor.

The New Testament does not make tithing binding on Christians, although many Christians practice it. Rather, the New Testament urged generous giving, proportionate to one's income. Wealthy Christians were expected to give generously to aid less fortunate brothers in the faith.

690. alms

It means giving to the poor—specifically, giving to beggars. The Old Testament set a high value on such generosity, as did Jesus and the apostles. But Jesus emphasized that alms-giving was to be done because it was good—*not* to win the praise of others (Matt. 6:2).

691. evangelism

The word comes from the common New Testament word *euangelos,* meaning "good news," but usually translated "gospel." It refers to the "good news" of Jesus as the Son of God and Savior of mankind from sin. The first disciples felt a powerful need to spread the faith in Jesus, and Matthew 28 records Jesus' "Great Commission," His command to go and teach their faith to all nations. The book of Acts and Paul's letters are evidence of how seriously the early Christians took the work of evangelizing the world.

692. excommunication

Torturing and executing heretics is not Christian, but, according to the Bible, shutting them out of the fellowship is. Jesus told His disciples that if one believer sins against another, he should be shown his fault, and if that doesn't reform him, take the case to the fellowship, and if he refuses to listen to them, then treat him "like a heathen and a tax collector" (Matt. 18:15–17). In other words, follow the path of mercy until the person proves stubborn, then shun him. As well as wronging a fellow Christian, other reasons for being cast out of the church included sexual immorality and false teaching (Gal. 6:1–2; 1 Cor. 5:1–12; 1 Tim. 6:3). Paul had much to say about the subject, concerned as he was for high moral standards among Christians: "Reject a divisive man after the first and second admonition, knowing that such a person is warped and sinning" (Titus 3:10–11).

Excommunication strikes modern readers as judgmental and coldhearted. But the early Christians placed a high value on following Christ, and they believed that faith and morals mattered more than "tolerance."

693. "brother"

In the New Testament, fellow Christians usually referred to each other as "brethren" or "brothers," the idea being that Christ's followers were a spiritual family. ("Brothers" is used much more often than "Christians" in the Bible.) Some churches still practice calling fellow members "brother" and "sister." Some churches refer to their pastor as "Brother So-and-so" instead of using "Reverend."

694. creeds

The most famous statements of faith, like the Apostles' Creed and the Nicene Creed, are based on the Bible but were formulated many years after the New Testament was written. The New Testament itself contains several short creeds or "statements of faith." Paul, in 1 Corinthians

15:3–7, makes a basic summary of Christian belief, and another in Philippians 2:6–11. Note Romans 10:9: "If you confess with your mouth the Lord Jesus and believe in your heart that God has raised Him from the dead, you will be saved." The same creed is found in 1 Corinthians 12:3, which suggests that "Jesus is Lord" was Christianity's original creed.

695. fasting

Denying oneself food for a certain period is mentioned many times in the Bible, notably in connection with the Day of Atonement, a mandatory fast for the Jews (Lev. 16:29). Depriving oneself was connected with consciousness of sin or grief, and wanting to obtain the Lord's favor.

Jesus did not emphasize fasting, and some of His enemies noticed this, taking it as a sign that He was not spiritual enough (Matt. 11:19; Luke 7:34). In Matthew 6:16–18, He made it clear that fasting is to please God, not to win applause from other people (which the Pharisees did). More important, in Matthew 9:14–17 Jesus said that fasting, associated with sadness, was not appropriate for the kingdom of God, which is a kingdom of joy.

The book of Acts shows that some early Christians did fast and pray (Acts 13:2–3; 14:23). But the apostle Paul never once mentions fasting.

696. transubstantiation

According to official Catholic teaching, the bread and wine used in holy Communion become the actual body and blood of Christ. Catholics base this teaching on Jesus' words at His Last Supper: When He gave His disciples bread and said, "This is My body" and gave them wine and said, "This is My blood," He meant His words literally, and the transubstantiation (meaning "change of substance") takes place in every Communion. This belief became widespread in the Middle Ages. In the 1500s the Protestants questioned the belief, leading the Catholics to decree once and for all that Christ's body and blood are "truly, really, and substantially contained" in the bread and wine, even though they *appear* to be nothing more than bread and wine.

697. confirmation

Churches that baptize infants usually practice confirmation, a ritual done around twelve years of age when the person "claims the faith" into which he has been baptized. The practice is traced back to Acts 8:14–17, which speaks of people who had been baptized and then, later, received the Spirit when the apostles laid hands on them. In confirmation services today, a bishop usually lays hands on the person. Most services include asking the person questions to assure that they understand the basic teachings of Christianity.

698. confession

The New Testament knows nothing of the practice of confessing sins to a priest or minister. However, the idea of moral accountability in the Christian fellowship is present.

James 5:16 mentions that believers should "confess your trespasses to one another, and pray for one another." And 1 John 1:9 states that "if we confess our sins, He is faithful and just to forgive us our sins and to cleanse us from all unrighteousness." But there is no mention of confessing to a minister.

699. saint

The Catholic church defines a saint as a person who is in heaven—made official by a church process called "canonization." But the New Testament applies "saint" to all believers, people called to be God's holy ones while living in the sinful world. Some saints are more "saintly" than others, but all believers whose lives are led by the Spirit are destined for eternal life. The New Testament Epistles make it clear that saints had to be reminded that they belonged to God and their lives should show it (Eph. 4:1; Col. 1:10; 2 Cor. 8:4).

700. baptism in the Holy Spirit

John the Baptist baptized people in water to symbolize repentance and turning to God. He predicted Someone greater who would "baptize you with the Holy Spirit" (Matt. 3:11). The prophecy of Spirit baptism was fulfilled in a dramatic way in Acts 2, when the twelve apostles "were all filled with the Holy Spirit and began to speak with other tongues, as the Spirit gave them utterance" (v. 4). One of the apostles, Peter, then preached a stirring sermon, ending it with these words: "Repent, and let every one of you be baptized in the name of Jesus Christ . . . and you shall receive the gift of the Holy Spirit" (Acts 2:38). Acts mentions baptism of the Spirit several times.

Baptism in the Spirit seems to refer to the person experiencing the active presence of God in his life. Some Christians believe that water baptism (particularly when used on infants) is only an outward sign and that the Spirit baptism is more significant. This belief has led to the growth of Pentecostal and charismatic churches (see 327 [Pentecostals] and 328 [charismatics]).

See 149 (speaking in tongues).

701. the keys of the kingdom

After Peter stated to His master, "You are the Christ, the Son of the living God," Jesus blessed him and said, "You are Peter, and on this rock I will build My church, and the gates of Hades shall not prevail against it. And I will give you the keys of the kingdom of heaven, and whatever you bind on earth will be bound in heaven, and whatever you loose on earth will be loosed in heaven" (Matt. 16:16–19). Catholics interpret this as Jesus' commissioning Peter as the first pope, with all popes afterward having "the power of the keys." Non-Catholics generally believe that the "rock" is the confession Peter (whose name means "rock") has just made. "The keys of the kingdom" definitely does not refer to earthly power (as some of the later popes believed) but to defining what is the Lord's will.

IDEAS ABOUT THE FUTURE

702. Day of the Lord

The prophets use this phrase to refer to a future time when God will intervene to punish sin and deliver His righteous ones. "The day of the LORD is great and very terrible; who can endure it?" (Joel 2:11).

The New Testament adds a new element: the return of Christ. Paul refers to the "day of the Lord Jesus" (2 Cor. 1:14). According to 2 Peter 3:10, the day will catch people by surprise and will be dramatic: "The day of the Lord will come as a thief in the night, in which the heavens will pass away with a great noise, and the elements will melt with fervent heat."

703. plowshares into swords

The phrase, used more than once in the Old Testament, refers to moving from a state of peace to a state of war. The prophet Joel used the phrase: "Beat your plowshares into swords and your pruning hooks into spears; let the weak say, 'I am strong'" (Joel 3:10). But the prophets Isaiah and Micah reversed the phrase, predicting a God-sent time of peace: "They shall beat their swords into plowshares, and their spears into pruning hooks; nation shall not lift up sword against nation, neither shall they learn war anymore" (Isa. 2:4; Mic. 4:3).

704. eschatology

This is the study of "the last things," and the Greek word *eschaton* means "end" or "last." Many parts of the Bible speak of "the day of the Lord" and Jesus' return to earth sometime in the future. Eschatology is the attempt to harmonize these different parts of the Bible and make sense of them all. The book of Revelation is important in eschatology, and so are Paul's statements in 1 Corinthians 15; 1 Thessalonians 4:13–5:11; and 2 Thessalonians 2:1–12. Jesus Himself spoke of the end times, notably in Mark 13; Matthew 24; and elsewhere. From the Old Testament, Daniel 7–12 is studied.

See 708 (Second Coming); 707 (Rapture).

705. the Millennium

It means "a thousand years," and is important in Christian thought because of Revelation 20, which speaks of a thousand-year reign of Christ and His saints on the earth. During this period Satan will be "bound," and Christ and His saints (including those who have died) will exist in a golden age, after which Satan will be released, but then will be defeated forevermore.

With its visions full of symbols and hidden meanings, Revelation has puzzled people for centuries. People who study it disagree about the timing of the Millennium. There are "premillennialists," "postmillennialists," and "amillennialists." The "pre" people believe Christ will return before the Millennium, while the "posts" believe He will return after it. "Amillennialists" take the "thousand years" symbolically, referring to the period between Christ's days on earth and His final return.

Much ink has been spilled over the matter of the Millennium.

706. the Tribulation

Before God and His saints finally triumph, evil will pull out all its stops. Jesus Himself predicted that in the end times "there will be great tribulation, such as has not been since the beginning of the world until this time, no, nor ever shall be" (Matt. 24:21). Naturally the book of Revelation, the great book of the end time, addresses this issue, depicting (in a symbolic way) the suffering of the saints under the powers of evil. Revelation 7:14 speaks of the period of persecution as "the great tribulation," and so the phrase passed into the Christian vocabulary.

While it is possible—perhaps likely—that the worst persecution still lies ahead, every day since the time of the apostles Christians have been tortured and killed on some part of the globe. It would be an injustice to say to the martyred dead that "the Tribulation has not yet happened."

707. the Rapture

The Rapture refers to Christians' being united with Christ at His second coming. The idea is based on Paul's words in 1 Thessalonians 4:16–17: "The Lord Himself will descend from heaven with a shout, with the voice of an archangel, and with the trumpet of God. And the dead in Christ will rise first. Then we who are alive and remain shall be caught up together with them in the clouds to meet the Lord in the air."

Jesus' classic statement on the Rapture is probably Matthew 24:40–41: "Then two men will be in the field: one will be taken and the other left. Two women will be grinding at the mill: one will be taken and the other left."

The word *Rapture* supposedly comes from the Latin *rapio*, "caught up," but obviously the normal meaning of *rapture*—a state of intense emotional excitement—is present also.

See 708 (the Second Coming).

708. the Second Coming

The early Christians knew Jesus had ascended to heaven and they expected that He would return from heaven for His people. We refer to this expected event as the second coming of Christ (although the term is never used in the Bible). Jesus foretold His return but made it clear that no one else could predict it (Matt. 24–25; John 14:3). Paul refers to the great hope many times: 1 Corinthians 15:23; Philippians 3:20; Colossians 3:4; 1 Thessalonians 4:15–17; and several other passages. The New Testament authors clearly expected the event in their own lifetimes. Just as clearly, the event has not yet occurred. No doubt the New Testament authors would repeat their message: Stay alert.

See 707 (Rapture).

709. eternal life in the Old Testament

The Israelites had no clear conception of an afterlife (see 869 [Sheol]). The one exception to this is the book of Daniel, one of the last Old Testament books to be written. Daniel 12:2–3, speaking of the end times, gives the one Old Testament glimpse of eternal life: "Many of those who sleep in the dust of the earth shall awake, some to everlasting life, some to shame and everlasting contempt."

ODD IDEAS

710. reincarnation

The Bible does not teach reincarnation, though some thinkers (such as Edgar Cayce) taught that it does. They interpret Jesus' words to Nicodemus—"You must be born again"—in the sense of being reborn into another body and life. Also, they point to the healing of the man born blind in John 9:2. Jesus' disciples asked Him, "Rabbi, who sinned, this man or his parents, that he was born blind?" Their question suggests (to people that already believe in reincarnation) that the man had lived a past life and his blindness was punishment for sins in that life.

711. snake handling

This provokes a lot of snickers from non-Christians, and even from many Christians. Mark 16:18 records the risen Jesus' words to His followers, telling them what they will be capable of: "They will take up serpents; and if they drink anything deadly, it will by no means hurt them." Did Jesus mean the words about snakes *literally?* Hard to say. Jesus did say, on another occasion, "You shall not tempt the LORD your God" (Matt. 4:7).

Acts 28 relates that Paul, shipwrecked on Malta, was bitten by a viper. He shook the poisonous snake off into the fire and suffered no ill effects. The people expected him to swell up or fall dead, but after waiting a long time and seeing nothing unusual happen to him, they believed he was a god. Note that in this situation Paul did not *deliberately* choose to handle the venomous snake.

Incidentally, George Went Hensley, the Tennessean who started the snake-handling ritual in 1909, died of snakebite.

712. bibliomancy

This is the name given to the practice of opening the Bible and reading a passage at random. Some people do this when they are looking for guidance in life. It is a foolish way to use the Bible. (After all, a person considering suicide might open to the passage that says, "Judas went away and hanged himself.")

IDEAS ABOUT MALE AND FEMALE

713. celibacy

Singleness was a rarity in ancient Israel, and most men and women expected to marry and produce children. A change in attitude occurs with the New Testament, for Jesus Himself was not (so far as we know) married, and Paul claimed he was unmarried (which does not rule out the possibility of his being widowed). We know that among the apostles Peter was married (Matt. 8:14), and in all likelihood the other apostles also. Jesus made the statement "There are eunuchs who were born thus from their mother's womb, and there are eunuchs who were made eunuchs by men, and there are eunuchs who have made themselves eunuchs for the kingdom of heaven's sake. He who is able to accept it, let him accept it" (Matt. 19:12). We can assume He was referring to the celibate state, not literal castration. Paul recommended celibacy, but recognized that it was "better to marry than to burn with passion" (1 Cor. 7:8–9).

Paul condemned false teachers who were "forbidding to marry, and commanding to abstain from foods which God created to be received with thanksgiving by those who believe and know the truth" (1 Tim. 4:3). Paul the celibate did not regard marriage as a bad thing.

Regarding celibacy for ministers: Paul wrote regarding the qualifications for ministers and mentions them as being married (1 Tim. 3; Titus 1:6). The Catholic requirement for celibate clergy is not based on the Bible and was not put into effect until A.D. 305. Even after that date there were numerous exceptions.

714. to "know" in the biblical sense

The first mention of sex in the Bible is in Genesis 4:1: "Adam knew Eve his wife; and she conceived, and bare

Cain" (KJV). Later, the perverted men of Sodom noticed that Lot had two male visitors and commanded him, "Bring them out unto us, that we may know them" (Gen. 19:5 KJV) "Know" and "knew" obviously refer to "carnal knowledge." This would have been clear to the original readers of the King James Version, but newer translations are, wisely, more direct: "Adam lay with his wife Eve, and she became pregnant and gave birth to Cain." "Bring them out to us so that we can have sex with them" (NIV).

715. concubines

In the New Testament period the rule was "one wife per man"—or one wife at a time, anyway, since it was possible to divorce then remarry.

But the Old Testament shows a bewildering array of marital options. No woman could have more than one husband at a time, but a man (if his assets allowed) could support a number of wives . . . and concubines.

Just what were "concubines"? We're told that the wealthy King Solomon had seven hundred wives of royal birth and three hundred concubines (1 Kings 11:3). (The common man could not afford such an extravagant household, naturally.) Generally, concubines were sort of secondary wives—often chosen from among slaves, servants, and captives of war. A concubine wasn't a "girlfriend" or "mistress" or "the other woman" that threatened to break up the marriage. The Israelites accepted that a man—particularly a wealthy one—could have certain female servants who provided sexual services in addition to their other duties. Children of concubines were not considered illegitimate.

716. divorce

The Old and New Testaments have radically different teachings on this subject. Christians believe that the New, because it reflects Jesus' teaching, is binding. Essentially the Old Testament left divorce to the husband's discretion—if she "finds no favor in his eyes because he has found some uncleanness in her" (Deut. 24:1). He wrote a "certificate of divorce," put it in her hand, and announced publicly, "She is not my wife, and I am not her husband." In the case of divorce, neither husband nor wife could remarry (thus one could not divorce in order to marry one's mistress).

Jesus set a stricter standard: no divorce at all (Mark 10:11–12; Luke 16:18) or (according to Matthew's version, 5:32), divorce only because of the other spouse's adultery. This obviously gave women a boost in status, since divorce was no longer a husband's prerogative.

The early church faced an interesting dilemma: What about a marriage where one partner becomes a believer but one does not? Paul dealt with this issue in 1 Corinthians 7, his classic statement on marriage. He was in accord with Jesus on a very important point: The divorced person must not remarry.

717. nakedness

The English Bible uses the word *naked* many times, but it doesn't always mean *stark* naked. Adam and Eve were, says

Genesis, "naked and not ashamed," and we can assume they were totally naked. And Noah, caught naked and drunk by his sons, was undoubtedly nude. But a man could be considered "naked" if he was, say, in his loincloth. Peter was "naked" while fishing (meaning he was stripped to the waist, not nude, John 21:7). The great prophet Isaiah walked around "naked" (but not nude) for three years (20:3), as did the prophet Micah, as a way of lamenting the people's sins (Mic. 1:8). King Saul, caught up in a religious frenzy, lay "naked" a whole day and night (1 Sam. 19).

OTHER IDEAS

718. anointing

Christ and *Messiah* both mean "the anointed one." Using the thumb or a finger, a person daubs an oil (usually olive oil) to mark a person or object as being special in some way. A sacred anointing meant the person or thing was being dedicated to God. The Old Testament records many things being anointed—stones, the tabernacle, prophets, priests, and kings. In time the marking with oil came to symbolize the Holy Spirit. It meant that person was set apart and empowered for a particular work in God's service. Samuel anointed King Saul and, later, David. David several times used the phrase "the LORD's anointed" to refer respectfully to Saul.

In the New Testament the "anointing with the Spirit" is a spiritual reality, not a matter of daubing oil. Jesus was said to be anointed with the Spirit, a fact the Gospels mention at His baptism. Jesus' disciples, through their spiritual union with Him, were also said to be anointed with the Spirit (2 Cor. 1:21; 1 John 3:20).

See 656 (Christ).

719. firstborn

It is hard for modern people to imagine the importance the ancient world gave to being the firstborn child (firstborn *son* especially). God told Moses, "Consecrate to Me all the firstborn . . . both of man and beast" (Ex. 13:2). The firstborn as an heir received a double portion of the inheritance. (A firstborn animal, on the other hand, was sacrificed.) The worst of God's ten plagues on the Egyptians was the death of the firstborn, which included Pharaoh's firstborn son (Ex. 12:29).

Sometimes "firstborn" was used figuratively, not literally. God told Moses that Israel was His firstborn son (Ex. 4:22), which referred to a position of preference, not physical descent. The New Testament refers several times to Christ as firstborn: "firstborn among many brethren" (Rom. 8:29); "firstborn over all creation" (Col. 1:15); "firstborn from the dead" (Col. 1:18; Rev. 1:5). As the first person to be resurrected, Jesus holds a special position. (And "firstborn from the dead" is an interesting play on words.)

720. Bible criticism

This type of criticism doesn't mean "put-downs." It means evaluating, explaining, critiquing. A movie critic is someone who reviews movies. In a similar way, a Bible critic "reviews" the Bible. They serve a useful purpose, since they study the Bible closely, often in the original Greek and Hebrew. Some of them make a career of knowing the Bible deeply, studying how it fit in with the ancient world, what the words meant in the original languages, etc. All this knowledge is a good thing.

The problem is, some of these critics really do become criticizers—people who knock the Bible and cast doubts on its divine origin. Studying the Bible closely builds up some people's faith. Unfortunately, in a few cases it has torn down people's faith. A Bible scholar can spend so much time with the Bible that it becomes "old hat." Instead of the inspired Word of God, the Bible is "just my job." It is sad, but true, that some of the Bible pros have come to study the Bible in the same way other scholars study the ancient writings of Greece and Rome—interesting writings, but not truly divine, and not really relevant to life today.

721. liberation theology

This theological movement was popular in the 1960s and 1970s. As everyone now admits, it was more influenced by Marxism than by the Bible. Liberation theologians played down the New Testament's teachings on mercy, kindness, and forgiving one's enemies and, instead, focused on the image of God as the divine liberator, freeing people from oppression as He did the Israelites in Exodus. Critics of liberation theology pointed out that Exodus shows God as the liberator but that the Israelites themselves did not use violence for their liberation—while liberation theologians condoned the use of violence. As Marxism has declined in popularity, so has liberation theology.

722. dispensationalism

This refers to a particular way of looking at the history of man from Adam to the present. Dispensationalists say that history is divided into seven dispensations (time periods), beginning with Dispensation 1, the age of innocence (Eden before the fall of man), through the present Dispensation 6, the age of grace, the church age. Dispensation 7 is the age of the kingdom, the millennial return of Christ. Following that is, of course, eternity. The theory behind dispensationalism is that in the seven ages God has used different ways of dealing with human beings.

Dispensationalism was popularized by C. I. Scofield's *Reference Bible,* which has gone through many editions.

723. pacifism

Many Christian groups, notably the Quakers and Mennonites, refuse to engage in war, claiming they take Jesus' words about nonviolence seriously. It is true that Jesus' Sermon on the Mount sets a goal of not resisting one's enemies—a standard most human beings, including most Christians, fail to meet. The only time Jesus Himself used physical force was in the cleansing of the temple (John 2:14–16), but His basic message was peace and gentleness (Matt. 5:38–48). Still, a Roman centurion, a military man, became a Christian, and the Bible gives no hint that he abandoned his vocation (Acts 10). In the early years of

Christianity, Christians never joined the army, but by A.D. 300 they were doing so. Should Christians avoid any military service? The Bible itself gives mixed messages, leaving the matter to an individual's conscience.

724. blessing

To bless is to wish good fortune and happiness upon someone. In the Bible, this was more than just speaking words, for most people believed there was power in words, and blessings and curses were taken seriously.

Blessing from God means bestowing His divine favor.

The most famous blessings in the Bible are Jesus' Beatitudes, found in Matthew 5 (see 394 [the Beatitudes]).

725. the right hand

The idea of the right side being the *best* side is centuries old. It is mentioned many times in the Bible, the place of honor being at a person's right hand. God's right hand (even though God, a Spirit, has no actual hands) is always mentioned as being powerful. Jesus ascended into heaven, and the New Testament mentions many times that He is now seated at "the right hand" of God (Mark 16:19; Acts 7:56; 2 Cor. 6:7; Col. 3:1). Jacob named his youngest son Benjamin, which means "son of the right hand" (Gen. 35:18).

726. dreams

People in the ancient world put great stock in dreams, which they believed came from the gods. The Bible reports that God did indeed send dreams to certain people. The most famous "dreamer" was Jacob's favorite son, Joseph, whose dreams of seeing his family bowing down to him angered his jealous brothers, who sold him into slavery. (The dreams came true, since later Joseph was promoted to high office and the brothers did indeed bow to him.) Joseph also had an ability to interpret the dreams of others, and centuries later Daniel was also a skilled interpreter. Matthew's gospel reports that a dream told Joseph that his betrothed, Mary, would bear the son of God. After Jesus' birth a dream told Joseph to flee Bethlehem, where Herod was slaughtering all infants.

727. stumbling block

It is anything that causes a person to trip or fall. Figuratively, it is something that causes material or spiritual ruin. The prophets preached that Israel's idolatry was a stumbling block (Jer. 18:15; Ezek. 14:3). Paul told Christians not to put any moral stumbling blocks in one another's paths (Rom. 14:13; 1 Cor. 8:9). Paul also said that because Jesus had been crucified, this was a stumbling block to Jews' accepting Him as Messiah (1 Cor. 7:23).

728. the environment

"Love Your Mother" say the bumper stickers, with their images of "Mother Earth." It's a popular sentiment, but doesn't square with the Bible's view of earth and mankind. The Bible's account of the Creation is clear on the central point that environmentalists find so scandalous: The earth was a gift from God for human use. In the Christian (and Jewish) tradition, nature by itself is not sacred and has no "rights." In fact, the Bible constantly drives home the point that God is *not* just nature, or a force of nature—He is *above* nature, the Creator. Even so, God gave man the task of caring for the earth—not polluting it or making it ugly.

729. divinity

In Greek religion and other ancient religions, there were "demigods" like Hercules and Achilles, the products of gods having intercourse with human women. The Bible has no such stories, and there is no divine (or half-divine) Being but God alone. Even so, God's "image" in man (see 686 [image of God]) means that man can be like God, at least in regard to love, justice, mercy, etc.

730. yoke

A yoke is a farm implement, a wooded frame placed on the necks of two or more draft animals. In the days of slavery, yokes were also used on humans. Figuratively, a yoke suggests slavery, hard labor, a burden, and the Bible uses the word often in this sense. Jesus thought religious Jews were overburdened with a "yoke" of too many legalistic rules. He told His followers, "Take My yoke upon you and learn from Me, for I am gentle and lowly in heart, and you will find rest for your souls. For My yoke is easy and My burden is light" (Matt. 11:29–30).

14

Literature, Theater, and Movies

LITERATURE

731. Mark Twain (1835–1910)

Born Samuel Clemens, Twain was a religious skeptic who enjoyed poking fun at Christianity and the Bible. He wrote *The Diary of Adam and Eve*, an amusing but not unkind look at the original human couple. Twain once said, "Most people are bothered by those Scripture passages they cannot understand. The passages which trouble me most are those which I *do* understand."

732. Charles Dickens (1812–1870)

England's best-loved novelist, author of such classics as *A Christmas Carol* and *David Copperfield*, also wrote for his children *The Life of Our Lord*, based on the Gospels. Dickens once wrote, "The New Testament is the best book the world has ever known or ever will know."

733. Robert Frost (1874–1963)

The great New England poet who wrote "Stopping by Woods on a Snowy Evening" and "The Road Not Taken" was not religious, but he knew the Bible well. Two of his works that deserve to be better known are based on the Bible. *A Masque of Reason* is an amusing dialogue between God, Job, and Job's wife. At the end of this long poem Frost writes, "Here endeth Chapter Forty-three of Job." (Job in the Bible has forty-two chapters.) Frost also wrote *A Masque of Mercy*, in which the "Fugitive" is the prophet Jonah, running away from God. He encounters the apostle Paul and a woman with the peculiar name of Jesse Bel (a takeoff on the name of wicked Queen Jezebel).

734. Oscar Wilde (1854–1900)

The witty Irish playwright gave the world such comedy classics as *The Importance of Being Earnest* as well as the novel *The Picture of Dorian Gray*. Wilde spent time in prison for his homosexual practices, and his reflection on his experiences was given a biblical title: *De Profundis*, Latin for "out of the depths," taken from Psalm 130:1: "Out of the depths I have cried to You, O LORD."

Witty Wilde wrote a tragic play on a Bible story, *Salome*. It tells the New Testament story of John the Baptist, imprisoned by the sinful ruler Herod and beheaded at the request of Herod's stepdaughter, Salome (Mark 6). Wilde's play served as the basis for Richard Strauss's opera of the same title.

See 272 (Salome).

735. Herman Melville (1819–1891)

The author of *Moby Dick* and other classic American novels was not a religious man, but like many great authors, he was fascinated by the Bible. At times Melville's prose seems to read like the King James Version. In his best-known novel, the captain who pursues Moby Dick, the white whale, is named Ahab, the name of a sinful king of Israel. The novel's narrator is Ishmael, the name of a rebellious wanderer in Genesis. Before Ishmael sets sail on Ahab's ship, he is warned not to by a man named Elijah, the name of a fiery Old Testament prophet. These are only a few of the many Bible references that Melville included in his classic. The book ends with a Bible quote, Job 1:15: "I only am escaped alone to tell thee" (KJV).

736. *Quo Vadis?*

Probably the best novel with biblical characters was written by Polish author Henryk Sienkiewicz, who won the Nobel prize for literature. This classic depicts the decadent Roman Empire and its persecution of Christians. The effeminate, snobbish Emperor Nero is a key character, and two important characters from the Bible are the apostles Peter and Paul, both of whom are executed by Nero. The 1951 movie version with Robert Taylor and Deborah Kerr was extremely popular.

737. John Steinbeck (1902–1968)

The popular author and winner of the Pulitzer prize and the Nobel prize was quite familiar with the Bible. His famous novel *East of Eden* takes its title from Genesis 4:16: "Cain went out from the presence of the LORD and dwelt in the land of Nod on the east of Eden." The novel is a retelling, in a modern setting, of the Cain and Abel story. Another novel, *To a God Unknown,* takes its title from Acts 17:23, in which the apostle Paul speaks to the people of Athens, mentioning an altar inscribed, "To the Unknown God." Steinbeck's most famous novel, *The Grapes of Wrath,* makes many references to the Bible.

738. Taylor Caldwell (1900–1985)

One best-seller after another came from the pen of Taylor Caldwell, including two popular novels about Bible characters. *Dear and Glorious Physician* (1959) is about the gospel writer Luke (called "the beloved physician" in Col. 4:14). *Great Lion of God* (1970) is about the apostle Paul.

739. John Milton (1608–1674)

England's great Christian poet was brilliant. He not only knew the Bible from cover to cover, but he also knew it in the original Hebrew and Greek. Milton's masterpiece was the long poem *Paradise Lost,* the story of the temptation of

Adam and Eve and God's promise of deliverance. Milton was able to make a book-length poem out of the third chapter of Genesis. He accomplished this by focusing on the serpent who tempted Adam and Eve. Milton (like most everyone else) identified the serpent with Satan, and *Paradise Lost* has a lot to say about Satan and his purposes in trying to corrupt mankind. Many of the pagan gods of the Old Testament (like Moloch) appear in the poem as demons. The poem contains the oft-quoted line "All hell broke loose."

Milton also wrote *Paradise Regained,* a long poem about Satan's temptation of Jesus, based on the Gospels.

Milton's other great poem based on the Bible is *Samson Agonistes,* telling of the Israelite strongman Samson, captured by the pagan Philistines. It is based on Judges.

740. William Faulkner (1897–1962)

The Nobel prize–winning author from Mississippi was very familiar with the Bible. One novel has a biblical title, *Absalom, Absalom,* taken from King David's lament over his wayward son Absalom (2 Sam. 18:33). The Pulitzer prize–winning novel *A Fable* concerns a young soldier who was born in a cow shed and whose body disappeared from his grave. Faulkner intended the story to parallel the life of Jesus.

741. Dante (1265–1321)

The Divine Comedy is one of the world's masterpieces. In it, the great Italian poet journeys through hell, purgatory, and finally heaven. Along the way he encounters people from the Bible, history, and even mythology, who speak about their lives on earth and the punishment they endure for their sins. Dante drew heavily from the Bible and its view of human sin.

742. Fyodor Dostoyevsky (1821–1881)

The great Russian novelist wrote many classics, including *The Possessed* (1871), a novel about political radicals. According to the author, he took the title from the Gospel account of Jesus healing a demon-possessed man (Mark 5:9).

743. Joseph Heller (b. 1923)

Catch-22 is the best-known work of American novelist Heller, but he also wrote *God Knows* (1984), an amusing retelling of the story of King David.

744. Ernest Hemingway (1899–1961)

One of America's best-known novelists, Hemingway despised Christianity, but he was familiar with the Bible. One of his best novels, *The Sun Also Rises,* takes its title from Ecclesiastes 1:5: "The sun also ariseth, and the sun goeth down" (KJV).

745. C. S. Lewis (1898–1963)

Lewis was a quiet English professor of literature, but he gained a reputation as "Apostle to Intellectuals." His brief, readable books on Christianity are still popular. *The Screwtape Letters, Miracles, Mere Christianity,* and others are much loved, as are his fiction works, The Chronicles of Narnia and his "space trilogy." All his works reflect Christian beliefs and a high view of the Bible. His one book dealing directly with the Bible was *Reflections on the Psalms.*

By an odd coincidence, Lewis died the same day as John F. Kennedy.

746. Isaac Asimov (1920–1992)

Both scientist and science fiction author, Asimov churned out a steady stream of popular science fiction but also found time to write *Asimov's Guide to the Bible.*

747. *Lord of the Flies*

William Golding (1911–1993) won a Nobel prize and is best known for *Lord of the Flies,* a disturbing novel about schoolboys who revert to savagery on a deserted island. The novel's title is a translation of the Hebrew word *Beelzebub,* a pagan god whose name is found in 2 Kings 1:2 and Matthew 12:24.

748. George Gordon, Lord Byron (1788–1824)

Byron the English poet led a colorful and (most people would say) immoral life. He was a religious skeptic but knew the Bible well. One of his long poems is *Cain, a Mystery,* in which he takes the side of the biblical Cain, who murdered his brother, Abel. Cain was a typical "Byronic hero," the defiant outcast who lives by his own code. But Byron also wrote "The Destruction of Sennacherib," celebrating the divine defeat of the Assyrian ruler Sennacherib, who had tried to conquer Jerusalem (2 Kings 19).

749. Lloyd Douglas (1877–1951)

A Lutheran pastor, Douglas wrote several popular novels about the early Christians, notably *The Robe* and *The Big Fisherman,* both of which were made into movies. *The Robe* followed the history of Christ's robe and its effects on those who possessed it, and *The Big Fisherman* is the tale of the apostle Peter.

750. Howard Fast (b. 1914)

This popular American novelist wrote one biblical novel, *Prince of Egypt,* the story of Moses.

751. *The Valley of Decision*

American novelists Edith Wharton and Marcia Davenport both wrote popular books with this title. It comes from Joel

3:14: "Multitudes, multitudes in the valley of decision! For the day of the LORD is near in the valley of decision "

752. Elmer Davis (1890–1958)

Davis was a notable journalist and radio commentator in the 1940s and 1950s. His novel *Giant Killer* tells the story of King David.

753. George Eliot (1819–1880)

Literary fans know that "George" was the pen name of Mary Ann Evans, author of such classics as *Silas Marner* and *Adam Bede*. She also wrote a poem, "The Death of Moses," and "The Legend of Jubal," a tale of the inventor of music, according to Genesis 4:21.

754. Thomas Mann (1875–1955)

Mann is considered one of Germany's greatest authors, and in 1929 he was awarded the Nobel prize in literature. He wrote a four-volume novel series based on the story of Joseph in Genesis, *Joseph and His Brothers*.

755. Anthony Burgess (1917–1993)

The author of the controversial novel *A Clockwork Orange* and other works, English author Burgess also wrote *Man of Nazareth*, a novel on the life of Jesus.

756. John Bunyan (1628–1688)

The Englishman who wrote *The Pilgrim's Progress* and other Christian classics was steeped in the Bible. His most famous book is an allegory full of biblical images: the narrow gate, the fiend Apollyon from the book of Revelation, the celestial city, and many others. For many years *Pilgrim's Progress* was, after the Bible itself, the most popular book in England and America.

757. John Dryden (1631–1700)

England's poet laureate wrote a comical and satirical poem *Absalom and Achitophel*, based on the story in 2 Samuel 15 of Absalom, who rebels against his father, King David. Dryden connected the biblical events with a recent rebellion of the Duke of Monmouth against his father, King Charles II.

758. Robert Browning (1812–1889)

England's great poet of the Victorian era became famous for his poetry collection *Bells and Pomegranates* (1841), which takes its title from the description of the high priest's robe (Ex. 28:34), which had colored pomegranate ornaments alternating with gold bells around the hem. Browning's long poem *Saul* is in the form of David's meditation upon King Saul.

759. Winston Churchill (1871–1947)

No, not Britain's prime minister, but a popular American novelist with the same name. Churchill, a Christian, was best known for historical novels, but he also examined religious issues in his writings. He also had the habit of choosing his books' titles from the Bible: *A Far Country* (from Luke 15:13), *The Inside of the Cup* (Matt. 23:25), *The Dwelling Place of Light* (Job 38:19).

760. T. S. Eliot (1888–1965)

One of the major poets of this century, Eliot is probably best known for the poems that became the lyrics of the musical *Cats*. But most of his work was serious, and he wrote as a Christian, basing many poems on the Bible, including "A Song for Simeon" (based on Luke 2:25–35) and "The Journey of the Magi."

761. Friedrich Nietzsche (1844–1900)

He was a pastor's son, but he became one of the most anti-Christian philosophers of modern times—and probably the most influential. Nietzsche knew the Bible well but believed it taught a "slave morality" of submission and passivity. He opposed this with his ideal of the "Superman" with the will and strength to rise above traditional morals. (His philosophy was read enthusiastically by the Nazis.) Nietzsche, who spent the last years of his life in an asylum, believed he was the Antichrist, a title he gave to one of his books. He also used another biblical title, *Ecce Homo* (see 860 [*ecce homo*]).

762. Lawrence of Arabia

T. E. Lawrence was famous for leading an Arab rebellion during World War I, a story told in the movie *Lawrence of Arabia*. Lawrence was also an author, and one of his books, *Seven Pillars of Wisdom*, takes its title from the Bible: "Wisdom has built her house, she has hewn out her seven pillars" (Prov. 9:1).

763. Leo Tolstoy (1828–1910)

The Russian genius who gave the world *War and Peace, Anna Karenina,* and other classics, was deeply influenced by the Bible. Though a wealthy aristocrat, his study of the New Testament, particularly Jesus' Sermon on the Mount, brought about a "conversion" to a "religion of love." He rejected traditional Christianity but pursued a lifestyle based on the teachings of Jesus. Jesus was, he said, the greatest moral teacher, not the Son of God. He abandoned belief in an afterlife or even a personal God. One of his philosophical books was titled *The Kingdom of God Is Within You,* taken from Luke 17:21. He referred to himself as "God's older brother."

764. Joseph Addison (1672–1719)

Addison and his friend Richard Steele were the great essayists of the early 1700s, contributing their elegant, sensible writing to the widely read *Spectator*. Addison wrote the still-popular hymn "The Spacious Firmament on High," his paraphrase of Psalm 19.

765. Christopher Smart (1722–1771)

Smart was a respected poet of his time, and also noted for his religious enthusiasm and his habit of praying in public places, which resulted in his being thrown into insane asylums for certain periods. (Christians in the 1700s were expected to be calm, not zealous.) Smart wrote some excellent poetry, much of it based on the Bible. His *Song to David* is superb, and he also produced a rhymed version of the Psalms.

766. Henry James (1843–1916)

The noted novelist's father was a theologian, so young Henry absorbed a lot of theology and the Bible in his youth. While he wasn't particularly religious, he did use the Bible in some of his novels' titles. *The Wings of the Dove* (made into a movie in 1997) takes its title from Psalm 55:6: "Oh, that I had wings like a dove!" The title of *The Silver Cord* is from Ecclesiastes 12:6: "Remember your Creator before the silver cord is loosed, or the golden bowl is broken."

767. Robert Heinlein (1907–1988)

The popular science fiction author was best known for the offbeat novel *Stranger in a Strange Land* (1961). Its title comes from the words of Moses in Exodus 2:22: "I have been a stranger in a strange land" (KJV).

768. Pär Lagerkvist (1891–1974)

One of Sweden's greatest authors and winner of a Nobel prize, Lagerkvist wrote *Barabbas,* a novel about the murderer who was released when Jesus was crucified.

769. Sholem Asch (1880–1957)

Jewish novelist Asch (who lived in America but wrote in Yiddish) wrote several notable biblical novels, including *The Nazarene* (about Jesus), *The Apostle* (about Paul), *Mary,* and *Moses.* Asch, a Jew, believed Christianity was the logical continuation of Judaism.

770. Upton Sinclair (1878–1968)

Novelist Sinclair won fame for *The Jungle,* exposing unsanitary practices in the meat industry. Most of his books were on contemporary social problems, but he also wrote a modern version of the story of Jesus, *They Call Me Carpenter,* with such characters as Mr. Carpenter (Jesus), Judge Ponty (Pilate), and Mary Magna (Mary Magdalene).

771. Pearl Buck (1892–1973)

The daughter of American missionaries in China, novelist Buck set many of her books there, including the classic *The Good Earth.* She published *The Story Bible* in 1971. Written for both children and adults, it tells the main Bible stories in seventy-two chapters, ending with Jesus' ascension. Buck claimed that her own parents never read the Bible to her because her father didn't like English translations and would only read the Hebrew and Greek originals.

772. Marjorie Holmes

The popular author of devotional books penned two best-selling novels based on the Gospels, *Two from Galilee*, about the young Mary and Joseph, and the sequel *Three from Galilee: The Young Man from Nazareth*, following up on Jesus' later life.

773. *Vanity Fair*

One of the classic novels of the 1800s was William Makepeace Thackeray's *Vanity Fair*, a comic tale of ambition and self-seeking. Thackeray ended his novel with some appropriate words from the Bible: *Vanitas Vanitatum!*, the Latin form of "Vanity of vanities," found in Ecclesiastes: "Vanity of vanities, saith the Preacher, . . . all is vanity" (1:2 KJV).

774. Blaise Pascal (1623–1662)

The Frenchman Pascal was a boy genius who became a noted scientist, inventor, and spokesman for Christianity. Pascal had a dramatic conversion in 1654, and he spent the rest of his life making notes for a book to be called *Apology for the Christian Religion*. He died before completing it, but his fascinating notes have been published as *Pensées*, meaning "Thoughts." Pascal knew the Bible by heart, and his notes support the basic truths of the Bible. He took

pains to show how Old Testament prophecies were fulfilled
in the New.

775. the Holy Grail

The New Testament tells the story of the Last Supper, in
which Jesus, dining with His disciples, refers to the cup of
wine with the words "This is My blood of the new
covenant" (Matt. 26:28). According to legend (not the
Bible itself), the cup Jesus used at the Last Supper was used
by one of His followers (Joseph of Arimathea) to catch the
blood of the crucified Jesus. The cup was passed on from
Joseph to others, and magical powers were associated with
it. Legends developed because the church in the Middle
Ages taught that the wine used in holy Communion
became the actual blood of Jesus. Christians assumed that if
their own cup of wine could magically become Jesus' blood,
imagine the power of the cup Jesus had used. The legend of
the cup—the Grail—became connected with the tales of
King Arthur and his Knights of the Round Table.
According to the Arthur legends, the knights sought the
Grail because it could heal diseases and wounds.

The Grail legend hit the big screen with *Indiana Jones
and the Last Crusade,* in which Indiana finds the Grail and
uses it to heal his wounded father.

STAGE AND FILM

776. *Jesus Christ Superstar*

One of the world's most popular musicals has aroused controversy, partly because it ends with Jesus' death, not His resurrection. Its Jesus is, unlike the Jesus of the Gospels, unsure about His divine mission, and its Judas is a good guy, not the evil betrayer in the Gospels. Andrew Lloyd Webber wrote the music and Tim Rice wrote the lyrics for *Superstar*, which was first staged in 1971, then filmed in 1973. The play does show that Jesus was (as the Bible makes clear) fully human, not just divine. But its Jesus is a far cry from the Jesus of the New Testament.

777. *Joseph and the Amazing Technicolor Dreamcoat*

Before composer Andrew Lloyd Webber and lyricist Tim Rice wrote *Jesus Christ Superstar*, they wrote another biblical musical, based on the story of Joseph and his jealous brothers, told in Genesis 37–50. While *Superstar* aroused controversy because it showed Jesus crucified but not resurrected, *Joseph* is noncontroversial. (In fact, some church groups have staged it.) The music is delightful, with songs ranging from rock to ballads to cabaret tunes. The Egyptian pharaoh does an Elvis impression (he's "the King"—get it?). The scene showing Potiphar's wife trying to seduce Joseph is hilarious (the lyrics say "It's all there in chapter 39 of Genesis"). The story of the boy sold into slavery by his brothers, only to later forgive them and rescue them from famine, has a universal appeal.

Note: Not once does the play mention God.

778. Ben-Hur

This popular novel became an even more popular movie. The novel was published in 1880 by Lew Wallace, a retired Civil War general who had intended to prove Christianity was a false religion. The more he read about Christianity and the Bible, the more he believed they were true. He ended up writing *Ben-Hur*, which has the subtitle *A Tale of the Christ*. While Christ is not the main character, He acts as an influence on the young Jewish aristocrat Ben-Hur (played by Charlton Heston in the movie version). In the movie version (which won several Academy Awards), Christ is shown only from behind. The viewer sees how people, including Ben-Hur, react to the presence of Christ.

See 82 (the Great Agnostic).

779. Godspell

It's billed as "a musical based on the Gospel according to St. Matthew," and it's probably one of the most popular musicals of our time. It presents us with a clownish, hippieish Jesus—warm and likable, but hardly awesome. Jesus is not crucified but strung up on a chainlink fence. At the end He is not resurrected but carried through the streets by His disciples.

Most of the lyrics are from old sources—notably the Bible. "On the Willows" is taken directly from Psalm 137 in the Bible. "Prepare Ye the Way of the Lord" is from Isaiah 40:3. "Bless the Lord" is from Psalm 103. "Light of the World" is from Jesus' Sermon on the Mount, Matthew 5:13–16. Jesus' stinging warning to hypocrites, "Alas for You," is from Matthew 23:13–36.

The name *Godspell* is Old English for "good news." It's where our word *gospel* comes from. It has the same meaning as the Greek word it translates: *evangel.*

780. Charlton Heston (b. 1924)

Many people who have never read the Bible's story of Moses believe that actor Charlton Heston *is* Moses. The 1956 film *The Ten Commandments* is still regularly shown on TV, and Heston's portrayal of Moses is probably the big screen's most familiar image of a Bible character. Heston's other great Bible role was the fiery wilderness prophet John the Baptist in *The Greatest Story Ever Told* (1965). Heston also played the title role in *Ben-Hur,* in which he encounters Jesus. The videotape series Charlton Heston Presents the Bible was published in 1998.

See 796 (Cecil B. DeMille).

781. *The Greatest Story Ever Told*

Jesus, a Jew born in Palestine, portrayed by a blond, blue-eyed Swedish actor? That's what happened in this 1965 movie epic, with Max von Sydow playing Jesus. Almost every star in Hollywood appeared in a "cameo," including John Wayne as a centurion at the Crucifixion (with only one line: "Truly this was the Son of God"). The title was taken

from a best-selling book on the life of Jesus by Fulton
Oursler.

782. *King of Kings*

No one has been really successful in making a satisfying
movie about Jesus, maybe because finding the right actor
for the part of Jesus is so difficult. *King of Kings,* released
in 1961, is probably one of the best Jesus films. Jeffrey
Hunter played Jesus fairly well, and Robert Ryan did a
good job as John the Baptist.

An earlier, silent version of *King of Kings* was released in
1927, directed by Cecil B. DeMille, even more famous for
The Ten Commandments.

"King of Kings" comes from Revelation 19:16, where
Christ is described as "King of kings, and Lord of lords."

783. *The Ten Commandments*

Probably the most popular film based on the Bible, this one
is still watchable. Charlton Heston played an excellent
Moses, and no one was better than director Cecil B.
DeMille at filming crowd scenes.

What is often overlooked about the 1956 film is that the
producers and scriptwriters "did their homework." The
costumes and scenery are historically accurate, and most of
the details square with what archaeologists have discovered
about ancient Egypt and the Israelites. A case in point: The
old pharaoh, who acts as a foster father to Moses, is called
Seti, while the new pharaoh (played by Yul Brynner) is

called Rameses. Most historians believe that the Exodus took place under Rameses II, whose predecessor was Seti I.

784. mystery plays

Theater in the Middle Ages was church-based, and "mystery plays" were dramas based on the Bible. They developed from reenactments of the life of Jesus and were done very reverently. Later, as they became more folksy, they were moved from the churches themselves to the church porch or courtyard. Some towns got caught up in producing the plays and turned them into elaborate pageants. In some areas a sequence of plays would be staged, following Bible history from the creation of the world to the resurrection of Jesus.

See 785 (passion plays).

785. passion plays

Dramas depicting Jesus' trial, crucifixion, and resurrection date back to the Middle Ages. Churches usually stage them around Good Friday and Easter, for obvious reasons. Probably the most famous passion play is the one staged in Oberammergau, Germany. The story is that in 1633 villagers prayed to be released from a plague epidemic and, if they were cured, would stage an elaborate passion play every ten years. The Oberammergau play still draws people from all over the world. Probably the most famous passion play in America is the Black Hills Passion Play, in that town with the amusing name, Spearfish, South Dakota. Presented every summer since 1939, it moves to its winter stage in Lake Wales, Florida.

786. Solomon and Sheba

Yul Brynner (with hair!) played King Solomon, and Gina Lollobrigida played the queen of Sheba in this 1959 movie.

787. Pier Paolo Pasolini (1922-1975)

This noted Italian film director was also a Communist. Curiously, he made a movie, *The Gospel According to St. Matthew* (1964), which is (considering the director was an atheist) a fairly reverent version of Matthew's gospel.

788. Two by Two

In 1970 Danny Kaye starred in the Broadway musical *Two by Two*, telling the story of Noah and the ark. ("Two by two" refers to the pairs of animals taken into the ark, of course.)

789. The Bible, according to Huston

The 1966 movie *The Bible*, directed by John Huston, covered only the first few chapters of Genesis, from the creation of the world to the life of Abraham. In the movie, director Huston played both Noah and the voice of God (which made it sound as if Noah were talking to himself).

790. Lillian Hellman (1905–1984)

An extremely talented playwright, she wrote a classic of the American theater, *The Little Foxes,* which takes its title from the Song of Solomon 2:15: "Catch us the foxes, the little foxes that spoil the vines, for our vines have tender grapes."

791. Christopher Fry (b. 1907)

English playwright Fry was popular in the 1940s and 1950s for such plays as *The Lady's Not for Burning* and *Venus Observed.* Fry was deeply influenced by the Bible and wrote a play, *The Firstborn,* about Moses.

792. Clifford Odets (1906–1963)

Odets was one of America's theatrical geniuses of this century, famous for *Golden Boy, Clash by Night,* and other dramas. He also wrote a play called *The Flowering Peach* about the Old Testament character Noah.

793. Don Marquis (1878–1937)

Humorist Marquis is best known for his stories about Archy the cockroach and Mehitabel the cat (noted for being typeset with no punctuation or capital letters). Marquis also wrote some serious works, including a play titled *The Dark Hours* about the last days of Jesus.

794. Edmond Rostand (1868–1918)

Cyrano de Bergerac was Rostand's theater masterpiece, but he wrote many other plays, including *The Woman of Samaria*, about the woman at the well whose life was changed after meeting Jesus (John 4).

795. *Damascus Road*

Townsend, Tennessee, in the Great Smoky Mountains, presents this outdoor drama on the life of the apostle Paul. Its title comes from Paul's dramatic conversion experience on the road to Damascus (Acts 9). The same theater presents the *Smoky Mountain Passion Play*, depicting the last days of Jesus.

796. Cecil B. DeMille (1881–1959)

When "Hollywood" and "the Bible" are mentioned together, inevitably people think of director Cecil B. DeMille. In the silent film era, DeMille directed *King of Kings* (1927), on the life of Jesus. He also directed a silent version of *The Ten Commandments* (1923), the story of Moses and the Israelite slaves' deliverance out of Egypt. In 1956 he remade *The Ten Commandments*, this time with sound, lavish color, and Charlton Heston as a dynamic Moses. It is probably one of the most-watched films of all time. DeMille's other great Bible epic was *Samson and Delilah* (1949), which concludes with Samson's destruction of the Philistines' temple. Referring to this impressive scene, DeMille said, "Credit is due to the book of Judges, not to me." DeMille also said, "The greatest source of material for motion pictures is the Bible."

797. Laurence Housman (1865–1959)

He was the brother of noted English poet A. E. Housman, but a popular author himself. He wrote two plays on biblical themes: *The Kingmaker*, on Samuel, Saul, and David; and *The Burden of Nineveh*, on the prophet Jonah.

798. Ingmar Bergman (b. 1918)

Sweden's most renowned movie director was a pastor's son and has often dealt with religious themes in his films. Two of his films have titles from the Bible: *The Seventh Seal* (referring to the seals opened by angels in Rev. 6–8) and *Through a Glass Darkly* (from Paul's words in 1 Cor. 13:12, "Now we see through a glass, darkly; but then face to face" [KJV]).

799. Peter and Paul

Anthony Hopkins played Paul and Robert Foxworth played Peter in this 1981 TV movie, which begins at Jesus' crucifixion and ends with both apostles being martyred under Roman emperor Nero.

800. Jesus of Nazareth

Director Franco Zefferelli assembled an all-star cast for his reverent and well-done TV movie (six hours long) first shown in 1977. Anne Bancroft was notable as Mary Magdalene. One departure from tradition: Joseph, Mary's husband, is young like his wife—not Joseph the older man as Christian tradition has always shown him.

801. *Moses the Lawgiver*

Actor Burt Lancaster has been notoriously hostile toward Christianity, but he played Moses in this six-hour 1974 TV movie. While never as appealing as Cecil B. DeMille's *The Ten Commandments,* it was well done and ought to be televised more often.

802. *The Green Pastures*

Imagine Old Testament stories acted out by a black preacher and his congregation. That is what *Green Pastures* is. Somehow it manages to be both reverent and humorous. The play by Marc Connelly was based on *Ol' Man Adam an' His Chillun,* a book by Roark Bradford, who also wrote *Ol' King David an' the Philistine Boys.* The movie version of *Green Pastures* was released in 1936 and featured Eddie "Rochester" Anderson as Noah.

803. Neil Simon (b. 1927)

Probably America's most successful comic playwright, Simon authored *The Odd Couple, Barefoot in the Park,* and other comedy classics. Simon also wrote *God's Favorite,* a wry retelling of the book of Job.

804. Thornton Wilder (1897–1975)

One of America's greatest playwrights, he is probably best known for *Our Town*. Wilder, who won three Pulitzer prizes, was noted for using phrases from the Bible in the titles of his plays. *The Skin of Our Teeth* takes its title from Job 19:20 ("I have escaped by the skin of my teeth"). *The Trumpet Shall Sound* comes from Paul's 1 Corinthians 15:52: "The trumpet will sound, and the dead will be raised incorruptible, and we shall be changed." *The Angel That Troubled the Waters* takes its title from John 5:4, describing a miraculous healing pool whose waters were stirred by an angel.

805. William Shakespeare (1564–1616)

England's great poet and playwright was deeply familiar with the Bible, and probably grew up reading the Geneva Bible, the most popular "household Bible" until the King James Version came along. Shakespeare's plays and poems are filled with references to the Bible. One example: In *Hamlet*, the prince says, "The devil hath power to assume a pleasing shape"—echoing Paul's statement that Satan masquerades as an angel of light (2 Cor. 11:14).

806. Archibald MacLeish (1892–1982)

American modernist poet MacLeish wrote *Nobodaddy* (1926), a verse play based on the story of Adam, Eve, Cain, and Abel, and also *J.B.* (1958), a modern version of the story of Job. It won a Pulitzer prize.

807. *Lazarus Laughed*

The Nobel prize–winning playwright Eugene O'Neill wrote this peculiar play about Lazarus, the friend whom Jesus raised from the dead. The play, written in 1927, deals with Lazarus's later life, when he teaches a new religion of love and life, symbolized by laughter. In Rome he is stabbed to death by the mad emperor Caligula.

808. Jean Racine (1639–1699)

He was, some say, France's greatest playwright, as admired by the French as Shakespeare is by the English. Most of his great tragedies were based on Greek mythology, but in his later years he wrote *Esther* and *Athaliah,* both based on the Bible.

809. Dorothy Sayers (1893–1957)

The public knows her best for her mystery novels featuring Lord Peter Wimsey. But Sayers, a Christian, wrote several religious works, including plays on biblical subjects. The Man Born to Be King is a twelve-play series about Christ. She was a friend of C. S. Lewis and J. R. R. Tolkien.

810. John Masefield (1878–1967)

England's poet laureate was both a poet and author of adventure novels. His verse drama, *A King's Daughter,* deals with the wicked Old Testament queen Jezebel.

15

Music and Art

THE GREAT COMPOSERS

811. George Frideric Handel (1685–1759)

What would Christmas be without Handel's *Messiah*? The great German composer gave the world one of its greatest choral works—and the words are taken entirely from the Bible. Handel's collaborator, Charles Jennens, assembled a sequence of Bible verses that would tell the story of mankind's sin and redemption through Jesus. *Messiah* opens with Isaiah 40:1 ("Comfort ye my people" [KJV]) and continues with verses from the Hebrew prophets, then the famous "Christmas section" and its verses from Luke. In fact, Handel didn't intend the work to be a Christmas project, and some parts of *Messiah* (particularly the parts having to do with the Resurrection) are more appropriate for Easter.

Messiah took Handel only a month to write. It was a deeply spiritual experience for him. He claimed that while writing the famous "Hallelujah Chorus" he "did see heaven opened, and the great God Himself."

Handel was a prolific composer, producing operas, concerti, and hundreds of other works. But his claim to fame is in the area of *oratorio,* a large-scale choral work. His *Messiah* and *Israel in Egypt* use words taken from the Bible. He also wrote the biblical oratorios *Samson, Saul, Solomon, Jephthah, Belshazzar,* and several others.

The correct title is *Messiah,* not *The Messiah.*

812. Johann Sebastian Bach (1685–1750)

Some music lovers believe Bach was the greatest composer ever. He was certainly one of the most productive, and one wonders how a man who fathered twenty children and held positions teaching and playing the church organ ever found time to compose.

Bach, a German, was an extremely devout Lutheran, and he believed all talent came from God. He inscribed his compositions—not just the religious ones but the secular ones as well—with such phrases as "In Praise of the Almighty's Will" and "To God Alone Be the Glory." Bach called the Bible "the great fountain of music, and every musician should play to the glory of its Author."

Many of Bach's great choral works are drawn from the Bible. He composed several "Passions," telling the events of Jesus' crucifixion. His *St. Matthew Passion* and *St. John Passion* are probably two of the greatest choral works ever written. Bach took the text from Martin Luther's German translation of the Bible. Bach also wrote a cantata based on the *Magnificat,* Mary's song of praise in Luke 1:46–55.

813. Franz Joseph Haydn (1732–1809)

The composer whom people lovingly called "Papa Haydn" wrote more than a hundred symphonies, plus operas, quartets, concerti, and almost every other form of music. He also wrote church music, including a choral work, *The Seven Last Words of Christ on the Cross*, with words taken from the four Gospels. After spending some time in England, Haydn became more familiar with the great oratorios of Handel, who wrote the famous *Messiah*. This prompted Haydn to write his own magnificent oratorio, *The Creation*, based on the book of Genesis and also on John Milton's poem *Paradise Lost*.

814. Ludwig van Beethoven (1770–1827)

The great German composer Beethoven wasn't deeply religious, but he did produce a few works based on the Bible. One was an oratorio, *Christ on the Mount of Olives*, based on Luke 22:39–46, which tells of Jesus' agony before His arrest and crucifixion.

815. Giuseppe Verdi's *Nabucco*

The great Italian opera composer who gave the world *Aida*, *Rigoletto*, and other masterworks also penned an opera with a biblical story, *Nabucco*, the story of the Jews' captivity under Babylonian king Nebuchadnezzar. The opera was first staged in 1842.

816. Gioacchino Rossini (1792–1868)

The Italian master of opera gave the world *The Barber of Seville* and *William Tell* (with its famous overture). He also wrote a biblical opera, *Moses in Egypt*, based on Exodus.

817. Hector Berlioz (1803–1869)

The acclaimed French composer, famous for his *Symphonie Fantastique*, also wrote a choral work known as *L'Enfance du Christ*, "The Childhood of Christ."

818. Felix Mendelssohn (1809–1847)

He is most famous for his symphonies, his *Hebrides Overture*, and his music for *A Midsummer Night's Dream*, but he also composed two grand oratorios from the Bible, *Elijah* and *St. Paul*. The great German composer died young, before he could complete his other biblical oratorio, *Christus*.

819. César Franck (1822–1890)

Franck was a world-famous organist but also a noted composer. He wrote several oratorios on biblical themes: *Ruth*, *The Tower of Babel*, *Redemption*, and *The Beatitudes*.

820. *Samson and Delilah*

The biblical story of lust, violence, and betrayal was an obvious subject for an opera. French composer Camille

Saint-Saëns wrote his opera in 1877, and it is still popular. The English did not allow it on the stage for many years because it was thought irreverent to base an opera on the Bible.

821. Edward Elgar (1857–1934)

His "Pomp and Circumstance" march is played at thousands of graduation ceremonies. The gifted English composer also wrote two oratorios based on the book of Acts, *The Apostles* and *The Kingdom*.

822. Arnold Schoenberg (1874–1951)

Schoenberg's music does not appeal to everyone, but he is one of the most notable modern composers of symphonic music. He wrote an interesting biblical opera, *Moses and Aaron*, with particularly interesting music in the scene of the Israelites worshiping the golden calf.

MUSIC FOR THE PEOPLE

823. "A Mighty Fortress Is Our God"

Reformation leader Martin Luther (see 574) wrote several hymns, and this is the best known. It is based on Psalm 46, which begins, "God is our refuge and strength, a very present help in trouble." Luther wrote the hymn (in German) sometime around 1520 and it has come to be called the "Battle Hymn of the Reformation."

824. Old Hundred

This is the name for one of the best-known tunes in the world, the tune to which people sing "Praise God from Whom All Blessings Flow," sometimes called simply the "doxology." The tune dates to 1551, where it was used with a rhymed version of Psalm 134. It was later used with Psalm 100, which it took its name from.

825. the doxology

The familiar "Praise God from whom all blessings flow" is actually the last verse of William Kethe's "All People That on Earth Do Dwell," which was his rhymed version of Psalm 100.

826. Isaac Watts (1674–1748)

Before Watts's day, the only songs that could be sung in English churches were rhymed versions of the Psalms. Watts, a pastor, wrote some of these himself, published as *Psalms of David Imitated*. Later he wrote such classic hymns as "When I Survey the Wondrous Cross" and "O God, Our Help in Ages Past" (his version of Psalm 90). His most famous song is probably "Joy to the World," a Christmas classic—even though it never mentions Christ or His birth and was actually Watts's version of Psalm 98.

827. Charles Wesley (1707–1788)

With his brother, John, he founded what became the Methodist church. He was one of the world's great hymn writers, and his words and phrases are often drawn directly from the Bible. Like many people, he found the worship in the Church of England dull and dry, so he and John launched the movement with a renewed emphasis on emotional involvement, studying the Bible, and singing the Bible. Among his hundreds of great hymns are "Hark, the Herald Angels Sing" and "O for a Thousand Tongues to Sing."

828. gospel songs

Most people refer to all Christian songs as "hymns." But in the many revivals in the 1800s a new type of song developed, the "gospel song," that had as a goal leading people to repentance, a kind of preparation for the preacher's call to come forward and accept Christ or to renew one's faith. While hymns generally praise God or Christ, gospel songs usually concentrate on the congregation, urging individuals to repent or to rededicate their lagging faith. Gospel songs reflect the Bible's many calls to repentance, such as Peter's sermon in Acts 2:14–41. Probably the most famous gospel song is "Just as I Am," popularized by Billy Graham's crusades.

829. "Abide with Me"

This favorite hymn with words by Henry Lyte was written in 1847 as he listened to a sermon on Luke 24:29, which deals with the risen Jesus and two disciples: "They constrained Him, saying, 'Abide with us, for it is toward evening, and the day is far spent.'" The opening words of the hymn are "Abide with me, fast falls the eventide, / The darkness deepens; Lord, with me abide."

830. "Turn, Turn, Turn"

In 1965 the folk-rock group the Byrds had a major hit with the song "Turn, Turn, Turn"—with the words taken right out of Ecclesiastes 3: "To every thing there is a season, and a time to every purpose under the heaven . . ." (KJV). Folksinger Pete Seeger had set the biblical text to music. The song has since been recorded countless times and is very much a Sixties classic.

831. the Statler Brothers

Country music's most durable quartet released a two-disk set of gospel songs in 1979, titled *The Holy Bible—The New and Old Testaments.*

832. the Jordanaires

The gospel quartet most noted for singing backup for Elvis Presley took their name from the Jordan River in Israel.

833. Johnny Cash

Country music's legendary "Man in Black" has recorded a number of gospel songs and toured with the Billy Graham crusades. He also published a novel on the life of Paul, *Man in White.* Cash and his wife, June, made the 1973 film *The Gospel Road,* tracing events in the life of Jesus.

834. "His Eye Is on the Sparrow"

Speaking of God's care for his children, Jesus said, "Are not two sparrows sold for a copper coin? And not one of them falls to the ground apart from your Father's will. . . . Do not fear therefore; you are of more value than many sparrows" (Matt. 10:29–31). The verse made its way into the popular gospel song "His Eye Is on the Sparrow." Music legend Ethel Waters, who toured with Billy Graham in her later years, titled her autobiography *His Eye Is on the Sparrow.*

835. "melody in your hearts"

The New Testament says a lot about Christians worshiping together, but it never mentions musical instruments in worship. This is the reason some churches—notably the Churches of Christ, which define themselves as "noninstrumental"—do not use organs, pianos, or any other instruments in worship. Some of these churches do have organs or pianos used for weddings or other services. Paul, in Ephesians 5:19, mentions "speaking to one another in psalms and hymns and spiritual songs, singing and making melody in your heart to the Lord." This is, apparently, the basis for the "noninstrumental" position.

836. "by the rivers of Babylon"

Psalm 137 is a song of people in exile, lamenting being away from their homeland, Jerusalem. Somehow this sad song of separation became popular when set to music. In recent years it has been recorded (in one form or another) by Don McLean, Linda Ronstadt, Boney M, and others. As the song "On the Willows," it was part of the musical *Godspell.*

THE ART MASTERS

837. Sandro Botticelli (1445–1510)

The Birth of Venus is a familiar artwork, showing the naked goddess rising from the sea. The Italian master who painted her painted many scenes from mythology, but later in life he experienced a religious conversion that led him to paint more spiritual subjects. Living in the worldly city of Florence, Botticelli got caught up in a religious revival. For a while the people of Florence, including the artist, took more interest in spiritual things. Some even went so far as to pile up their jewelry, makeup, and flashy clothes and burn them in "bonfires of the vanities." With his mind on eternity, Botticelli created masterpieces like the *Mystic Nativity,* showing the familiar Christmas scene of the newborn Jesus but also showing airy angels dancing in a golden heaven. On this painting the artist wrote (in Greek, for some reason) a message indicating that the end of the world was near and that the prophecies in the book of Revelation were coming to pass.

838. Hieronymous Bosch (1450–1516)

Bosch is best known as a "fantasy painter," famous for such unusual pictures as *The Garden of Earthly Delights* and *Ship of Fools*. But he was also a noted religious painter. His *Christ Mocked* and *Carrying of the Cross* are striking, and he also painted scenes of heaven and hell.

839. Leonardo da Vinci (1452–1519)

His best-known painting is *Mona Lisa,* but another of his paintings, *The Last Supper,* is probably the most familiar biblical painting in the world. While thousands of artists have painted the Last Supper (showing Christ and His twelve disciples at their last meal before Christ's arrest), da Vinci's has somehow become *the* Last Supper. Curiously, the famous painting barely survived. Leonardo liked to experiment with new painting techniques and his *Last Supper,* painted on the dining room wall of a monastery near Milan, Italy, started to fall apart during the artist's lifetime. Thanks to some cleaning and restoration, it now looks better than it has for centuries.

Like most artists of his time, Leonardo painted many biblical scenes, including a famous *Adoration of the Magi.* But *The Last Supper* is probably his masterwork.

840. Albrecht Dürer (1471–1528)

The famous "Praying Hands" picture is Dürer's (the actual title is *Hands of an Apostle*). Dürer was a superb painter, but was most noted for woodcuts and engravings of Bible scenes. He illustrated most key events in the life of Jesus, but his most ambitious—and most disturbing—work was his set of illustrations for the book of Revelation, his *Apocalypse*. The book, with its images of angels, dragons, devils, plagues, and the "four horsemen," comes to vivid life in Dürer's pictures.

841. Michelangelo (1475–1564)

He excelled at painting, sculpture, architecture, and poetry—a true Renaissance man, and one whose art was deeply influenced by the Bible. Michelangelo was fascinated by the human body, and his driving ambition was to re-create it in stone. He succeeded, and his statue of the biblical *David* is familiar to everyone. (The David in the statue is not circumcised. Michelangelo must have known that the Hebrew David definitely *would* have been circumcised.) Michelangelo also sculpted a famous *Moses*, with the great leader holding the Ten Commandments. But Michelangelo is probably most famous for his biblical paintings in the Vatican in Rome. People who know nothing about art are familiar with the image of the gray-bearded God reaching out His finger to the newly created naked Adam. This, along with other scenes from the book of Genesis, appears on the ceiling of the Vatican's Sistine Chapel, unveiled in

1512. On a wall of that chapel he painted *The Last Judgment,* showing sinners getting their just deserts in hell.

842. Raphael (1483–1520)

He was truly a Christian painter, not only because of his subject matter, but because of his gentle and loving personality. Most of his many paintings have a biblical subject: *Transfiguration, Deposition from the Cross,* and many others painted in his short life.

843. Titian (1490–1576)

Like most notable artists of his time, Titian painted both the Bible and mythological subjects. He excelled in both, and his biblical paintings found in museums around the world are awe-inspiring. His *St. John the Evangelist on Patmos,* painted on a ceiling, is a stunning depiction of John receiving the Revelation from heaven. Titian's *Crowning with Thorns* and *Entombment of Christ* are majestic.

844. Jacopo Tintoretto (1518–1594)

The great Italian painter studied under the famous Titian, and almost all his works had a biblical theme. His masterpieces include a stunning *Last Supper, Washing of the Feet, Paradise,* and (in Washington, D.C.'s National Gallery) *Christ at the Sea of Galilee.*

845. Pieter Brueghel (1525–1569)

He made his reputation with his scenes of peasant life, but Brueghel was a master of biblical scenes, notably *Massacre of the Innocents*, *Tower of Babel*, and *Fall of the Rebel Angels*.

846. Caravaggio (1573–1610)

He was known for using *chiaroscuro* in his paintings—deep contrasts of light and dark. His *Conversion of Saul* dramatically shows the divine light falling on the face of the blinded Paul. Other paintings like *The Beheading of John the Baptist* and *The Supper at Emmaus* are equally dramatic, as if the great biblical figures were in a kind of spotlight.

847. Nicolas Poussin (1594–1665)

Poussin was a French painter living in Rome, and was best known for his paintings of Greek mythology. But he also painted some impressive and dramatic biblical scenes, such as *The Adoration of the Golden Calf*, *Moses Striking the Rock*, and *St. John on Patmos*. He was one of the first painters to try to make his biblical characters look authentic in their clothing and surroundings, instead of dressing them like his own contemporaries.

848. Rembrandt (1606–1669)

This Dutch master was, some say, the greatest artist of all time. He was certainly one of the best where paintings of Bible scenes are concerned. Like most Dutch painters,

Rembrandt excelled in realism, making everyday objects and people seem interesting. He used himself, his wife, his son, even street people as models in his paintings, and even used a beggar as a model for a king of Israel. In *The Raising of the Cross*, he shows himself as one of the people helping to crucify Jesus. *The Return of the Prodigal Son* is filled with a deeply felt humanity. He painted dozens of other Bible scenes: *The Supper at Emmaus, Joseph Accused by Potiphar's Wife, Belshazzar's Feast*, and many others.

849. William Blake (1757–1827)

Blake was poet, painter, and mystic—and his religious beliefs were offbeat, to say the least. His poetry is some of England's best and best known—the famous line "Tiger, tiger, burning bright," for example, from his most noted book, *Songs of Innocence and Experience*. Blake illustrated his poem with copper-plate engravings, and he also made engravings for the book of Job—probably some of the most bizarre (but certainly *interesting*) Bible illustrations ever made.

850. the Nazarenes

Around 1810, several talented German artists formed a Christian art brotherhood that became known as the Nazarenes (named for Jesus' hometown, Nazareth). The group produced *The Bible in Pictures* and other excellent religious works of art.

851. Holman Hunt (1827-1910)

Hunt, an Englishman, traveled in Egypt and Palestine so he could give an authentic flavor to his paintings of Bible scenes. His most famous painting is of Christ, titled *The Light of the World*. His paintings were popular in Christian homes throughout America and Britain.

852. Gustave Doré (1832-1883)

Doré's illustrations for the Bible are probably the most popular ones available, notably because they can be reproduced for free. The great French artist also did some notable illustrations for *Don Quixote* and *The Divine Comedy*, but his Bible pictures made his reputation.

853. Georges Rouault (1871-1958)

He was a stained-glass window maker, and his paintings actually resemble church windows, with heavy black lines separating parts of the pictures. Rouault was a devout Catholic and painted many scenes from the Bible, particularly the life of Jesus. Notable paintings are *Christ and the High Priest*, *The Holy Face*, and *Christ Mocked by Soldiers*.

854. Salvador Dali (1904-1989)

Noted for his surrealist paintings, the Spanish artist enjoyed his reputation as an eccentric. Hardly religious, he did paint a few biblical scenes. Like their creator, they are peculiar. His *Sacrament of the Last Supper* shows a beardless, pale-skinned Jesus presiding over His disciples in white robes in a sort of glass room. His *Christ of St. John of the Cross* shows the crucified Jesus from directly overhead—an unusual view, but, one might say, the divine view.

PICTURING THE BIBLE

855. halo

Christian artwork often shows a halo around the head of Jesus, the apostles, or other saintly persons. The early Christian artists borrowed the concept from pictures of Roman emperors. No one actually believed that saintly people really had visible halos.

856. the Nativity

Despite all the legal battles every Christmas regarding Nativity scenes on public property, they remain popular with private citizens. It is hard to imagine Christmas without scenes of Mary, Joseph, baby Jesus, shepherds, angels, and wise men.

Nativity comes from the Latin *nativitas*, meaning "birth." Another popular word for the Nativity scene, *créche*, is a French word meaning "manger." According to Luke's gospel, Mary placed the newborn Jesus in a manger (a food box for livestock).

Nativity scenes are based on Matthew's and Luke's accounts of the birth of Jesus. He was born in Bethlehem, and Luke says the family was forced to stay in a stable "because there was no room for them in the inn." Luke tells of how angels announced to shepherds that Christ the Savior had been born in Bethlehem, and that they would find the child in a manger in a stable. Matthew tells of the story of the wise men (or "magi") who came from the East to see the newborn "King of the Jews." Interestingly, Matthew speaks of the family being in "a house," not in a stable. It's probable that the wise men's visit occurred some time after the birth in the stable. So the Nativity scenes that show shepherds and the wise men together are probably taking some liberties with the facts—not that anyone minds much.

See 617 (Christmas); 507 (wise men).

857. INRI

Thousands of paintings show Jesus hanging on a cross, and many of them show over His head a sort of placard inscribed with the letters INRI. All four Gospels mention this placard (or "notice"), which declares that Jesus was "King of the Jews." According to John 19:19, Pilate, the Roman governor, had a notice prepared and fastened to the cross. It read: "Jesus of Nazareth, the King of the Jews." In Latin (the Romans' official language) the inscription would be IESUS NAZARENUS, REX IUDAEORUM. The abbreviation for the Latin inscription is INRI. It was Roman custom for crucified criminals to have their offense displayed on the cross.

The Jews who had agitated for Jesus' crucifixion weren't happy with the inscription. The chief priests of the Jews protested to Pilate, "Do not write, 'The King of the Jews,' but, 'He said, "I am the King of the Jews."'" Pilate replied, "What I have written, I have written" (John 19:21–22).

858. the Adoration

The shepherds who came to see the newborn Jesus after hearing the announcement from angels are a favorite subject for artists, as well as part of millions of Nativity scenes. Artists usually give this scene the title "Adoration of the shepherds" or sometimes just "Adoration."

859. Academy of St. Luke

According to an old tradition, Luke, the author of Luke and Acts, became a friend of Jesus' mother, Mary, and painted a portrait of her. For this reason Luke became the patron saint of artists. Art academies were sometimes named for him, and there was a famous Academy of St. Luke in Rome and one in Paris.

860. ecce homo

This Latin phrase means "Behold the man." John 19 describes the Roman governor, Pilate, saying these words while displaying the arrested Jesus to the angry mob of Jews in Jerusalem. The Roman soldiers have arrayed Jesus in a purple robe and a crown of thorns. A purple robe is a sign of royalty, but the soldiers are being sarcastic, and the crown of thorns is clearly intended to cause pain. Apparently Pilate (who believes Jesus is an innocent man) hopes that this degradation will make the Jews happy, but instead they begin shouting "Crucify!"

Many great artists have painted this painful scene, showing the silent and innocent Jesus surrounded by sneering Romans and the angry Jewish mob. Such paintings are always titled *Ecce Homo*.

861. Jesse window

Jesse's sole claim to fame in the Bible is that he was King David's father, and thus an ancestor of Jesus. Isaiah 11 contains an interesting prophecy: "There shall come forth a Rod from the stem of Jesse, and a Branch shall grow out of his roots. The Spirit of the LORD shall rest upon Him" (vv. 1–2). Christians believed this "shoot" (descendant, obviously) was Jesus. Artists liked to depict a "Jesse tree," showing the sleeping Jesse with a tree coming up from his loins—a literal "family tree" with the kings of Israel and, of course, Jesus. It was a favorite subject for stained-glass windows, and many an old church has a "Jesse window."

862. Deposition from the cross

Artists have painted thousands of pictures of Jesus on the cross, but also of His body being taken down from it—the "Deposition." According to the Gospels, Joseph of Arimathea, Nicodemus, and others were responsible for taking the body down, wrapping it in graveclothes, and placing it in Joseph's tomb.

863. Moses with horns

Michelangelo's famous statue of Moses possesses an oddity: Moses has two horns on his head. Did Michelangelo think Moses was on Mount Sinai so long that he turned into a mountain goat? Exodus 34 tells of Moses' coming down from the mountain with the commandments from God. Having been in God's presence, his face literally glowed. The Hebrew words that we translate as "glowing" or "radiant" are related to the Hebrew word for "horn." The Vulgate, the old Latin Bible, does state that Moses had "horns" projecting from him. Michelangelo was one of many artists to show a "horned" Moses.

864. man, ox, lion, eagle

An old tradition connects each of the four Gospels with a symbol: Matthew with a man, Mark with a lion, Luke with an ox, and John with an eagle. Artworks sometimes show the Gospel writers accompanied by these symbols. The four symbols are based, oddly, on the prophet Ezekiel's vision of the four "living creatures" (or "cherubim"): Each of them had the face of a man, a lion, an ox, and an eagle (Ezek. 1:10). Some imaginative Christian decided, centuries ago, that the four faces of the creatures represented the four Gospels.

865. "I stand at the door and knock"

Many Christian homes have a picture of Jesus knocking on a door. That popular image is based on Jesus' words in

Revelation 3:20: "Behold, I stand at the door and knock. If anyone hears My voice and opens the door, I will come in to him and dine with him, and he with Me."

866. the four horsemen of the Apocalypse

In one of Revelation's visions are four figures mounted on horses: conquest on a white horse, war on a red horse, famine on a black horse, and death on a pale horse. "Pale" is actually a poor translation, since the Greek word *chloros* here is more like "sickly green"—an appropriate color for death (Rev. 6:1–8).

The four horsemen symbolize the horrors that will occur at the end of time. They have been depicted in many artworks, notably a frightening engraving by the great Albrecht Dürer. *The Four Horsemen of the Apocalypse* was used as the title of a World War I novel by the Spanish author Blasco Ibáñez made into a classic silent movie with Rudolph Valentino.

867. Bob Jones (1883–1968)

A noted evangelist in his day, Jones decided to start his own college promoting fundamentalist Christianity. That college, Bob Jones University in Greenville, South Carolina, is still in operation, making no apologies for its conservative view of the Bible and Christianity. What many people don't know about the university is that it has an exceptional art museum, the Sacred Art Gallery, probably one of the greatest collections of art on biblical themes. The school also has a noted Bible Lands Museum.

16

Places

PLACES NOT ON THE MAP

868. heaven and hell

The Old Testament says very little about the afterlife. For the people of Israel, the main goal in life was to live on earth and have a good relationship with God and with other human beings. After death . . . what? Most of the Israelites did not speculate about that. They focused on this life.

But the New Testament makes it clear that God designs human beings for an afterlife—a happy, joyous afterlife with Him (heaven) or an unhappy, despairing afterlife apart from Him (hell). Jesus says a lot about God's love and kindness, but also a lot about what happens to us when we reject that love. By our own choice we come running to God, sorry for our failures and wishing to be forgiven and accepted. Or we choose to live strictly for ourselves, ignoring God and neglecting our duties to other people. Hell is like locking ourselves up in a closet, shutting out God and other people.

Is hell a hot furnace, and is heaven a cloudy place with harps and golden streets? The Bible says little about the physical attributes of either place. The book of Revelation does paint a picture of heaven as a beautiful city with streets of gold, pearly gates, and praising God. Revelation uses these images to communicate the ideas of beauty, order, and fellowship with God. Revelation also refers to the devil and all evil people being destroyed in a lake of fire. Jesus Himself spoke of the fire of hell—the idea being that the person apart from God is in agony. Is it a "literal" fire? That question misses the point. The point is that the person who chooses to separate himself from God is in the worst possible circumstance.

869. Sheol

The Old Testament has no doctrine of hell in the sense of a place of eternal punishment. It does refer many times to *Sheol,* a Hebrew word found over sixty times, and usually translated as "the grave." The King James Version sometimes translates *Sheol* as "hell," but in fact the Israelites thought of Sheol as the place *everyone* went after death. The basic belief of Israel is summarized in Psalm 6:5: "In death there is no remembrance of You; in the grave [Sheol] who will give You thanks?" After the Old Testament period a fuller belief in reward for the righteous and punishment for the wicked developed. For the Old Testament Israelites, the horror of Sheol was being cut off from all that one loved, including fellowship with God.

870. Gehenna / Hell

Why is hell pictured as a place of fire? The Valley of Ben Hinnom outside Jerusalem was noted as a place of slaughter, where children were sacrificed (by burning) to the god Moloch. The good king Josiah put a stop to these horrors, but for years people remembered the site as a place of idol worship and death. In the period between the Old and New Testaments some Jewish writers claimed Ben Hinnom was the gateway to hell. The Hebrew name Ben Hinnom passed into Greek as *Gehenna*. In the Greek New Testament, the word *Gehenna* signified the place of eternal punishment— which we translate "hell." Jesus Himself used the word several times. To Him, and probably to everyone who used the word, it brought to mind the sacrificial fires of the gruesome god Moloch. Also, years later, it was used as Jerusalem's garbage dump and kept continually burning. No wonder that Gehenna indicated a horrible place of unending fire. The New Testament uses other expressions besides Gehenna: "furnace of fire" (Matt. 13:42); "lake of fire" (Rev. 19:20); and "eternal fire" (Jude 7). The word translated "hell" in 2 Peter 2:4 is *Tartaros*—a word the Greeks used to refer to the place of punishment for the wicked.

See 227 (Moloch); 868 (heaven and hell).

871. paradise

We use it as a synonym for "heaven," and that is how the Bible uses it. Jesus on the cross promised the repentant thief crucified near Him, "I say to you, today you will be with

Me in Paradise" (Luke 23:43). Paul, in 2 Corinthians 12, speaks of a man (himself, apparently) who was caught up to paradise and who heard inexpressible things. Paul, it seems, had had a glimpse of heaven. Revelation 2:7 mentions "the tree of life, which is in the midst of the Paradise of God." The word is from the Greek *paradeisos*, meaning "parkland."

872. purgatory

Heaven and hell are, according to the New Testament, the two final destinations for human beings. Catholic tradition teaches that there is another state after death, purgatory, where people whose eventual destination is heaven must spend time "purging away" sins they have accumulated in their earthly lives. Catholics seem to base this teaching on a section in the Apocrypha, 2 Maccabees 12:39–45, which speaks of offering sacrifices for dead persons "that they might be released from their sin." Part of the teaching regarding purgatory is that people still alive can do deeds to benefit people in purgatory. Since the Reformation, Protestants have rejected the belief in purgatory.

873. the Holy Land

You won't find it on the map, but many tour operators could take you on a "Holy Land tour." Jews, Christians, and Muslims can all point to places associated with their religious history in the nation of Israel and nearby nations. The ancient city of Jerusalem, in particular, has sites that each of the three religions honor.

Technically, Christians don't have "holy places"—God and Christ are not tied to any land, city, or building. But for centuries Christians have enjoyed visiting—"making pilgrimages" to—sites associated with Jesus, Paul, David, and other biblical figures.

See 879 (Canaan); 274 (Israelites); 932 (Palestine); 900 (Zion).

874. Eden

The name means "delight," and it was mankind's original home, a garden watered by four rivers (two of which, the Tigris and Euphrates, can be found on the map). Man's original occupation was tending the beautiful Garden (Gen. 2:15). The Garden had all kinds of "trees that were pleasing to the eye and good for food" (Gen. 2:9 NIV). God told Adam he was free to eat from any tree in the Garden except the Tree of Knowledge of Good and Evil, for when he ate from it he would die. The serpent tempted Adam and Eve, they ate the forbidden fruit, and because they disobeyed God, they were banished from Eden, the gate guarded by an angel with a flaming sword.

The prophet Isaiah comforted the exiled Israelites by telling them that God would "make her wilderness like Eden, and her desert like the garden of the LORD" (51:3). The prophet Ezekiel referred several times to "Eden, the garden of God."

PLACES ON THE MAP

875. Tigris and Euphrates

The two great rivers are found in Iraq today. In the ancient world the ground between them was called "Mesopotamia," the "land between the rivers." This was the area of the mighty Assyrian and Babylonian Empires.

The two rivers are mentioned early in the Bible, in connection with the Garden of Eden, which has led people to believe that the site of Eden was not Israel but Mesopotamia.

876. Mount Ararat

The extinct volcano Mount Ararat is in what is now Turkey. Genesis 8:4 states that Noah's ark came to rest "on the mountains of Ararat" after the worldwide flood had receded. "Mountains" is plural here, so it may mean the general area of Ararat, not the one specific mountain.

877. Ur

This ancient city was known for being the home of Abraham when God called him to be the father of His chosen nation (Gen. 11:28). It was in what is now Iraq and was excavated by archaeologists in 1922. The excavations show that the people there worshiped many gods. God's call to Abraham to leave Ur and settle in Canaan meant that Abraham was leaving a land of idol worship to pursue a new life of serving only one God.

878. the promised land

Israel was the promised land, "promised" because when God called Abraham from the pagan land of Ur, He promised Canaan (later called Israel) to Abraham's descendants (Gen. 12:7). Their residency in the region ended when Jacob and his twelve sons moved to Egypt to escape a famine. Exodus relates that Jacob's descendants lived peacefully in Egypt until the Egyptians made them into slaves. Moses led them from Egypt back to Canaan—a journey that took forty years. After several centuries in the land, the people were deported to Assyria and Babylonia. They returned eventually, but after the final Jewish war with Rome in A.D. 135, the Jews were again displaced from their promised land.

879. Canaan

Many old hymns refer to "Canaan land." "Canaan" in the Old Testament referred to the general area occupied by the Israelites—roughly the same area as is occupied today by the nation Israel. The "Canaanites" referred to the land's original inhabitants, idol worshipers who were driven out when the Israelites settled in the area.

A familiar, and poetic, name for Canaan was "the promised land." This refers to the promise—mentioned dozens of times in the Bible—that the patriarch Abraham and his descendants (the Hebrews) would possess the land of Canaan, "a land flowing with milk and honey" (Deut. 26:15). The Jews who live today in the modern nation of

Israel still believe the promise that Abraham's descendants would possess that piece of land.

See 873 (Holy Land); 274 (Israelites); 932 (Palestine); 277 (patriarchs); 900 (Zion).

880. the cities of the plain

Genesis 13 and 19 refer to the immoral cities of Sodom, Gomorrah, and neighboring cities as the "cities of the plain," which God destroyed with fire from heaven. *Sodom* is the root of the word *sodomy,* meaning homosexual practices. French novelist Marcel Proust wrote a novel about homosexuality among aristocrats, giving it the title (in French) *Sodome et Gomorrhe.* Its English translation is titled *Cities of the Plain.*

881. Hebron

This was a key city in the Old Testament. Abraham lived there a while and buried his beloved wife, Sarah, there (Gen. 13; 23). David was anointed king there and made it his capital before moving the capital to Jerusalem (2 Sam. 2:4).

882. Salem

The Hebrew word means "peace," which is part of the reason the name is a popular one for cities. It is mentioned only in Genesis 14:18 as being the place where the priest-king Melchizedek ruled (see 486 [Melchizedek]). Jewish tradition says that Salem was an earlier name for Jerusalem.

883. Bethel

The name in Hebrew means "house of God." Jacob, with his head on a stone pillow, had a dream of angels on a stairway to heaven, a dream in which God promised blessings on his offspring. In the dream God is reaffirming His covenant with Jacob's grandfather, Abraham. Jacob awoke and said, "Surely the LORD is in this place," and he named the place Bethel (Gen. 28). Later, God ordered him to settle there, and Jacob erected an altar to God.

Bethel became important centuries later when Israel split into a northern kingdom (Israel) and a southern kingdom (Judah). With no temple (which was at Jerusalem, in Judah), King Jeroboam of Israel set up worship centers at Dan and Bethel. Much to the vexation of the prophets, Jeroboam set up golden calf idols at both places (1 Kings 12). Hosea, Amos, and others condemned the worship centers repeatedly.

884. Egypt

Excepting Israel itself, no nation is mentioned more often in the Bible than Egypt. The ancient civilization along the Nile River was connected with the key event in Israel's history, the exodus from slavery, led by Moses. Because of the years of bondage in Egypt, and because the pharaoh resisted their liberation, Israel always had a low opinion of Egypt. Besides being an oppressor nation, Egypt was also notorious for worshiping dozens of gods in the shapes of animals, something the Israelites abhorred.

Egypt was still a powerful empire long after the Israelites left. The saintly king Josiah was killed while battling Egyptian forces. When the Babylonians conquered Judah in 586 B.C., many of the Jews, including the prophet Jeremiah, fled to Egypt. And, much later, Joseph, Mary, and the infant Jesus fled to Egypt for a while to avoid the massacre of the infants of Bethlehem by King Herod.

885. Goshen

This was the section of Egypt where Israelites lived, first as a free people, later as slaves. The settlement occurred while Joseph, Jacob's son, was Egypt's prime minister, a time when their homeland was enduring a famine (Gen. 46–50). Later, as Exodus 1 painfully relates, the Egyptians turned the Israelites into slaves. Moses, Israel's deliverer, was born there. During the ten plagues that God sent on the Egyptians, the region of Goshen was unharmed.

886. the Nile

The Bible mentions Egypt many times, but never actually names the great Nile, the world's longest river. It is referred to by the Hebrew word *ye'or*, meaning "the river." The book of Exodus takes place mostly in Egypt, and the river is referred to many times: Pharaoh orders the Hebrew infants thrown there, Pharaoh's daughter finds the infant Moses there, and the plagues God sends upon the Egyptians often affect the river (for example, the waters turning to blood). Some modern translations read "the

Nile," but in fact the King James Version translates the Hebrew more correctly by simply calling it "the river."

887. the Red Sea

Thanks to the movie *The Ten Commandments,* the miraculous parting of the Red Sea is one Bible event that people are familiar with. But it never happened. "Red Sea" is an error in translation of the Hebrew. The Israelites, led by Moses, crossed a smaller body of water known as the "Sea of Reeds" or "Marsh Sea." Of course, the parting of the waters, the Israelites crossing over on dry land, and then the drowning of the Egyptians in the waters were still amazing miracles. But the actual Red Sea, the huge body of water between Egypt and Arabia, was not what was parted.

That crossing was one of the great events of the Bible, one that Israel constantly reminded itself of, proof that God cared for the nation.

888. Mount Sinai

The Bible's most famous mountain was where God delivered His divine law to Moses and the Israelites. This dramatic encounter is described in Exodus 19: "Mount Sinai was completely in smoke, because the LORD descended upon it in fire. Its smoke ascended like the smoke of a furnace, and the whole mountain quaked greatly . . . Then the LORD came down upon Mount Sinai, on the top of the mountain. And the LORD called Moses to the top" (vv. 18, 20). The laws in Exodus, Leviticus, and part of Numbers were delivered by God at the site. After a long stay in the plain around the mount, the Israelites moved on toward Canaan.

Curiously, no one is sure today just what mountain was the holy mount of Sinai. It seems probable that Horeb may be another name for Sinai (see 889 [Horeb]).

For more on God's covenant with Israel at Sinai, see 635 (Sinai covenant).

889. Horeb

Was it Horeb or Sinai where God delivered the commandments to Moses? The Old Testament uses both names for the mount, so we can assume it was called by both names. Horeb is mentioned as the site where Moses first encountered God in the burning bush (Ex. 3) (see 341).

Horeb was also the place where the prophet Elijah fled from the wrath of wicked Queen Jezebel (1 Kings 19). Elijah, totally disheartened, received encouragement from the Lord, who reminded him that he was not the only true believer left in Israel. The encounter with God involved an earthquake, a wind, and a fire from heaven. "And after the fire a still small voice," the voice of God (v. 12).

890. Mount Nebo

Poor Moses! He led the Israelites out of their captivity in Egypt, spent forty painful years with them in the wilderness, then, because of his one act of disobeying God, could not enter the promised land himself. Deuteronomy 34 relates that he climbed Mount Nebo to get his one glimpse of the land God had promised to Abraham and his descendants.

God let him see the land but would not allow him to cross over into it. Moses soon died in that region of Moab, and to this day no one knows where his grave is.

891. the Jordan River

It is Israel's largest river, though not large by world standards. It is connected with some of the most important events in the Bible.

Most notable is the Israelites' crossing it while at flood stage. According to Joshua 3, the water from upstream stopped flowing as the people, led by priests carrying the ark of the covenant, crossed over on dry land. The great prophet Elijah, just before he was taken into heaven, struck the Jordan with his cloak and the waters parted. His successor prophet, Elisha, healed the Aramean military leader Naaman of leprosy by having him wash in the Jordan.

In the New Testament, the Jordan was the site where John the Baptist baptized repentant sinners. Most important, it was where John baptized Jesus (Matt. 3:13–17; Luke 3:21–22). This event has been for centuries one of the most popular subjects for artists, so the Jordan River is probably one of the most painted rivers in the world.

The Jordan empties into the Dead Sea.

892. the Dead Sea

It is also called the Salt Sea, and its heavy salt content is why it is dead—almost no plants or animals living in it. (The saltiness makes it easy to float and swim in, as tourists discover.) It is the lowest point on earth, 1,290 feet below sea level, and the area is desolate. It is mentioned many times in the Bible, mostly as a reference point in geography, not as a place where people lived.

893. cities of refuge

Unlike the other eleven tribes of Israel, the tribe of Levi received no land in Israel, but did have forty-eight towns scattered through the land. Six of these served a special purpose as places of refuge where someone who killed another person accidentally could flee. These cities of refuge were not a permanent escape from punishment, but a temporary sanctuary so that the victim's family could not immediately take revenge. The killer would stand trial and if the death was ruled accidental, he would remain in the city of refuge. If he set foot outside the city of refuge, the "blood avenger" of the victim could then legally take revenge.

Peculiar as this custom sounds, it was a compassionate way of aiding people who had killed accidentally, protecting them from a swift kind of "frontier justice" without a fair trial.

894. Shechem

This ancient city was the site where the Israelites, led by Joshua after Moses' death, renewed their promise to worship the God who delivered them from Egypt (Josh. 24). In this they promised never to worship other gods (a promise Israel frequently broke). Centuries later, when Israel split into two separate kingdoms, Shechem was made the capital of the northern kingdom by Jeroboam (1 Kings 12).

895. Shiloh

Before David made Jerusalem the political and spiritual capital of Israel, Shiloh was the center of worship, with the tabernacle and the ark of the covenant remaining there most of the time. The site was associated with the great judge and prophet Samuel: "The LORD revealed Himself to Samuel in Shiloh by the word of the LORD" (1 Sam. 3:21).

896. "from Dan to Beersheba"

This was a poetic way of saying "all of Israel." Dan was in the far north and Beersheba in the far south, so "from Dan to Beersheba" meant the whole country, or all the people.

897. Jerusalem

No city is mentioned more often in the Bible, and the Bible's last chapters, Revelation 21–22, are a stunning picture of the *New* Jerusalem (heaven, that is), a perfectly holy place where God's saints dwell. It contrasts with the earthly Jerusalem, the site of Israel's temple, but a city noted for its moral backsliding.

King David made the city his capital. His son Solomon made the city great by building the temple and the royal dwellings. In 586 B.C. the Babylonians sacked and burned the city and deported most of the people. Jerusalem sat in ruins until some exiles returned and rebuilt the temple and the rest of the city. By Jesus' day, Herod the Great had lavishly renovated the temple, and Jews from across the Roman Empire tried to visit the city on the Jewish holy days. Most of Jesus' life and ministry was spent in His native region, Galilee, but in the last days of His life He visited Jerusalem, where He provoked the Jewish establishment, leading to His crucifixion. Jesus lamented that the chief city of the Jews was opposed to true spirituality: "O Jerusalem, Jerusalem, the one who kills the prophets and stones those who are sent to her!" (Matt. 23:37).

Jerusalem was sacked by the Romans in A.D. 70 and the temple destroyed.

898. the temple

Israel began as a "nation on the move," since they only came together while making their way from Egypt to the homeland God had promised them. For the forty years while they were "in the wilderness," rituals centered around a large but portable holy place, the tabernacle (see 115). Even after the Israelites were settled, the Tabernacle was still in use, until King Solomon, who had wealth at his disposal, built an elaborate temple in Jerusalem. The building and the impressive dedication service are described in 1 Kings 5–8.

Any building containing expensive furnishings is apt to be plundered. This occurred often as invading nations sacked Jerusalem and its temple. The crowning blow came when Nebuchadnezzar of Babylon conquered Jerusalem, carrying off the temple furnishings and torching the building.

With Jerusalem in ruins and many people carried off to exile in Babylon, religious life no longer centered around the temple. A new development came in the life of the scattered Jews: the synagogue (see 132).

The temple ruins sat for many years until a rebuilding took place under Zerubbabel, who was given permission by the Persian ruler Cyrus to renovate Jerusalem. The renovated temple (sometimes called "the Second Temple"—Solomon's was the first) was further enlarged and beautified under Herod the Great (see 234). This was the temple that Jesus and the first Christians were familiar with. Jesus prophesied that the magnificent building would one day be destroyed, with not one stone left upon another (Luke 21:6). The prophecy came true in A.D. 70, when the Romans destroyed the temple. All that remains of it is the Western Wall, better known as the Wailing Wall.

899. Mount Moriah

This was (says 2 Chron. 3:1) the site of Solomon's temple in Jerusalem. Much earlier Moriah was the site where Abraham was told by God to sacrifice his only son, Isaac (see 370 [the sacrifice of Isaac]. Happily, God restrained Abraham at the last moment (Gen. 22). For some reason Moriah is a popular name for churches in the South.

900. Zion

Zion is one of the hills of the city of Jerusalem. Israel's King David captured it from the tribe of Jebusites and brought the famous ark of the covenant there, which gave the site a special significance. Over time the name Zion came to stand for the whole city of Jerusalem, and when the Old

Testament refers to Zion, it is usually referring to all of Jerusalem, or even to all Israel. The New Testament gave the name Zion a spiritual significance, and over time it came to suggest heaven, not just the earthly Jerusalem. Hundreds of Christian hymns refer to Zion.

In the 1890s, when Jews around the world began to plan on establishing their own nation in Palestine, the movement took the name *Zionism*. The name is still used today to refer to Jews (or their supporters) who want to maintain the Jewish nation of Israel.

See 897 (Jerusalem).

901. Mount Carmel

Carmel lies just south of the modern city of Haifa in Israel, on the coast. It is most famous as the site of the showdown between the Lord's faithful prophet, Elijah, and the 450 prophets of the pagan god Baal, whose cult was being promoted by wicked Queen Jezebel (1 Kings 18). Elijah—or God, rather—won the contest. Afterward, from the mountaintop Elijah sighted a rain cloud—a hopeful sign, since Elijah had predicted a long drought, now ended.

The Israelites were impressed with Carmel's beauty, which is mentioned several times in the Old Testament.

902. Edom

The Edomites were descended from Esau (whose other name was Edom), the brother of Jacob (also called Israel). The Edomites and Israelites regarded each other as related, but there was frequent warfare between the two nations.

When the Israelites left Egypt and journeyed to their new homeland in Canaan, the king of Edom refused them permission to pass through his land (Num. 20:14–21). When the Babylonians sacked Jerusalem and depopulated the area in 586 B.C., the Edomites rejoiced and took over parts of the area, something the Hebrew prophets condemned heartily). The book of Obadiah is one long rant against the Edomite raiders.

When the Romans conquered the region, they gave it the name Idumea. Herod the Great (see 234) was an Idumean.

903. Tyre

This famous coastal city was built by the Phoenicians, famous as navigators and traders. Hiram of Tyre was a friend of Israel's kings David and Solomon, and he supplied them with timber, gold, and other articles for use in building palaces and the Lord's temple, plus craftsmen to do the work. Israel's commercial partnership with Tyre allowed Solomon to spend lavishly.

The Hebrew prophets had harsh words for Tyre, aware of the city's materialism. Isaiah called the city "the crowning city," but also "a harlot" who plies her trade with all the kingdoms (Isa. 23). Isaiah, Ezekiel, and other prophets predicted ruin for Tyre. The prophecies came true when Alexander the Great conquered the region.

904. Judah and Israel

Judah, one of the largest of the twelve tribes of Israel, was the tribe that the great king David came from. Israel's capital,

Jerusalem, was in the territory of Judah. After the death of King Solomon (David's son), the ten northern tribes split off, calling themselves Israel. Judah, along with the smaller tribe of Benjamin, became the kingdom of Judah. When Israel was conquered by the brutal Assyrians, the ten northern tribes ceased to exist. (In literature you'll sometimes see a reference to the "lost tribes" of Israel. This refers to the ten tribes conquered by the Assyrians.)

People living in the territory of Judah came to be called Jews. Jesus was descended from the tribe of Judah. Paul, the great missionary in the New Testament, was from the tribe of Benjamin, which was also part of the kingdom of Judah.

905. Samaria

When the kingdom of Israel split into two kingdoms (Israel in the north, Judah in the south), the north was left without a capital, since Jerusalem was in Judah. Omri, a powerful king of Israel, built a new capital city, Samaria. Most of the kings of Israel were a sorry lot, prone to worship false gods, and the prophets frequently condemned Samaria. Ahab was one of the worst kings, and his famous enemy was God's faithful prophet, Elijah.

Unlike Jerusalem, Samaria never had a temple dedicated to the Lord. In 722 B.C. the king of Assyria destroyed Samaria and deported the Israelites (2 Kings 17). Assyria resettled the area with foreigners, and the northern kingdom of Israel came to an end.

See 301 (Samaritans).

906. Assyria

We know it as Iraq today, but in the past the area was occupied by a number of mighty empires, notably Assyria. Israel's relations with the warlike Assyrians began under King Menahem when Pul, king of Assyria, invaded the land (2 Kings 15:19). Later, King Ahaz of Judah felt compelled to strip the Lord's temple of its gold and silver and send it to the Assyrian king Tiglath-Pileser (2 Kings 16). Israel, the kingdom consisting of the ten northern tribes, ended in 722 B.C. when the Assyrian king Shalmaneser captured the capital (Samaria) and deported the people. The Assyrians, following their usual policy, settled foreigners in Israel.

The southern kingdom of Judah remained, and Assyria was a thorn in its side. The arrogant King Sennacherib besieged Jerusalem, but Hezekiah, Judah's king, learned from the prophet Isaiah that Sennacherib would not triumph. As told in 2 Kings 19:35–37, an angel killed 185,000 Assyrian soldiers. Sennacherib withdrew and later, worshiping in the temple of his god Nisroch, his own sons murdered him. Assyria was never again a menace to Judah—but the next empire, Babylon, was.

God's prophets, particularly Isaiah, frequently denounced Assyria's cruelty. The book of Nahum is one long tirade against Assyria and a prophecy of its doom.

Assyria's famous capital was Nineveh (see 907).

907. Nineveh

One of the grand cities of the ancient world, it was the capital of the Assyrian Empire. It is mentioned many times in the Old Testament, notably in the book of Jonah (see 956 [the sign of Jonah]). Jonah was God's reluctant prophet told to preach repentance to Nineveh (and Jonah acted very peevish when the city actually repented!). The prophet Nahum's book is a rant against Nineveh and the Assyrians' cruelty. He prophesied its doom, and in 612 B.C. the mighty city fell to the Babylonians. No one knew where the site was until 1845 when the ruins were discovered. Jesus mentioned Nineveh as a city that repented when a prophet preached to it, unlike the Jewish towns that were rejecting Him.

908. Babylon

Israel faced many hostile empires, and in the Bible the most damaging one was Babylon. Jerusalem fell to Nebuchadnezzar of Babylon in 586 B.C. He destroyed the temple, sacked the city, and deported most of the people to Babylon, where they stayed in exile for decades. Later the relatively merciful Persians (who conquered the Babylonians) allowed the Jews to return home. The Jews always recalled Babylon as incredibly cruel—a mighty and prosperous empire built on evil.

In the New Testament period Babylon had ceased to exist. But the name Babylon was used several times, sometimes as a kind of code name for Rome, but sometimes as a figurative name for any evil power. Peter, in his first epistles, sends his greetings from "Babylon," which probably meant Rome (1 Peter 5:13). The book of Revelation, depicting the final showdown between God and evil, mentions Babylon many times. The author may have been thinking of

Rome, with its wealth and its persecution of Christians. But he may also have been thinking of any persecuting power, which he says will eventually fall: "Babylon is fallen, is fallen, that great city" (14:8).

909. Persia

We call it Iran today, but for centuries it was known as Persia. It was the last of the great empires in the Old Testament, the one that conquered the Babylonians and their territories. Compared to Assyria and Babylon, Persia was fairly humane toward people it conquered. The books of Ezra and Nehemiah relate how Cyrus, Persia's ruler, allowed the exiled Jews to return to their homeland and rebuild their temple. Nehemiah was cupbearer (meaning a chief aide) to the Persian ruler Artaxerxes, who allowed Nehemiah to return to Jerusalem and repair the city walls. The book of Esther takes place at the Persian court, where the ruler Ahasuerus (called Xerxes in some versions) chose a Jewish wife, Esther, who used her position to save the Jews from an extermination plot. Part of the story of Daniel takes place in Persia (see 353 [Daniel in the lions' den]).

The Persians receive more favorable coverage in the Bible than any foreign power. Cyrus, who allowed the Jews to return home, even gave them back the temple treasures that the Babylonians had plundered. Isaiah 45:1 refers to Cyrus as the Lord's "anointed." The Jews may also have respected the Persians for worshiping only one god, their "wise Lord." Between the Old and New Testaments, Persia fell to the Greek leader Alexander the Great.

910. Bethlehem

Thanks to Christmas, Bethlehem is probably one of the best known of Bible towns. It was the birthplace of Israel's great king, David, and, centuries later, the birthplace of Jesus. According to the Gospels, Mary and Joseph were residents of Nazareth, but they came to Bethlehem because of a Roman census, which required men to report to their hometowns. Joseph, a descendant of David, took the pregnant Mary to Bethlehem where, because the inns were crowded, Jesus was born in a stable and visited by shepherds and, later, the wise men.

Matthew's gospel says that Herod had the boy babies of Bethlehem slaughtered after hearing from the wise men that a "King of the Jews" had been born in Bethlehem. Herod's court scholars quoted to him from the prophet Micah, who had predicted that a great ruler of Israel would come from the town of Bethlehem (Mic. 5:2).

Centuries later, the Roman emperor Constantine built the Church of the Nativity over the site where Jesus was supposed to have been born.

911. Nazareth

Had it not been Jesus' hometown, no one would ever have heard of this unimportant place. Jesus was born in Bethlehem but grew up in Nazareth, the home of Mary and Joseph. It was not highly regarded in Jesus' lifetime, and John 1:46 records the skepticism of Nathaniel who, when told that a great prophet had come from Nazareth, replied, "can anything good come out of Nazareth?"

After Jesus began His ministry, His hometown was hardly supportive, and sometimes even hostile. On a trip to the town He visited the synagogue, read from the prophet Isaiah a prophecy of one anointed with the Spirit who would heal and free people, then told His hometown audience, "Today this Scripture is fulfilled in your hearing." The people became furious and drove Him out of town, even attempting (unsuccessfully) to push Him over a cliff (Luke 4:14–30). Jesus' famous quotation about the incident: "No prophet is accepted in his own country."

Throughout the Gospels and Acts, Jesus was usually referred to as "Jesus of Nazareth." (In a day when no one had last names, and the name Jesus was fairly common, a geographical "handle" was useful in identifying a person.) Acts records that the Jews sometimes referred to the early Christians as "the Nazarene sect."

912. the Sea of Galilee

It isn't a sea but a large lake, also called the Lake of Gennesaret (Luke 5:1), the Sea of Tiberias (John 6:1), and, in the Old Testament, the Sea of Kinnereth. Its importance is its connections with episodes in the life of Jesus. By its shores Jesus called His first disciples, who were fishermen (Luke 5:1–11). Jesus stilled a violent storm on the lake (Mark 4:39), and, according to Matthew 14:22–34, during another storm He walked on its waters.

The famous Jordan River (see 891) flows into the lake. On its shores were several noted towns, including Capernaum (home to the disciples Peter, Andrew, and Matthew), Magdala (home of Jesus' follower Mary

Magdalene), and Bethsaida (also home to some of the disciples).

913. Galilee

As Jesus' homeland, Galilee is mentioned often in the Bible. In the New Testament period it was a province of the Roman Empire, north of Judea and Samaria. Jesus' hometown of Nazareth was in Galilee. The Jews of Judea, with the capital at Jerusalem, looked down on the Jews of Galilee—partly as "country bumpkins," partly because Galilee had a large Gentile population. Most of Jesus' teaching and healing took place in this area, and all His disciples (except, possibly, Judas) were Galileans. Jesus claimed that He was sent to the "lost sheep" of Israel (Matt. 15:24), and the Jews and Gentiles of Galilee were more receptive to Him than the "establishment" Jews in Judea.

914. Capernaum

The Gospels show that Jesus was constantly on the move as He preached and healed. But He had a "base" in Galilee—not His hometown of Nazareth (which rejected Him) but the town of Capernaum (Matt. 4:13). Jesus did many miracles there, and it was there that He called the tax collector Matthew to be His disciple. Even so, Jesus considered the town unrepentant in spite of His miracles there, and He predicted the complete ruin of the place (Matt. 11:23). The prophecy came true, for the town has completely disappeared.

915. Caesarea Philippi

As the name indicates, this city was named for Caesar, and also for Herod the Great's son Philip the Tetrarch. It is notable in the life of Jesus because it was there that Jesus asked His disciples, "Who do men say that I, the Son of Man, am?" They replied, "Some say John the Baptist, some Elijah, and others Jeremiah or one of the prophets." But Peter answered, "You are the Christ, the Son of the living God." Jesus blessed Peter for this answer, but, for reasons of His own, told the disciples not to tell anyone He was the Christ (Matt. 16).

The incident (often called "Peter's confession") is important for being the first time the disciples acknowledged that they understood who their Master was.

916. Bethany

This village outside Jerusalem was an important place in Jesus' life. His friends Martha, Mary, and Lazarus lived there, and it must have been nearby that Jesus raised Lazarus from the dead (John 11). Bethany was also where Jesus dined in the home of Simon the leper, and a woman anointed Jesus' feet with expensive perfume (Matt. 26:6–13). Luke says that it was at Bethany that Jesus ascended into heaven (Luke 24:50).

917. the Upper Room

This was the room, somewhere in Jerusalem, where Jesus and His disciples celebrated the Last Supper, which began as their celebration of the traditional Jewish Passover (Luke 22:12). Because thousands of artists have depicted the scene of the Last Supper, the Upper Room is probably the most painted room in history.

918. Gethsemane

The word has come to mean, as *Webster's* puts it, "a place or occasion of great mental or spiritual suffering." Gethsemane was a sort of garden or park near Jerusalem. Jesus and His disciples went there the night He was arrested. Before the arrest, Jesus—who knew what was about to happen—went by Himself to pray, begging God, "Father, if it is possible, let this cup pass from Me; nevertheless, not as I will but as You will" (Matt. 26:39). The "cup" meant the "cup of suffering" he was about to drink from. While Jesus prayed, the disciples, who were supposed to keep watch, had fallen asleep. A mob appeared, and Judas, the traitor, gave his Master, Jesus, a kiss, the sign to the mob that He was the one to arrest.

The scene of Jesus praying in Gethsemane has been a favorite one for artists, who often gave their painting the title *The Agony in the Garden*. Usually the picture shows the disciples sleeping nearby, emphasizing that Jesus was truly alone as He faced death.

919. Golgotha

The place of Jesus' crucifixion was called in the local language (Aramaic) Golgotha, which the Gospels translate as "the place of the Skull." Presumably there was something about the locale that reminded people of a skull—or, if it was commonly used as a place of execution, the name may refer to its connection with death. (The Gospels do not say it was a *hill*, by the way.) It was outside, but near, the city of Jerusalem. The Romans, to instill fear in the people they ruled, usually crucified criminals in highly visible places, so Golgotha was likely near a well-traveled road. No one is certain where the actual site is.

See 920 (Calvary).

920. the hill of Calvary

The name Calvary is made known wherever Christians go, often used as the name of churches, Christian schools, and cemeteries. It is famous as the name of the hill where Jesus was crucified. But the name does *not* occur in the Bible. The Bible also does *not* say that the Crucifixion occurred on a hill. The Gospels call the place of Jesus' crucifixion "the place of the Skull," also called in Aramaic (the language most Jews spoke at that time) "Golgotha."

The Latin word *Calvaria* means "skull." In some versions of the Bible, Luke 23:33 mentions the site as "Calvary," but the more accurate translation into English is "the place called the Skull."

921. the Field of Blood

Judas Iscariot used the money he received for betraying Jesus to buy a field. He killed himself there, and so people called the field Akel Dama, meaning "Field of Blood" (Acts 1:19). Matthew tells the story slightly differently: Judas returned the "blood money" to the priests, then hanged himself. The priests used the money to buy a "potter's field," a burial place for foreigners. Afterward it was called the Field of Blood (Matt. 27:3–10).

922. Damascus

It is Syria's capital and one of the oldest inhabited cities in the world. It was chief city of the Arameans, a people hostile to Israel.

The ancient city is important in the New Testament because of incidents in the life of Paul. He was on his way to Damascus to persecute Christians there. Near Damascus he was struck by a blinding light and heard Jesus asking, "Why are you persecuting Me?" In Damascus, a Christian named Ananias helped Paul regain his sight. Paul, a changed man, was baptized and spent some time with the Christians of Damascus (Acts 9). The Jews, feeling betrayed by Paul, conspired to kill him, but his friends lowered him over the city walls in a basket and he escaped. Afterward, Paul spoke many times of his conversion on the road to Damascus.

923. Caesarea

This important city was built by Herod the Great and named for his benefactor, Caesar Augustus. It figures prominently in the book of Acts. Cornelius, the Roman centurion converted to the faith by Peter, was stationed there (Acts 10). Philip the evangelist and his prophesying daughters lived there (Acts 21:8–9). Paul was a prisoner there for two years, and it was where he witnessed to the faith before cynical King Agrippa (Acts 23:31–26:32).

924. Rome

Rome in central Italy dominated an empire covering much of Europe, northern Africa, and the Middle East, including Israel. The action of the Gospels takes place in the Roman provinces of Judea, Samaria, and Galilee. Several Jewish rulers (such as Herod) had authority, but the real power was held by the Roman governor. The governor Pilate was the one who reluctantly gave in to the Jews and ordered Jesus' crucifixion.

Romans were great builders and efficient politicians and soldiers. But they could be cruel when dealing with the people they conquered. Most Romans despised the Jews for being unruly and practicing their strange religion of one God. But the Romans also made some concessions to Jewish feelings—for example, not setting up statues, which the Jews regarded as idols.

Because of the Roman roads and the relative safety of traveling in the empire, Christian missionaries were better able to spread the new faith.

Crucifixion was not invented by the Romans, but they did use it effectively.

In A.D. 70 a Jewish revolt against Rome resulted in the sacking and burning of Jerusalem, ending forever the Jewish priesthood and temple.

925. Asia

This refers not to the whole continent of Asia but to a province of the Roman Empire, roughly the area that we now call Turkey. Asia's capital was Ephesus, a city connected with the apostle Paul's missionary work, and the city where he sent one of the New Testament letters. Revelation 1–3 includes messages to "the seven churches in Asia."

926. Greece

In the period between the Old and New Testaments, Greece became a world power, with Alexander the Great conquering lands from Egypt to India, spreading Greek language and culture. By the New Testament period his former territories, including Israel, belonged to the Roman Empire. The area we now call Greece was the Roman provinces of Achaia and Macedonia. Paul carried the Christian faith to those provinces, the first time the gospel was preached in Europe.

927. Corinth

It was the capital and chief city of the Roman province of Achaia (that is, Greece), more important than the more cultured city of Athens. As a cosmopolitan port city, it was notoriously immoral, and for many people a "Corinthian" was another way of saying "prostitute." It had wealth, luxury, and immorality—but also a large community of Christians. Paul worked as a missionary in the sinful city and addressed two of his most important epistles to the

Christians there. Not surprisingly, the Christians in Corinth faced numerous moral difficulties, particularly in regard to sex.

928. Athens

The cultural capital of Greece was, in the New Testament period, under Roman rule, but the Greeks were still proud of their traditions of art and philosophy. The apostle Paul traveled there, but had little luck evangelizing the skeptical Athenians. Acts 17:16–34 reports that Paul debated with Epicurean and Stoic philosophers, who thought him a "babbler." Even so, he preached a fine sermon, observing that the city had statues of numerous gods, even an altar inscribed "To the Unknown God." Paul told the Athenians that it was this God he came to proclaim to them. He did make a few converts there.

929. Philadelphia

As William Penn was aware, the name means (in Greek) "brotherly love." In the New Testament it was a city in Asia (modern-day Turkey), mentioned in Revelation 3 as having a faithful Christian community.

930. Alexandria

The great coastal city in Egypt was only one of many cities the conqueror Alexander the Great named for himself. It was a cosmopolitan city with a large Jewish community and reputation for learning. Some Jews from Alexandria helped bring about the stoning of the Christian martyr Stephen (Acts 6–7). Apollos, an eloquent Christian preacher and friend of Paul, was from Alexandria (Acts 18:24).

931. Patmos

This tiny, rocky island off the coast of Turkey has one claim to fame: It was the place of exile for John, who lived on Patmos when he received the visions he wrote down in the book of Revelation. Artists have enjoyed painting the apostle on the barren isle while over his head are the bizarre visions of his book.

932. Palestine

Thanks to the political turmoil in the Middle East, we hear a lot about Palestine (as in Palestine Liberation Organization, the PLO). In the past, the name referred to the region that was also called by many other names, depending on the time period—Canaan, Israel, Judea, the Holy Land, the promised land, etc.

The name comes from *Philistine*, the name of a warlike people who were a constant thorn in Israel's side. The old name *Palestina* means "land of the Philistines." The Romans, who conquered the region, first made the name an official place on the map. The name has nothing to do with Arabs, by the way. The Philistines—and the Israelites—lived in the region long, long before the Arabs (or the religion of Islam) existed. The name was revived by the British, who governed the area beginning in World War I.

See 879 (Canaan); 873 (the Holy Land); 274 (Israelites).

17

Odds and Ends, Mostly Fascinating

933. B.C. and A.D.

B.C. means "before Christ," and A.D. means *Anno Domini,* Latin for "year of our Lord." The practice of dating years from the time of Jesus' birth has been around for centuries. Strangely enough, it is slightly wrong. A Christian scholar named Dionysius Exiguus, living in the sixth century, calculated the year of the birth, but was off a few years. We now feel fairly certain that Jesus was born around 5 B.C. We know that Herod the Great died in 4 B.C., and that Jesus' birth occurred before that (see Matt. 2). We also feel fairly certain that Jesus' crucifixion and resurrection occurred in A.D. 30.

Using the phrase "the year of our Lord" was common for centuries and is still sometimes used.

There was no year 0. The year 1 B.C. was followed by A.D. 1.

934. Ab-, Abba

The Hebrew *ab* means "father," and it is found in hundreds of names in the Old Testament, often at the beginning of a name, sometimes at the end. Some of the more famous *ab* names were Abraham ("father of a multitude") and Absalom ("father is peace").

In the New Testament the word *abba* is used several times, notably by Jesus, who frequently referred to God as "Father." *Abba* was a more intimate form of *ab*, with a meaning something like "dear Father." Jesus used it in the Garden of Gethsemane, when He was in agony over His approaching death: "'Abba, Father, all things are possible for You. Take this cup away from Me; nevertheless, not what I will, but what You will'" (Mark 14:36).

Paul the apostle used the term in his letters, reminding his readers that, as beloved children of God, we are free to approach God, saying "Abba, Father" (Rom. 8:15; Gal. 4:6).

935. the language of Jesus

The Old Testament is written mostly in Hebrew, the New Testament in Greek. But a third ancient language was in use in Bible lands, Aramaic. It was similar to Hebrew, and parts of the books of Ezra, Jeremiah, and Daniel are in Aramaic. It was a widely used diplomatic and commercial language in the Assyrian, Babylonian, and Persian Empires. More important, by the time of Jesus it was the common language of the Jews. So it was the everyday language of Jesus and His first followers. Since the New Testament was written in Greek, most of its authors were writing in their second language, since they probably spoke Aramaic in their homes. The New Testament was largely addressed to people throughout the Roman Empire, people who did *not* speak Aramaic, so on several occasions the authors felt the need to translate an Aramaic word or phrase. John's gospel has several of these occurrences. Examples: "'You are Simon son of John. You will be called Cephas' (which, when translated, is Peter)," "a pool, which in Aramaic is called Bethesda," "the place of the Skull (which in Aramaic is called Golgotha)." Paul stated that during his dramatic conversion experience he heard the voice of Christ saying to him in Aramaic, "Saul, Saul, why are you persecuting Me?" (Acts 26:14).

936. Hebrew

The word *Hebrew* refers to:

1. The language of the people of Israel. Most of the Old Testament was written in this language. A form of it is the national language of Israel today, and it is studied by Jews and Christians who want to read the Old Testament in the original.

2. An Israelite. The first person called *Hebrew* is the patriarch Abraham. *Hebrew* means essentially the same as *Israelite*, although *Israelite* is much more commonly used in the Old Testament.

3. The group of Christians who received the letter to the Hebrews, found in the New Testament. The author of this letter probably meant the word in a figurative sense—that is, in the Old Testament the Hebrews were "God's chosen people," so the Christians, now God's chosen people, are the "new Hebrews."

See 275 [the twelve tribes of Israel].

937. Jehovah

Did you ever wonder who Jehovah was (as in "Jehovah's Witnesses")? It is an older form of the name for God. In the original Hebrew Old Testament, God's name is *Yahweh,* a name meaning (probably) "I Cause to Be" or "I Am What I Am." Most English Bibles now translate Yahweh as "the LORD." But some older Bibles (the King James Version, for example) sometimes used the name Jehovah—which, believe it or not, is a form of the name Yahweh. (If you have a King James Bible, you'll find Jehovah in Ex. 6:3; Ps. 83:18; and Isa. 12:2.) Most newer translations do not use Jehovah at all. The name occurs in a lot of old hymns.

See 631 (Lord).

938. the shortest verse

It's only two words, "Jesus wept," found in John 11:35. He wept over the death of His friend Lazarus, whom He then raised from the dead.

939. the shortest books

The shortest book in the Old Testament is the one-chapter book of Obadiah. The shortest book in the New Testament—and the entire Bible—is 3 John. Philemon, 2 John, and Jude are also one-chapter books.

940. six books from three

Six books in the Old Testament were originally just three. First and 2 Samuel, 1 and 2 Kings, and 1 and 2 Chronicles were originally just Samuel, Kings, and Chronicles. Because they were so large and bulky in the form of scrolls, they were each divided in two.

941. "a psalm of David"

There are 150 psalms, and 73 are attributed to David, Israel's king. The Old Testament makes it clear that David had musical and poetic gifts (1 Sam. 16:16–18; 2 Sam. 1:19–27; 3:33–34). In 2 Samuel 23:1, David is called "the sweet psalmist of Israel." Some of the best-loved psalms— such as Psalm 23, the "shepherd Psalm," and Psalm 51, the "confession Psalm"—are labeled "psalms of David." Psalm 18 is almost exactly like David's song in 1 Samuel 22.

942. Songs of Ascents

Psalms 120 through 134 are labeled "Songs of Ascents." Tradition says these were sung or recited as worshipers made their way up the steps of the temple in Jerusalem.

943. lengthy book and chapter

The longest book in the Bible is Psalms, with 150 chapters (individual psalms, actually). The longest chapter in the Bible is Psalm 119, with 176 verses. It is a meditation on the delights of following God's law.

944. the quotable Old Testament

The New Testament authors were not conscious of any break with the religion of Israel. They believed that Jesus was the promised Messiah the Jews had hoped for. They accepted, as did the Jews, the Old Testament as sacred Scripture. For that reason the Old Testament is quoted (or referred to) repeatedly in the New. The most quoted book is Isaiah (419 times), followed by Psalms (414), Genesis (260), Exodus (250), Deuteronomy (208), Ezekiel (141), and Daniel (133).

Only a few Old Testament books are *not* quoted or referred to in the New: 2 Chronicles, Ezra, Esther, Song of Solomon, Lamentations, Obadiah, Nahum, and Zephaniah.

945. the synoptic Gospels

Matthew, Mark, and Luke are known as the "synoptic Gospels." The Greek word *synoptikos* means "to see together." The three do indeed "see together," reporting most of the same acts and teachings of Jesus, often using the same wording. They differ in several ways from John's gospel, which records a number of events and teachings that the Synoptics leave out.

Of the three Synoptics, only Matthew was written by one of Jesus' disciples. Mark, written by the Mark mentioned in the book of Acts, was (according to a very old tradition) based on information Mark obtained from the disciple Peter. Luke, who also wrote Acts, was the only Bible author who was not a Jew.

946. the Minor Prophets

The twelve books at the end of the Old Testament—Hosea through Malachi—constitute the Minor Prophets. The name comes not from their importance, but from the size of their books, which are much briefer than the books of the major prophets, Isaiah, Jeremiah, and Ezekiel.

947. the Writings

For the Jews of yesterday and today, the most important part of the Bible is the Torah (see 117), the first five books. Following them in importance are the Prophets (which include not just the books named for the various prophets, but also Joshua, Judges, 1 and 2 Samuel, and 1 and 2 Kings, which we consider historical books, not prophecy). Everything in the Old Testament that is not Torah or Prophets falls into the group known as the Writings. It includes Ruth, 1 and 2 Chronicles, Ezra, Nehemiah, Esther, Job, Psalms, Proverbs, Ecclesiastes, Song of Solomon, Lamentations, and Daniel. Jews and Christians consider these to be holy Scripture, inspired by God, but the Writings took much longer to be accepted as sacred than did the Torah and the Prophets. Esther and the Song of

Solomon, the two books that do not mention God, took the longest time to be accepted as sacred.

Probably the most-read book of the Old Testament is Psalms, which, along with Job and Proverbs, is one of the most popular Writings.

948. Scripture

Scripture means, simply, "written things." Many Bible study aids use "Scripture" or "the Scriptures" to mean exactly the same thing as "the Bible." Just as the Bible is often referred to as "the Holy Bible," it is also called "the holy Scriptures." (The adjective forms are "biblical" and "scriptural." So you'll find books referring to "biblical times" and "scriptural teachings," and so forth. They mean the same thing.)

You won't actually find "the Bible" in the Bible (except on the title page). But in the New Testament you will find the words *Scripture* and *the Scriptures*. Every time you see these words in the New Testament, they refer to the Old Testament, which the early Christians believed to be the holy and authoritative revelation of God to mankind. Later, Christians also accepted the New Testament as Scripture.

949. Agrapha

It means "things not written" and refers to sayings of Jesus not found in the four Gospels. Although the four tell us all we need to know about Jesus, they did not (and probably could not) write down *everything* He ever said or did. In Acts 20:35, Paul quotes Jesus as saying, "It is more blessed to give than to receive"—a saying not found in the Gospels, but no doubt a genuine saying that Paul learned about from Jesus' disciples.

950. the "we" passages

Acts, like the gospel of Luke, was written by Luke, whom the apostle Paul calls "Luke the beloved physician" (Col. 4:14). In several passages of Acts, Luke writes in the first person plural—"we." The "we" passages are 16:10–17; 20:5–15; 21:18; and 27:1–28:16. All the "we" sections focus on the activity of Paul, so he and Luke were apparently fellow missionaries. The fact that Luke was an eyewitness of these events adds a nice touch of authenticity.

951. letters or epistles?

Is there a difference? A letter is usually one person's private communication to another. An epistle is more "public," addressed to a group or designed to be circulated. The first parts of the New Testament to be written were Paul's epistles to the various Christian communities he visited. In these letters he gave moral advice, explained Christian beliefs, and dealt with questions and controversies he had heard of. Most epistles thus seem more like sermons than letters, though the writers often added personal notes at the end, speaking to individuals they knew.

It is correct to say either "Paul's letter to the Romans" or "Paul's epistle to the Romans," but, technically, Romans is more of an epistle than a letter.

952. Bible paper

This is the thin but durable (and relatively expensive) paper used in Bibles and some other books. (It's also called "India paper.") In our own day, acid-free paper means that most books will hold up well as they age. But, as a look at old books in libraries will prove, earlier papers aged horribly, yellowing and falling to shreds—except for Bible paper, which did and does last.

953. study Bibles

Some Bibles are "just Bible," the text of the Old and New Testaments and nothing else. But most contain some aids to the reader—at the minimum, footnotes explaining difficult phrases. Study Bibles with extensive footnotes and introductions to the various books in the Bible are very popular now, and they have been popular ever since the printing press made Bibles available to the general public. The Reformation in the 1500s opened the Bible to the laity, and most readers liked some notes to aid their understanding. The trend today seems to be "niche markets" for study Bibles—geared for mothers, fathers, teens, senior adults, and so on.

954. red-letter Bibles

In a "red-letter Bible," the words of Christ are printed in red (presumably because they are of special importance). The first red-letter Bible appeared in 1928, and they are still available. In recent years one Bible publisher decided (correctly) that red print is hard to read, so a new "green-letter Bible" was published. It has yet to replace the old standby, the red-letter.

955. concordance

A concordance to the Bible is a reference book with alphabetical word lists, showing the places in the Bible where each word occurs. They are extremely useful for pastors, teachers, and Bible readers in general. Alexander Cruden (see 203 [Alexander the Corrector]) produced the first, and most famous, concordance for the King James Version. There are concordances for all major English versions, many of them available as computer software.

956. the sign of Jonah

According to the book of Jonah, the prophet was in the whale's belly three days and three nights. Matthew relates that some Pharisees asked Jesus to show them some miraculous sign. Jesus replied, "An evil and adulterous generation seeks after a sign, and no sign will be given to it except the sign of the prophet Jonah. For as Jonah was three days and three nights in the belly of the great fish, so will the Son of Man be three days and three nights in the heart of the earth" (Matt. 12:39–40). He was predicting His own death, burial, and resurrection.

957. the Koran

The Muslims' holy book (also spelled Qur'an) shows that their prophet Muhammad was familiar with Jewish and Christian beliefs, though he never actually read the Bible. The Koran refers to the angel Gabriel, Adam, Noah, Abraham, Moses, David, and Jesus, who is called "the son of Mary, the apostle of God" and also "Messiah." But, "the Messiah the son of Mary is only a prophet." Muslims do not accept Jesus as the Son of God. Muhammad thought (wrongly) that Christians believed in a Trinity of God the Father, Mary the Mother, and Jesus the Son.

958. *The War Cry*

Isaiah 8:9 reads, "Raise the war cry, you nations, and be shattered!" (NIV). For many years the official magazine of the Salvation Army has been named *The War Cry*. It is appropriate that an *army* (though a spiritual one) would have a magazine with *war* in the title.

959. the stone of Scone

British rulers are crowned over the ancient rock known as the "stone of Scone" or "stone of destiny." It sits beneath the coronation chair in England's Westminster Abbey. A centuries-old legend says it is the stone pillow that Jacob rested his head on while he had his dream of angels on a stairway to heaven (Gen. 28).

960. census

A census is taken for many reasons, such as for taxation or for counting the available fighting men. The Old Testament mentions a census of the Israelites at Mount Sinai (which is where the book of Numbers got its name). David, for military purposes, made a census of Israel (2 Sam. 24). The most famous census was that ordered by the Roman emperor Augustus, a census that resulted in Joseph and Mary being in Bethlehem, where Jesus was born (Luke 1).

961. the honeymoon law

Readers find the regulations in the Old Testament Law bewildering. How, we wonder, could people live with so many stifling rules?

In fact, some of the rules were quite sensible—and humane. There were laws, for example, to ensure the happiness of newlyweds and engaged couples:

"What man is there who is betrothed to a woman and has not married her? Let him go and return to his house, lest he die in the battle and another man marry her" (Deut. 20:7).

"When a man has taken a new wife, he shall not go out to war or be charged with any business; he shall be free at home one year, and bring happiness to his wife whom he has taken" (Deut. 24:5).

962. giants in the earth

In many translations, Genesis 6:4 reads, "There were giants on the earth in those days." The Hebrew word translated "giants" is *Nephilim,* and it is used in Numbers 13 to describe the hulking inhabitants of Canaan, who so impressed the Israelite reconnaissance men. *Nephilim* may not mean giants of supernatural origin, but simply a tribe of large-framed, powerful men. When military strength was a man's most important asset, such men were, of course, feared and respected.

963. the sons of God

Bible scholars run into some problems that just cannot be solved. One is found in Genesis 6:1–4: "When men began to multiply on the face of the earth, and daughters were born to them, . . . the sons of God saw the daughters of men, that they were beautiful . . . The sons of God came in to the daughters of men and they bore children to them. Those were the mighty men who were of old, men of renown." Just who were these "sons of God"? No one knows for sure. The best guess is that they were kings and chieftains, the bigwigs in a primitive warrior society.

964. pearly gates and streets of gold

People are so accustomed to thinking of heaven as having pearly gates and streets of gold that we wonder, Is that in the Bible? It is indeed, part of a description of the New Jerusalem (heaven) in Revelation 21:21: "The twelve gates were twelve pearls: each individual gate was of one pearl. And the street of the city was pure gold."

965. harps and white robes

The popular image of heaven is of white-robed people playing harps. This image comes from Revelation 15:2, which describes the saints who held harps given to them by God. And the white robes? Revelation 7:9: "Behold, a great multitude which no one could number, of all nations, tribes, peoples, and tongues . . . clothed with white robes." White robes symbolize purity, and the harps symbolize the music of peace and harmony.

966. martyrs

It now means "one who dies for his faith," but in the New Testament the Greek word *martus* meant "witness" or "one who testifies." Many of the witnesses for faith did indeed die for their belief. Jesus Himself suffered death, and He predicted that His followers, like the faithful prophets of old, would be injured and even killed (Matt. 5:11–12; 24:9; Luke 11:49). This certainly came true, as Stephen became the first of many Christian martyrs (Acts 6–7). James became the first of the apostles to be killed (Acts 12:2), and Paul was stoned and left for dead, though he did recover (Acts 14:19). Revelation 17:6 refers to "the blood of the martyrs of Jesus." Tradition says that both Peter and Paul were executed during the persecutions under the Roman emperor Nero.

967. sour grapes

Our expression "sour grapes" is based on a fable of Aesop. But the Bible has its own sour grapes proverb, quoted by both Jeremiah and Ezekiel: "In those days they shall say no more: 'The fathers have eaten sour grapes, and the children's teeth are set on edge'" (Jer. 31:29). "What do you mean when you use this proverb concerning the land of Israel, saying: 'The fathers have eaten sour grapes, and the children's teeth are set on edge'?" (Ezek. 18:2). The old proverb meant that children suffer for the parents' sins. Both prophets looked forward to a new age when each individual would suffer punishment only for his own sins.

968. kissing

Kissing in Bible times was not necessarily romantic. People kissed idols of the gods they worshiped, kissed relatives or old friends, and (as in the case of Judas Iscariot and Jesus) kissed their teachers. There *was* romantic kissing, as found in the Song of Solomon (1:2; 8:1).

Among the early Christians, a "holy kiss" (probably a peck on the cheek) was common practice. Paul closed several of his letters with the instructions "Greet one another with a holy kiss" (see Rom. 16:16).

The common expression "kiss of death" comes, of course, from the kiss Judas gave Jesus as a signal to the authorities to arrest Jesus. Another treacherous kiss: Military man Joab gave a friendship kiss to Amasa—then fatally stabbed him in the belly (2 Sam. 20).

969. laughter

Laughter is mentioned many times in the Bible—but *almost never* in connection with merriment or joking. The laughter mentioned is the laughter of scorn, mocking, or sarcasm. Psalm 37:13 speaks of God laughing, but it is a scornful laugh: "The LORD laughs at him [the wicked], for He sees that his day is coming." The first laugh mentioned in the Bible is Abraham's, who laughed when told his wife—age ninety—would bear a child. Appropriately, when the child was born they named it Isaac, meaning "he laughs."

The Bible is not anti-laughter, however. Proverbs has cheerful words about being merry: "He who is of a merry heart has a continual feast" (15:15). "A merry heart does good, like medicine" (17:22).

970. last names

People in Bible times had no last names, so it was customary to refer to someone as the "son of" or "daughter of" their father. We read of "Saul son of Kish" and "David son of Jesse"—a convenient way of connecting the person's first name with a family.

A curiosity: The great prophet Elijah was never referred to as "son of" anyone. He is only referred to as "Elijah the Tishbite," meaning he came from a place called Tishbe. Bible readers have enjoyed speculating that the great prophet who did not die but was taken to heaven in a fiery chariot (2 Kings 2) is not mentioned as having any earthly father, as almost all men were.

971. Abraham's bosom

Abraham was spiritually and physically the ancestor of Israel, the "father of the faithful." As Israel began to believe in a blessed afterlife for the faithful, they naturally believed the godly Abraham would be in heaven. The phrase "in Abraham's bosom" (or "at Abraham's side") had the same meaning as "in heaven." Jesus mentioned the phrase in His parable of the rich man and the beggar (Luke 16:22–23). The dead beggar Lazarus is "in Abraham's bosom" while the rich man is in hell.

972. bread

Bread was the basic item of one's daily diet in Bible times, and "bread" often means "food in general." When the Lord's Prayer says "Give us this day our daily bread," it means "Give us the basic material things we need today."

Israel's tabernacle (and later the temple) had a special table for the "bread of the Presence" (or "showbread" in some translations). The twelve small loaves symbolized Israel's twelve tribes and were a reminder of God's presence among the people as their Sustainer. Jesus referred to Himself as the "bread of life," the food that meets man's deepest needs (John 6:35).

973. widows and orphans

Widows and orphans are mentioned many times as people in need of special concern. (Presumably a widower could take care of himself.) A good summary of the Bible's compassionate attitude toward them is in James 1:27: "Pure and undefiled religion before God and the Father is this: to visit orphans and widows in their trouble, and to keep oneself unspotted from the world."

UNPLEASANT THINGS

974. blood

The Old Testament books of Joshua and Judges show the tribes of Israel settling in the land of Canaan—and butchering the original dwellers. Is this Christian behavior? Hardly—but then, this slaughter predates Jesus and His teaching on love and nonviolence. But would God really command His people, the Israelites, to slaughter other people?

Consider what the Israelites faced: tribes that worshiped gods of nature and fertility. Worship of these gods—Baal, Ashtaroth, Molech—often consisted of sex with temple prostitutes and even sacrifice of children. The religion of Israel had no place for such horrors. The Israelites were constantly tempted to fall into the heathen worship. The only way they saw to keep their religion pure was to exterminate the heathen.

A word about blood: Until fairly recently, most human beings had a fair amount of exposure to blood—usually in the butchering of animals. The book of Leviticus strikes some people as gross in its bluntness about sacrificing animals. But in fact, our own squeaky clean society, where we seldom see an animal bleed, is unusual in the world's history. In Bible times, and in many parts of the world today, people got a lot of exposure not only to animal blood but to human blood as well.

975. famine

It was common in ancient times, when food storage was more difficult. The most famous famine was the one in Canaan that forced Jacob's sons to visit Egypt for food. There they fatefully encountered their brother Joseph, whom they had sold into slavery years before. Joseph had become Egypt's prime minister, also administrator of food supplies during famine. The book of Ruth tells of a famine during the days of the judges, forcing an Israelite family to move to Moab, where the Moabite woman Ruth became part of the family.

976. leprosy, lepers

Modern medicine can cure or alleviate most skin diseases, but in ancient times there were few cures. People feared that leprosy (a generic name for a variety of loathsome skin diseases) was infectious, and probably the ugliness of it made people more fearful. Leviticus 13 gives detailed instructions on quarantining lepers. A leper had to call out "Unclean! Unclean!" to warn others of his presence. He had to live in isolation, "outside the camp."

The prophet Elisha caused the healing of Naaman, the Aramean military man, by having him bathe in the Jordan River.

Leprosy could sometimes be a punishment from God. Miriam, Moses' sister, was struck with leprosy for opposing

Moses (Num. 12). Gehazi, servant of the prophet Elisha, be
came a leper after stealing and lying to his master (2 Kings
5). King Uzziah dared to burn incense on the altar (something only priests were allowed), so God afflicted him with
leprosy (2 Chron. 26).

Jesus healed several lepers. In one notable instance, He
healed ten lepers at once, but only one bothered to thank
Him (Luke 17:11–19).

977. stoning

Before the days of gas chambers, lethal injections, and electric chairs, the Israelites used what was available: stones.
The Old Testament prescribed execution by stoning as the
punishment for blasphemy, idolatry, profaning the Sabbath,
human sacrifice, occultism, and other offenses. Some genuine offenders were executed, but Jesus lamented that Israel
had also stoned true prophets (Matt. 23:37). John 8:1–11
records the story of a woman about to be stoned for adultery; Jesus uttered His famous words, "He who is without
sin among you, let him throw a stone at her first," and the
mob dispersed. More than once the Jews decided to stone
Jesus Himself for blasphemy. If His execution had been
Jewish instead of Roman, He would have been stoned
instead of crucified.

Stephen, the first Christian martyr, was stoned for blasphemy (Acts 7:54–60). On one occasion Paul was stoned
and left for dead, though he recovered (Acts 14:19–20).

Stoning was a kind of "community execution," with the
people as a group stoning the offender.

978. burial

The Bible does not forbid cremation or other means of disposing of the dead, but traditionally Christians have been buried. This is partly a heritage from the Jews, who hold firmly to the tradition. Unlike some other world religions, Christianity and Judaism are not anti-body or anti-matter. Jesus Himself was buried, and the New Testament makes it clear that each individual believer will be resurrected in a "spiritual body" like the body of Jesus after His resurrection. This belief has inclined Christians to keep each body intact.

Only one person—Joseph in Egypt—is mentioned as being buried in a coffin (Gen. 50:26).

979. sackcloth and ashes

Sackcloth was a rough dark cloth, usually made of goat's hair, with a texture like (but probably rougher than) burlap. Wearing only a rough sackcloth tunic was a sign of grief or repentance (2 Sam. 3:31; 2 Kings 19:1; Isa. 20:2; Luke 10:13). Wearing sackcloth was often accompanied by smearing ashes on one's face or body (2 Sam. 13:19; Esther 4:1; Isa. 58:5).

980. rending the garments

Tearing one's clothes (or "rending the garments," in some translations) was a sign of sorrow, mourning, or repentance, practiced in Israel and still practiced by Jews today. Jacob tore his clothes when he believed his son Joseph dead (Gen.

37:34). King Ahab, chastised by Elijah because of his sins, tore his clothes (1 Kings 21:27). At Jesus' trial, the high priest, believing Jesus a blasphemer, tore his clothes (Matt. 26:25).

The prophet Joel told the people that sorrow over sin should be an inward thing, not an outward thing: "Rend your heart, and not your garments" (Joel 2:13).

981. barrenness

Inability to bear children was considered the most horrible fate that could befall a woman in Bible times. Being "fruit-ful" was a sign of divine blessing. The Bible has many sto-ries of women whose barren state was miraculously changed by God, often when the woman was old. Examples: Sarah, wife of Abraham, bore Isaac when she was ninety; Jacob's unloved wife Leah bore children while the beloved Rachel was long barren; Manoah's long-barren wife gave birth to Samson; Hannah gave birth to Samuel; the Virgin Mary's elderly relative Elizabeth gave birth to John the Baptist.

982. baldness

Normal baldness (as in "male pattern baldness") is hardly mentioned in the Bible, where baldness is usually the result of some disease. The prophet Elisha is the only man men-tioned as being bald. The teens who poked fun of his bald-ness were punished severely for the insult: Bears came and mauled them (2 Kings 2).

NATURE WALK

983. fig leaf

The leaves of the fig plant are a memorable part of the Adam and Eve story. Tempted by the serpent to eat the forbidden fruit, Adam and Eve got more than they bargained for: "Then the eyes of both of them were opened, and they knew that they were naked; and they sewed fig leaves together and made themselves coverings" (Gen. 3:7).

984. rose of Sharon

The Song of Solomon, not one of the most quoted of Bible books, says in 2:1, "I am the rose of Sharon." Sharon was not a woman's name, but the name of Israel's coastal plain. Rose of Sharon is now a common name for the flowering garden shrub *Hibiscus syriacus*.

985. lily of the valley

Song of Solomon 2:1 says, "I am the rose of Sharon, and the lily of the valleys." Lily of the valley is the common name for the plant *Convallaria majalis,* not a true lily, but a low-growing plant with white bell-shaped flowers.

986. the tree of life

It existed in the Garden of Eden, and after Adam and Eve disobeyed God, God was concerned that they might eat its fruit "and live forever" (Gen. 3:22). Whatever the tree was (or represented), God banished the couple from Eden forever. But the tree of life is mentioned again much later, in Revelation's description of heaven, the New Jerusalem (22:2). There the faithful are free to eat of its fruit.

987. olive trees

These are mentioned in the Bible more than any other tree. They were important mostly for their oil, but also for the wood. Olive oil was used not only in cooking but also in lamps. Mixed with fragrant herbs, olive oil was used for anointing. The olive tree may be the oldest tree cultivated by man.

988. cedars of Lebanon

The national flag of Lebanon features the enormous cedar tree known as (appropriately) the cedar of Lebanon. The area was known in Bible times for the enormous cedar trees there, and they supplied the timber used in Jerusalem's temple and palaces. The wood was both durable and fragrant. Cedars of Lebanon are now grown around the world as shade trees.

989. vineyard

Most ancient peoples loved their vineyards, and in the Bible sitting under one's own is a sign of security (since they don't bear fruit until they've been planted several years). In a figurative sense, the Bible authors often compared Israel to a vine or vineyard (Ps. 80:9–10; Isa. 5:1–7; Hos. 10:1).

Jeremiah reports God saying to Israel, "I had planted you a noble vine, a seed of highest quality. How then have you turned before Me into the degenerate plant of an alien vine?" (2:21). As God's vineyard, Israel was supposed to pay back His tender care by bearing fruit (spiritually speaking).

In John's gospel, Jesus says He is the true vine, and His disciples, dependent on Him, are branches of the vine. God the Father is the gardener (John 15:1–8). So in the New Testament view, the vineyard is not Israel but any persons who are spiritually dependent on God.

990. wormwood and gall

Wormwood was a bitter plant, and gall was a bitter herb mixed with a drink as a sort of painkiller. Both were used, figuratively, to refer to deep bitterness and sorrow (Ps. 69:21; Prov. 5:4; Lam. 3:19). Jesus on the cross was offered wine mixed with gall to relieve His pain, but He refused it (Matt. 27:34).

991. doves

The Bible's first dove of note is the one Noah sent out from the ark. When it returned with an olive branch in its beak, Noah knew that dry land was appearing on the flooded earth.

Doves were common in Israel, and Israel's ritual law made them the "poor man's sacrifice" for those who could not afford to sacrifice a lamb. When Jesus drove the merchants from the temple, the Gospels specifically mention the sellers of the sacrificial doves (Mark 11:5).

Doves had a reputation for being gentle, innocent creatures, which lies beyond Jesus' words to His disciples to "be wise as serpents and harmless as doves" (Matt. 10:16).

The most famous dove of all was the Holy Spirit, which appeared over Jesus in the shape of a dove at His baptism (John 1:32). Based on the story of Jesus' baptism, the Holy Spirit has always been symbolized by a dove.

992. ravens

These bulky black birds, relatives of crows, appear at several crucial points in the Bible. Noah in the ark sent out a raven, which did not return. Ravens played an important role in the life of the faithful prophet Elijah, who lived in the wilderness and was fed, at God's command, by ravens who brought him bread and meat every morning and evening (1 Kings 17:6). Based on this story, ravens have become a symbol of God's care.

993. bears

Of all the wild animals of Bible times, the bear was probably the most dangerous to man. David, while a shepherd boy, had killed both a bear and a lion that threatened his sheep (1 Sam. 17:34–37). A she-bear whose cubs were threatened was known to be especially dangerous (2 Sam. 17:8).

994. baboons and peacocks

Hebrew is not always an easy language to translate, and some Old Testament words are "iffy" when translated. A word in 1 Kings 10:22 is translated "peacock" in the King James Version and several others, but translated "baboon" in some versions. Neither animal was native to Israel, but 1 Kings 10 reports the animal (whichever it was) as part of Solomon's royal zoo.

NUMBERS

995. seven

Why is seven considered a lucky number? Certainly it is a significant number in the Bible. God created everything in six days, then rested on the seventh, so seven symbolizes completion. Israel was required to observe the Sabbath also. Seven occurs in other contexts. Mourning was for seven days. Priests sprinkled sacrificial blood seven times. Seven priests marched around Jericho seven times, then the city's walls fell. Every seventh year was a "sabbatical" year, and after seven times seven years (forty-nine) came the "jubilee" years. Jesus told His disciples to forgive people "seventy times seven" times. He miraculously fed four thousand people with seven loaves of bread. The Christian fellowship chose seven men as deacons.

See 608 (Sabbath).

996. twelve

Twelve, like seven, was a significant number for the Israelites. Why? It isn't a logical "body" number like ten. (Does anyone need to ask why ten is a significant number?) No, the significance of twelve lies in the stars—literally. The Israelites and other people of the Middle East divided the calendar into twelve months, based on the changes of the moon. The nations of the Middle East also were aware of the twelve signs of the zodiac. Israel did not dabble in astrology as its neighbor nations did, but people were aware of the zodiac.

Because of its significance in the calendar, twelve became a key number. Jacob, also named Israel, had twelve sons, each one the founder of one of the "tribes" of Israel. Jesus chose twelve men to be disciples, and when one (the traitor, Judas) killed himself, the remaining eleven felt obligated to replace him. The disciples are sometimes referred to as "the Twelve." The letter of James, addressed to Christians throughout the world, goes out to "the twelve tribes scattered among the nations."

The book of Revelation, with its visions and symbols, paints a picture of heaven that is filled with twelves—twelve pearl gates, twelve angels, twelve gems, twelve foundations, twelve kinds of fruit on the tree of life, the names of the twelve apostles, and the twelve tribes of Israel.

See 995 (seven); 275 (tribes).

997. Friday the thirteenth

Twelve is a "good" number in the Bible (see 996 [twelve]), but there is no suggestion that thirteen is unlucky. Many people believe that "unlucky thirteen" is based on the Last Supper of Jesus and His twelve disciples. The traitor Judas Iscariot was clearly the "bad luck charm" at this dinner for thirteen. Since Judas's treachery led to Jesus' crucifixion (on a *Friday*), the combination of thirteen and Friday is considered especially unlucky. (And yet we call it *Good* Friday .)

998. forty

Forty, like seven and twelve, is one of the great "Bible numbers." Several significant events took forty days: Noah's Flood, Moses' time on Mount Sinai, the time of Moses' spies scoping out Canaan, Elijah's flight from Jezebel, Jesus' time of temptation, the period Jesus was on earth after His resurrection, etc. Forty years was significant as the time the Israelites wandered after leaving Egypt, and the period that a number of Israel's leaders ruled (Eli, David, Solomon, Joash). For the Israelites, forty seemed to be a good round number that suggested a generation.

MEASUREMENTS

999. shekel

The shekel is the unit of currency in Israel today. It was so in the Old Testament also, but more a unit of weight than of currency. The Hebrew word *shekel* means "weight." Pieces of gold, silver, bronze, and even iron were weighed to determine their value. When Genesis 20:16 mentions "a thousand shekels of silver" (NIV), we can probably calculate this at about twenty-five pounds of silver. During most of the Old Testament period money was *not* in the form of coins, but only lumps of metal, which had to be weighed to determine value. Later on, shekel coins came into use. In the New Testament period, three thousand shekels equaled one *talent* of silver, and a *mina* equaled one hundred shekels. Talents and minas are both mentioned in the Gospels.

1,000. cubit

This is the most common unit of measurement in the Bible. A cubit was the length of a man's forearm, roughly eighteen inches. Many contemporary Bible translations are thoughtful enough to give measurements in cubits then, in a footnote, give the equivalent in feet and inches.

1,001. hour

A day divided into twenty-four hours of sixty minutes was not known in Old Testament times. The New Testament has the Greek word *hora* many times, and each day had twelve of these, not twenty-four. Mark 15:25 says that Jesus was crucified at "the third hour," probably about six in the morning (the "sixth hour" was noon). However, the Romans used a different system from the Greeks and divided the day into twenty-four hours, numbering them (as we do) from midnight and noon. John's gospel uses the Roman system of time, so when it mentions "the tenth hour" being during daylight (John 1:39), it is referring to 10:00 A.M.

Index

Numbers refer to the 1,001 entry numbers, not to page numbers.